# The Core *of* Christianity

# Neil T. Anderson

HARVEST HOUSE PUBLISHERS

EUGENE, OREGON

*Cover by Dugan Design Group, Bloomington, Minnesota*

**THE CORE OF CHRISTIANITY**
Copyright © 2003/2010 by Neil T. Anderson
Published by Harvest House Publishers
Eugene, Oregon 97402
www.harvesthousepublishers.com

Library of Congress Cataloging-in-Publication Data
    Anderson, Neil T., 1942-
    The core of Christianity / Neil T. Anderson.
      p. cm.
    ISBN 978-0-7369-2506-8 (pbk.)
    1. Christian life. 2. Theology, Doctrinal—Popular works. I. Title.
    BV4501.3.A537 2010
    248.4—dc22

2009017186

10  11  12  13  14  15  16  17  18  / VP-SK /  10  9  8  7  6  5  4  3

*To Joanne, my wife,*
*with all my respect and love*

## Acknowledgments

For 65-plus years people have been building into my life. Books by authors I never met and tapes by people I never knew have contributed to my growth in Christ. I'm grateful for all the teachers I have had over the years. I'm sure each one has contributed something to this book.

What I write affects the staff of Freedom in Christ Ministries around the world. So I have asked them for feedback on this manuscript, and I am grateful for their response, even though I am responsible for the content. This book reflects my own journey to the center of God's will. I long for that spiritual resonance that comes from abiding in Christ and being led by the Holy Spirit. Whatever is true or balanced in this book is to be credited to His guidance.

I especially want to thank my wife, Joanne. She has been my faithful companion for over 40 years and has cared enough for me to give me honest feedback. She is the best editor that any writer could hope for. Joanne was educated as a home economist, but she missed her calling. Literature is her love, and she devours books on a variety of subjects. The breadth of her knowledge is challenging to me, especially her contribution from ancient Christian literature.

Neil T. Anderson

# Contents

# United in Christ

I think God intends the church to function like an orchestra playing a symphony. Gifted musicians take their seats and play their assigned parts. Every instrument is needed in order for the resultant sound to be what the Creator intends. Some instruments have longer parts to play, while the cymbals may crash together only once or twice—and yet the music wouldn't be the same without them. Some seemingly lesser instruments cannot be heard above the others, and yet their combined effect added to that of the rest of the musicians makes a contribution that cannot come about in any other way.

Occasionally one instrument may be called to solo, but its primary role is to be a part of the whole. Great musicians work hard to perfect their performance skills and then pass them on to the next generation. They don't consider their instrument to be better than any of the others, because they realize they are just part of something greater. They are grateful for the privilege to play, because they are fulfilling their purpose in a grand performance.

Before the conductor appears onstage each player tunes their instrument independently of others. They are preparing to play their part. To the listener the result is a cacophony—a harsh or discordant noise. Then the lead violinist stands and plays a single note, and all the instruments join in. Suddenly there is harmony where there was just noise. The conductor walks onstage, picks up his baton, and the music begins as the musicians willingly submit to the conductor's leadership.

The music sours, however, when players pay little attention to the conductor and split into duets, trios, and quartets. And when the symphony starts sounding like a cacophony, the attendance dwindles. Then self-appointed critics usurp the role of the maestro by correcting the other players. Rather than more critics, what's needed at this point is a humble lead violinist to stand, play the right note, and set the stage for the conductor, who is patiently waiting in the wings.

Can you see the parallel here? When the church is out of harmony nobody is more grieved than the One who is praying for its unity. Many Christians long for spiritual renewal—and rightly so. It is wonderful when harmony happens. When such times are precipitated by genuine repentance and faith in God, barriers disappear between brothers and sisters as they become one in Christ. When they are filled with the Holy Spirit and when the word of Christ richly dwells within them, they sing psalms, hymns, and spiritual songs and make melody in their hearts to the Lord (Ephesians 5:18-20; Colossians 3:15-16). That is spiritual rhythm.

## Understanding the Cacophony

Over the years I have been invited to speak to a wide variety of churches with different theological perspectives. I have seen many good and some not so good expressions of Christianity. When the fellowship is good, the unifying factor is a love and devotion to Christ. I have also come to recognize the forces that draw Christians away from Christ and estrange them from other believers, namely the world, the flesh, and the devil. Concerning the latter the apostle Paul wrote, "I am afraid that, as the serpent deceived Eve by his craftiness, your minds will be led astray from the simplicity and purity of devotion to Christ" (2 Corinthians 11:3). In what ways have we in the church been influenced by the world, indulged the flesh, and been deceived by the father of lies? To begin answering that question consider the following diagram:

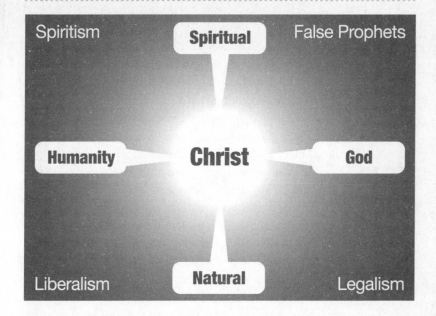

Keep in mind that I am not pitting the spiritual against the natural, or God against humanity. The above diagram is just a grid by which one can evaluate various expressions of Christianity. God is the ultimate reality, and Christ is the perfectly balanced God-man. After speaking the world into existence God created Adam and Eve in His image. They were to be fruitful, multiply, and subdue the earth. There was perfect harmony in the Garden until Adam chose to act independently of the "Conductor." The result was that sin separated Adam and his descendants (us) from God. The Law couldn't reconcile sinful man to God. Only Christ could reconcile us to God and so He does for those who choose to repent and believe in Him. Then, as believers, Christ should be at the center of our existence, our marriages, and our ministries.

The church falls out of harmony with God when it moves away from the center (Christ) in any direction. Historically, the Western church has been biased substantially toward the natural, but that is changing as we are being challenged by the New Age movement, the influence of Eastern religions, and the advent of postmodernism.

Jesus gave us an example and called us to follow in His steps. What He demonstrated was a life totally dependent upon His heavenly Father. In the high-priestly prayer He said, "Now they have come to know that everything

You have given Me is from You" (John 17:7; see also John 5:30; 6:57a; 8:42; 14:10). Jesus showed us how a spiritually alive person could live a righteous life and stay "in tune" by maintaining a dependent relationship with God the Father. Temptation is an attempt to get us to live independently of God.

Growing Christians are moving toward the center of the diagram—towards Christ—and overcoming the forces that would pull them away. This requires repentance and a growing faith in God. Jesus said, "The time is fulfilled, and the kingdom of God is at hand; repent and believe in the gospel" (Mark 1:15). There are many opportunities around the world to grow in our faith, but few opportunities to repent. Consequently, many new believers stay connected to the world, which impedes their growth in Christ.

We should be tolerant of those coming out of the world and accept them as new creations in Christ. That is why I show a "tolerance circle" around the center in the diagram, and don't expect new believers to be perfect overnight. The apostle Paul wrote, "Accept one another, just as Christ also accepted us to the glory of God" (Romans 15:7). I am eternally grateful that when I was still a sinner Christ died for me, and that same unconditional love and acceptance is what I want to extend to every believer I meet.

## Examining the Four Quadrants

People are coming to Christ from all four quadrants shown in the above diagram, and there are healthy expressions of Christianity in each quadrant if they are growing toward the center. There are staff members of Freedom in Christ Ministries in each quadrant who are helping others draw closer to Christ. What characterizes those closest to the center (Christ) is humility and godly character. What characterizes those outside the tolerance circle is usually biblical ignorance, or pride and arrogance. Let me briefly describe each quadrant and then expand upon them in the chapters that follow.

### God/Natural

In this book I am going to focus on issues and stay off personalities, except to illustrate good examples. Two good examples of those in this quadrant are Dr. Wayne Grudem and Dr. Dallas Willard. Both are highly intelligent and godly men. From my perspective Dr. Grudem's *Systematic Theology* has a balanced perspective on the reality of the spiritual world.

Those who are outside the tolerance circle tend to be legalistic and theologically arrogant. The problem is, you can know theology and be arrogant, but you cannot know God and be arrogant. The apostle Paul tells us that "knowledge makes arrogant, but love edifies" (1 Corinthians 8:1), and warns the church about latter-day Pharisees:

> Realize this, that in the last days difficult times will come. For men will be lovers of self…holding to a form of godliness, although they have denied its power; Avoid such men as these…[who are] always learning and never able to come to the knowledge of the truth (2 Timothy 3:1,5,7).

### Natural/Humanity

Psychologist Dr. Larry Crabb and Dr. David Stevens, the president of the American Association of Christian Doctors and Dentists, are two good examples of Christian men who come from this quadrant who are encouraging others to become like Christ. The lower-left quadrant reflects the medical and psychological models that have dominated the helping professions in the Western world. Humanity and nature are the dominant players outside the tolerance circle, with humanism the dominant philosophy.

Liberal churches fall into this category when they show little respect for the authority of God's Word, and almost no regard for the reality of the spiritual world. Those farthest from Christ are marked by scientific and philosophical pride. The apostle Paul warns the church about such liberal leanings in Colossians 2:8: "See to it that no one takes you captive through philosophy and empty deception, according to the tradition of men, according to the elementary principles of the world, rather than according to Christ." Paul is even more direct when he writes in 2 Timothy 4:1-4,

> I solemnly charge you in the presence of God and of Christ Jesus, who is to judge the living and the dead, and by His appearing and His kingdom: preach the word; be ready in season and out of season; reprove, rebuke, exhort, with great patience and instruction. For the time will come when they will not endure sound doctrine; but wanting to have their ears tickled, they will accumulate for themselves teachers in accordance to their own desires, and will turn away their ears from the truth and will turn aside to myths.

### Humanity/Spiritual

The late John Wimber is a good example of someone in this quadrant.

John had an infectious love for God and concern for humanity. He fully embraced the reality of the spiritual world and wanted the church to glorify God by manifesting His presence. Outside the tolerance circle there has been a dramatic shift as worldly philosophies move upward on the left side of the diagram.

Tragically, this spiritual emphasis does not always reflect a Christian worldview, but rather a New Age or spiritist worldview. In the absence of spiritual discernment and an adequate theology, these people have no clue what they are getting involved in. They make demons acceptable by calling them spirit guides. Mediums are called channelers and a gullible public accepts this enticing label. Liberal churches are dying and humanism as a viable philosophy is waning in the West as spiritism and New Age philosophies are becoming a dominant secular religion in America. Such "enlightened" ones are marked by spiritual pride. Paul warned us about moving in this direction away from the center in 1 Timothy 4:1: "The Spirit explicitly says that in later times some will fall away from the faith, paying attention to deceitful spirits and doctrines of demons." That is presently happening all over the world.

### Spiritual/God

I know of no better example from this quadrant than Dr. Jack Hayford. This godly man has been a positive influence across many denominations and a credible representative of the Pentecostal movement. The upward movement on the right side of the diagram has been rapid in Christian circles. Much of the growth in foreign missions has been Pentecostal. A growing awareness of the Holy Spirit has been sorely needed in the church, but distortions are evident when this emphasis becomes unbalanced. The apostle Paul has also warned us about that possibility in 2 Corinthians 11:13-15:

> Such men are false apostles, deceitful workers, disguising themselves as apostles of Christ. No wonder, for even Satan disguises himself as an angel of light. Therefore it is not surprising if his servants also disguise themselves as servants of righteousness, whose end will be according to their deeds.

Those outside the tolerance circle are marked by ecclesiastical pride, claiming to be apostles and prophets. The apostle Peter also warned us about this possibility in 2 Peter 2:1-2:

> False prophets also arose among the people, just as there will be
> false teachers among you, who will secretly introduce destructive
> heresies, even denying the Master who bought them, bringing swift
> destruction upon themselves. Many will follow their sensuality, and
> because of them the way of truth will be maligned.

False prophets have an independent spirit and despise authority (verse 10). They don't want to answer to anyone.

## Where Do You Fall?

The inner circle constitutes orthodox teaching and practices by those who hold to the authority of Scripture and devotion to God. If only God was interpreting His Word, the circle would be a dot. But for us, it must be a circle, because there will always be disagreements even among the most intellectually gifted theologians. No person other than Christ will ever be able to achieve omniscience or perfect holiness.

Where you would fall on the inner circle may also be affected by giftedness. Those with the gift of prophecy would probably be more oriented to the right, because they are calling for holiness; the administrators would be closer to the bottom, because they work in the more natural world of facts and figures; those who have the gift of helps would be to the left because they are motivated to serve people, and so on.

However, where you would be on the diagram is mostly determined by your education and spiritual upbringing. We are all born dead in our trespasses and sins according to Ephesians 2:1. That means we were born physically alive, but spiritually dead. Before we came to Christ, we had neither the presence of God in our lives nor the knowledge of His ways. So we all learned to live our lives independently of God. Then by the grace of God we were born again, and became new creations in Christ, but that did not clear all that we previously learned from our minds. That is why Paul wrote in Romans 12:2, "Do not conform any longer to the pattern of this world, but be transformed by the renewing of your mind. Then you will be able to test and approve what God's will is—his good, pleasing and perfect will" (NIV).

Your introduction to Christianity may have happened in an Evangelical, Charismatic, Pentecostal, mainline Protestant, liturgical, or sacramental church. All would claim to be the true church or at least a representative of the true church, and the leadership would likely believe they are living a balanced Christian life. If you ask anyone in these churches who is radically out of balance in their Christian walk to please stand up, you will get a lot of smiles, but probably nobody standing. Nobody thinks they are radically out of balance, or else they would be making serious moves about re-educating themselves or relocating where they attend church. Most pastors are going to preach their brand of Christianity and convey the belief that they are right and imply that you would do best by believing what they are teaching.

That is not entirely wrong if they are committed to teaching God's Word. However, pastors have been taught a certain theological perspective as well. Jesus said, "A pupil is not above his teacher; but everyone, after he has been fully trained, will be like his teacher" (Luke 6:40). If you never leave your original denomination or church, you may never know that there are equally valid expressions of Christianity outside the realm of your experience and exposure. Most church attenders are in balance to their own educational system, but not necessarily in balance from God's perspective.

### New Perspectives

I was raised in a mainline denomination that has since become quite liberal. So I was exposed to the lower left quadrant of the diagram. I never found Christ there, although I am thankful for the Bible studies and moral standards that were taught. My wife, Joanne, was raised Lutheran and switched to Catholicism. We became Episcopalians when we got married, but we still didn't know the Lord. I was introduced to Christ through the ministry of Campus Crusade for Christ, and a friend at work invited us to the Baptist church he was attending. At that church I grew like a fertilized weed, and two years later sensed God calling me to full-time ministry.

Since leaving the pastorate to teach at Talbot School of Theology and later becoming the founder of Freedom in Christ Ministries, Joanne and I have fellowshipped in a variety of denominations. We even attended an Eastern Orthodox church to gain experience and exposure to ancient Christianity. I am somewhat embarrassed to say that in my pastoral experience the church calendar was mostly understood to be a calendar of events showing our schedule for the year. In the sacramental churches the church calendar depicts great moments in church history and is celebrated in worship throughout the year.

I have also been invited to present my ministry in a wide variety of denominations. I have found them to be far more similar in what they teach and practice than the stereotypes they have been branded with would indicate. I personally think it is unfortunate that every Christian hasn't had the same exposure to the larger body of Christ that has been so beneficial to me. We may be driving our own cars, but we are driving them in the same kingdom and getting our gas from the same station.

Since many of you haven't had that exposure, you may be challenged by my analysis and find yourselves supporting some things I write and questioning others. In chapter one, I will show the delicate balance between Western rationalism and Eastern mysticism, with Christ at the center.

In chapters two through five, I will examine the four quadrants shown earlier and explain what may be hindering some believers from drawing closer to God and keeping them from fellowshipping with the whole body of Christ. The rest of the book is on knowing God, receiving divine guidance, exercising discernment, and knowing how to survive the dark times of life. In the epilogue I will speak briefly to the problem of our disunity, make an appeal to be more tolerant of other Christian expressions, and offer a plan to draw you and your church closer to God.

I have included study questions for your own use or for discussion in small groups. The purpose of this book is to expose you to other perspectives in the larger body of Christ, enhance your relationship with God, show you how to stay in tune with the Conductor, and sharpen your senses to discern between good and evil. What I hope will happen is illustrated by the e-mail I received from a pastor friend in Holland:

> I would like to thank you personally for your teaching. As you know it is well received in the Netherlands. It has had a great influence in our ministry. We were mainly focused on power struggles rather than a truth confrontation. Our prayers for deliverance were more characteristic of a battle that needed to be won, rather than a peace that has already been achieved. For hours on end we would engage in battle against evil spirits by singing victory songs and quoting warlike texts from the Bible, but now we overcome the darkness through love and truth.
>
> Many doors have opened for us and we can't contain our ministry any more. The Holy Spirit is working in a very special way in this once so divided country of the Netherlands. We are able to train teams in Evangelical churches, Catholic churches, and Pentecostal churches.

Do you remember drawing me a diagram with Christ at the center (shown earlier), with the message that a church that falls into extremes is in danger of becoming liberal or "charismagical"? This diagram touched me greatly. We went down on our knees and confessed any form of thinking, speaking, and acting exclusively in our own lives and ministries. God does not think exclusively, but inclusively. This has led to bringing together national leaders from most of the major churches in the Netherlands in a movement that is choosing to be united in Christ.

Part One:

# Moving Toward the Center

*He is discovered to be the only God who created all things, who alone is Omnipotent, and who is the only Father. He founded and formed all things…He has fitted and arranged all things by His wisdom. He contains all things, but He Himself can be contained by no one…There is only one God, the Creator. He is above every principality, power, dominion, and virtue. He is Father; He is God; He is Founder; He is Maker; He is Creator. He made those things by Himself, that is, through His Word and His Wisdom…He is the God of Abraham, the God of Isaac, and the God of Jacob…He is the Father of our Lord Jesus Christ. Through His Word, who is His Son, through Him, He is revealed and manifested to all to whom He is revealed. For [only] those know Him to whom the Son has been revealed. But the Son, eternally co-existing with the Father, from of old, yes, from the beginning, always reveals the Father.*[1]

IRENAEUS (C. 180)

# Chapter One

# Defining the Center

*I, the prisoner of the Lord, implore you to walk in a manner worthy
of the calling with which you have been called, with all humility
and gentleness, with patience, showing tolerance for one another in
love, being diligent to preserve the unity of the Spirit in the bond of
peace. There is one body and one Spirit, just as also you were called
in one hope of your calling; one Lord, one faith, one baptism, one
God and Father of all who is over all and through all and in all.*

EPHESIANS 4:1-6

*The purpose for which the Spirit was given was to bring into unity
all who remain separated by different ethnic and cultural divisions;
young and old, rich and poor, women and men…Thus he wants us to
be bound together with one another, not only to be at peace, not only
to be friends, but to be all one, a single soul. Beautiful is this bond.
With this bond we bind ourselves together both to one another and to
God. This is not a chain that bruises. It does not cramp the hands. It
leaves them free, gives them ample room and greater courage.*[2]

CHRYSOSTOM, "HOMILY ON EPHESIANS 4:1-3"

Imagine a factory that is interconnected by a sophisticated arrangement
of gears meshing together. Everything works decently and in order, provided that each gear is turning properly in a concentric fashion. *Concentric*
means to have a common center. When one gear loses its bearings, the gear
takes an elliptical path. Damage is inevitable not only to that gear, but to
every other gear it interfaces with.

So delicate is the nature of the church that one person out of fellowship
can affect many others. If one root of bitterness springs up, many are defiled

(Hebrews 12:15). If the beliefs or practices of any given church body are not centered in Christ, the focus is off. Participants will be slightly out of balance, and it will hinder their spiritual potential. Heresy doesn't always begin with blatant error. It often begins with truth out of balance.

Paul's instruction to be diligent in preserving the unity of the Spirit implies that the church is already united. There can only be one basis for that unity, and that is our common spiritual heritage—our identity and position in Christ. Jesus is the one common core of the church. When anything else defines us, we become elliptical and out of balance to some extent, major or minor.

## Brothers and Sisters in Christ

God is the Creator and center of the universe and our existence, and we are called to be in a righteous relationship with Him. When asked what the great commandment in the Law is, Jesus said,

> "You shall love the Lord your God with all your heart, and with all your soul, and with all your mind." This is the great and foremost commandment. The second is like it, "You shall love your neighbor as yourself." On these two commandments depend the whole Law and the Prophets (Matthew 22:37-40).

In other words, we have fulfilled the Law of God if we love the Lord and our neighbor. The purpose of divine revelation is to govern our relationship with God and others. The Pharisees didn't ask Jesus for the second great commandment, but He shared it anyway because our relationship with God is inextricably bound up in our relationship with others. Christianity is all about relationships, and we cannot be rightly related to God to the exclusion of others. "If someone says, 'I love God,' and hates his brother, he is a liar; for the one who does not love his brother whom he has seen, cannot love God whom he has not seen" (1 John 4:20).

Over the years I have seen diverse people come together in Christ, and I have seen the walls that separate us come down. C.S. Lewis wrote, "I believe that in the present divided state of Christendom, those who are at the heart of each division are all closer to one another than those who are at the fringes."[3] I agree. I have ministered in a wide variety of churches, and I have observed that what we believe and what we have in common is far greater than the issues that divide us.

Various denominations and churches take on different shapes, as illustrated in the following diagram. Notice that they all have a common core. Those closest to the center have little problem relating to individuals in other groups who are also close to Christ. Those furthest from the center (Christ) typically find their identity in their religious preferences, practices, and denominational distinctives, which serve as barriers to fellowship with those who have different labels and distinctives.

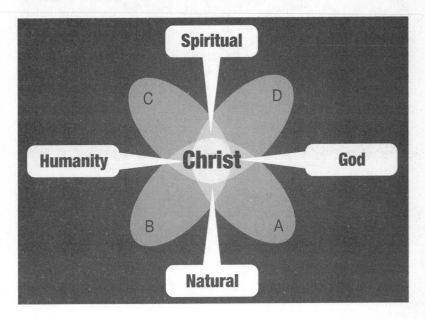

To illustrate, consider groups A and C with X representing the norm for each group as shown on the next page. Those in group A may consider themselves Evangelical, and those in group C may consider themselves Charismatic. Those farthest from the center in group A tend toward legalism. They have a tendency to be intellectually arrogant and staunchly anticharismatic. Those farthest from the center in group C tend toward spiritism. They have a tendency to be spiritually arrogant and want little to do with what they see as dead orthodoxy. Those near the center point of any group marked by X tend to stay in their own groups and are somewhat tolerant of other Christian persuasions. Those closest to the center have learned to appreciate other perspectives and find their identity in Christ.

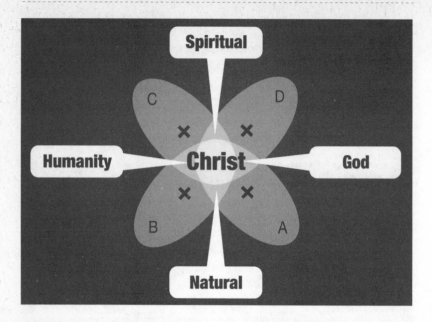

Every Christian has one thing in common: "As many as received Him, to them He gave the right to become children of God, even to those who believe in His name" (John 1:12). God is our Father, and we are His children. The church is the body of Christ, the spiritual family of God.

Pause for a moment and think about that. All those believers in one of the other three quadrants of Christianity are your brothers and sisters in Christ. You may be tempted to question their beliefs, practices, and even their salvation. Likely they are being tempted to question yours. It is a mistake to see the errors in others when they're measured against our own standards. We should first consider the errors of our own ways as measured against God's standards.

If we are truly reconciled to God, the Holy Spirit will lead us to be reconciled with one another. God has given the church the ministry of reconciliation,[4] which must start with our being reconciled to God. What we have freely received in Christ, we then freely extend to others. "Beloved, if God so loved us, we also ought to love one another" (1 John 4:11). We are to be merciful as God has been merciful to us (Luke 6:36). We are to forgive as Christ has forgiven us (Ephesians 4:32). When we are reconciled to God, the life of Christ flows through us to others.

## The Great Schism

Pentecost is generally acknowledged by Christians to be the origin of the church age, which is characterized by the New Covenant of grace. Most of what we know about the first 25 years of the church is described in the book of Acts. In his letter to Timothy, the apostle Paul wrote, "The things which you have heard from me in the presence of many witnesses, entrust these to faithful men who will be able to teach others also" (2 Timothy 2:2). Initially such teaching was passed on by oral tradition. The only Scripture the early Christians had was the Old Testament.

There was only one visible manifestation of the church for about the first millennium, and when disputes arose, the bishops in a given area would gather in council, just as the apostles did in Jerusalem (see Acts 15). In AD 313 the Roman Emperor Constantine granted Christianity legal status, which ended the age of persecution, but other opposition arose to challenge the church. The threat was not from the outside, but from within, perpetuated by apostate priests and bishops such as Arius, Eutyches, and Nestorius. These heretical teachers were opposed by such great men of the church as Athanasius, Gregory of Nazianzus, Basil the Great, Hilary, John Chrysostom, Ambrose, Cyril of Alexandria, Leo of Rome, and hundreds of others.

### Ecumenical Councils

For the next 450 years, from 325 to 787, leaders from all over the world gathered on seven different occasions to combat false teachings and put forth the true belief of the church. These were later called the Seven Ecumenical Councils. The word *ecumenical* comes from a Greek word meaning "all the inhabited earth," which implies that these councils represented and defined the Christian faith as it was held throughout the world.

The first council, in 325, resulted in the Nicene Creed, which Christians profess to this day. The Council of Carthage in 397 confirmed the authoritative books that make up the Bible. It is important to note that the council did not *establish* them as authoritative; rather, it *acknowledged* them as authoritative. God is the ultimate authority, and the church collectively recognizes that.

We are indebted and grateful to these Church Fathers who fought for and preserved the true historical church and presented us with the correct doctrine of Christ and the infallible Word of God. The critical doctrine then and still today is the Trinitarian nature of God, and the divine and human natures manifested in the one person of Christ.

As the second millennium approached, a schism arose between the East and the West. The Roman Empire had morally rotted from within and crumbled under the attack of invading tribes. The Eastern Roman Empire had survived these invasions and eventually became known as the Byzantine Empire. The churches of the West were aligned with Rome; the churches of the East remained under their respective patriarchs.

This schism had an effect upon the churches—oneness of mind and the desire and ability to come together in council was gradually lost. Doctrinal changes took place in Rome that further divided fellowship between the East and the West, such as the Immaculate Conception of Mary, the celibacy of the priesthood, the idea of purgatory, and the declaration of the Pope as the single visible leader of the church. These remain formidable barriers to reconciling the East with the West.

### The Reformation

The selling of indulgences and other practices tolerated or initiated by the Roman Church led to the Reformation. Initially Martin Luther (1483-1546) attempted to rediscover what had been lost in the West. He wasn't protesting against the Orthodox Church. Nor did he want to leave the Catholic Church, but he and other protestors were excommunicated, resulting in the formation of the Lutheran Church.

Subsequently, the most prominent reformer was John Calvin (1509-1564) who did not agree with Luther. So another schism occurred laying the foundation for the Presbyterian and Reformed Churches. The Anabaptists were yet another splinter group, resulting in the Amish, Mennonites, and Quakers, who now have many divisions within themselves, as do the Lutherans, Baptists, and Presbyterians. In the mid-1500s King Henry VIII of England wouldn't accept the Pope's refusal to grant the marriage annulment he wanted, so he broke from Rome and started the Anglican church. The Puritans and Methodists then broke from the Anglicans.

Our lack of intimacy with our heavenly Father is revealed by our inability to live in harmony with one another. Divisions are inevitable when that is the case. The apostle Paul explains why:

> Now I mean this, that each one of you is saying, "I am of Paul,"
> and "I of Apollos," and "I of Cephas," and "I of Christ." Has Christ
> been divided? (1 Corinthians 1:12-13)

Christ hasn't been divided, but the visible church has been and will continue to be as long as we find our identity in someone or something other than Christ.

## Rationalism vs. Mysticism

The schism between the Orthodox and Roman Catholic Churches, made official in AD 1054, paralleled the rise of scholasticism in the West, exemplified by scholars such as Thomas Aquinas. The pursuit of scholarship is still a prized Western value. The Eastern Orthodox Church does not lack scholarship, but is more inclined to accept the notion of mystery. *Mystery* does not mean "mysterious." It means that God has not previously or fully revealed something. It implies that we cannot fully comprehend the mysteries of God.

I believe we serve a rational God. However, our own ability to reason is limited on three counts. First, we can never be sure we have all the facts. Second, we can never be sure we are perfectly interpreting the facts. Finally, we can never be sure what the consequences will be when we decide upon a course of action. Consequently, we will always need divine guidance. We will never know so much that we will no longer need God. On the contrary, the more I know God and His Word, the more dependent on Him I have become. The apostle Paul's words illustrate why we need to recognize our limitations:

> Where is the wise man? Where is the scribe? Where is the debater of
> this age? Has not God made foolish the wisdom of the world? For
> since in the wisdom of God the world through its wisdom did not
> come to know God, God was well-pleased through the foolishness
> of the message preached to save those who believe (1 Corinthians
> 1:20-21).

## The Middle Ground of Truth

We cannot abandon our God-given ability to reason, but we must accept the fact that mystery is part of the church. Now we see dimly, but someday we shall see fully. Jesus is the Truth and stands at the apex of the bell-shaped curve shown below.

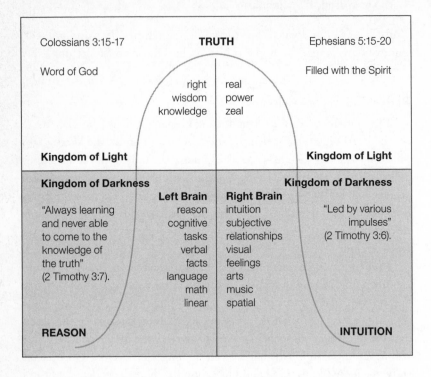

As an aerospace engineer I was so left-brained that my head probably tilted slightly to the left! It's no surprise then that when I became a Christian, I charged up the Western slopes of rationalism. As the truth became more personal and real, however, I slowed to a crawl. I wanted to be able to explain everything. To think that we have everything defined gives a false sense of security. My emotions were guarded, and I wasn't sure how real I was prepared to be. Being vulnerable is risky. Thankfully, such thinking has become more and more a part of my past, but I am aware that my natural bent is to be on the left side of center.

A friend of mine graduated from Dallas Theological Seminary and continued with a degree in psychology. Now he is a professional counselor. I asked him, "If you had to explain in one word why Western theologians and most evangelical pastors and teachers are so skewed to the left in the above diagram, what would that word be?" He said, "Control." I think he is right. I know that was the case for me.

When I taught evangelism in seminary, I had the students respond to the following three directives, without asking for any clarification. First, *Have you ever met God?* The question was a little more subjective than what they were used to. A few said no, thinking it was a trick question. Second, *Describe the experience.* Third, *How did you know it was God you met?* At least 90 percent had a subjective answer to the last question: "I just knew it was God" or, "I sensed a peace!" Is such subjective confirmation wrong? It isn't wrong if 90 percent of my students were assured of their salvation through the personal witness of the Holy Spirit. "The Spirit Himself testifies with our spirit that we are children of God" (Romans 8:16).

## Our Whole-Hemisphere God

The idea of "left-brained" vs. "right-brained" is supported by some secular researchers. They believe our brains have two hemispheres, which function as follows:

| Left Brain | Right Brain |
| --- | --- |
| reason | intuition |
| cognitive | subjective |
| tasks | relationships |
| verbal | visual |
| facts | feelings |
| language | arts |
| math | music |
| linear | spatial |

God does His work through the church, and He doesn't bypass our minds. Neither does He favor one hemisphere at the expense of the other. We have one brain and one mind, and we have a whole-hemisphere God. Without Christ, rationalists are "always learning and never able to come to the knowledge of the truth" (2 Timothy 3:7). Without Christ, intuitive people are "led on by various impulses" (2 Timothy 3:6). Cultures can vary in the same way. "Jews ask for signs and Greeks for wisdom" (1 Corinthians 1:22).

We don't come to Christ by reason or intuition. Jesus said, "No one can come to Me unless the Father who sent Me draws him; and I will raise him up on the last day" (John 6:44). He draws both the rationalist and the mystic to Himself when they choose not to lean on their own understanding or follow their subjective feelings.

When we receive Christ by faith, we are transferred out of the kingdom of darkness into the kingdom of God's beloved Son. Christian rationalists searching for wisdom and knowledge may find it difficult to be intimate in relationships and to be real. The truth is, we can't be right with God and *not* be real. If necessary, God may have to make us real in order to be right with Him. On the other hand, Christian mystics may be real, expressive, and personal, but may become defensive when objective truth calls their experiences into question.

Drawing close to Christ is neither a question of just having more information nor a question of having another subjective experience. It is not getting to know more *about* God, it is getting to *know* God. The apostle Paul knew all about God when Christ struck him down on the Damascus road. On the other hand, if you know nothing about Him, you may end up following a counterfeit Jesus. Faith has an object, and with little knowledge of that object, there can be only little faith. We need objective truth and discernment, but most of all we need the "more" that Paul exemplified in Philippians 3:8-10:

> *More* than that, I count all things to be loss in view of the surpassing value of knowing Christ Jesus my Lord, for whom I have suffered the loss of all things, and count them but rubbish so that I may gain Christ, and may be found in Him, not having a righteousness of my own derived from the law, but that which is through faith in Christ, the righteousness which comes from God on the basis of faith, that I may know Him and the power of His resurrection and the fellowship of His sufferings, being conformed to His death; in order that I may attain to the resurrection from the dead.

The sister epistles of Colossians and Ephesians reflect this balance. According to Ephesians 5:15-20, in order to stop being foolish and know what the will of God is, a Christian should be filled with the Holy Spirit. Spirit-filled Christians will sing and make melody in their hearts to the Lord. According to Colossians 3:15-17, the way to know the will of God is to let the Word of Christ richly dwell within us. The result is the same—singing and making melody in our hearts. It's not either/or. It is both/and! Being filled with the Spirit and letting the Word richly dwell within us are two sides of the same coin.

The Holy Spirit doesn't work in just the right brain, and the Word doesn't dwell only in the left brain. There is only one brain and only one mind— and only one God. The Holy Spirit will lead us into all truth, and the Word is a living reality. We must strive to be both right and real. We need both wisdom and power; our zeal should be rooted in the knowledge of God's Word. Being biblically balanced is our goal—not just knowing what the right balance is, but experiencing it in our daily lives.

### The Center Line Defines Us

Many Christians have never ventured outside their Protestant denomination, or the Catholic or Orthodox Church. Consequently they believe, or would like to believe, that their faith and practice is the right one. If you desire to move up in the ranks of any one Christian persuasion, you cannot stray too far from the "party line." The members of every religious group represent a bell-shaped curve, and the leaders are those closest to the center, as illustrated below:

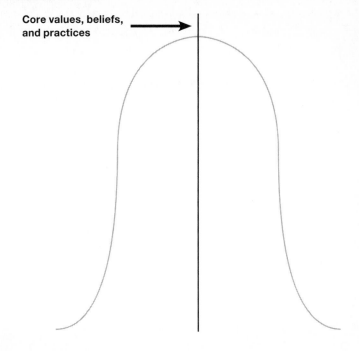

**Core values, beliefs, and practices**

Those who are closest to the center represent the party line. Those who stray too far to the left or to the right are marginalized. This is also true for any social group, including those defined by schools, workplaces, secular institutions, and even political parties. As elections draw near the candidates start moving to the center to gain more votes. The centrists win, and the extremists keep their day jobs.

Consider one schism among Protestant believers, that being the Pentecostal or Charismatic movement. If you want to move up in their organizational structure, you need to believe in a second work of grace, which they believe is made evident by the gift of tongues. That may get you thrown out of some Evangelical circles, or limit your ability to expand your influence.

In the past 15 years roughly half the conferences I have conducted were in Pentecostal, or Charismatic churches, and the other half were in Evangelical churches, of which some were doctrinally Arminian and the others Calvinist. I have been blessed to be able to do that. I think the reason is because I try to stay off the issues that divide us and focus on those that unite us, which is Christ crucified and risen. I have also discovered that this wonderful truth is all I need to teach in order to carry out the ministry of reconciliation with God.

Who is a Charismatic—someone who speaks in tongues or places a greater prominence on spiritual gifts? Spiritual gifts have always been a part of the church. The apostle Paul asked, "All do not speak with tongues, do they?" (1 Corinthians 12:30)? It's a rhetorical question, but the obvious answer is, no, they don't. Who is a Pentecostal—someone who places a greater emphasis on the work of the Holy Spirit? There is no church without the Holy Spirit. Who is an Evangelical—someone who believes in the authority of God's Word and a conversion experience? Has that not always been true for the church? On the other hand, didn't the apostle Paul also write, "Do not forbid to speak in tongues" (1 Corinthians 14:39)? That is a very clear statement that doesn't require enlightenment from others to understand. Neither the "can't have" or the "got to have" positions seem to be the right balance. There is a lot of theological diversity within Evangelical, Charismatic, and Pentecostal circles, and these circles are very overlapping. I wish we could do away with the labels that separate us.

I respect and have fellowship with almost every biblically conservative Christian group, but the question of who is right or wrong is not the only issue—and maybe not the critical issue. The biggest issue is, What defines us, or by what or whom are we identified? Every group claims Christ as the head of their church or denomination, yet what defines the center of these bell-shaped curves is never Christ. What identifies Christian groups, or what makes them different from other groups, is their unique beliefs and practices. That is usually what separates them from the others.

A Baptist theologian friend of mine shared a personal story that illustrates the point. It was the first day of a semester, and his students were all new to the seminary. He asked them, "Why are we Baptists?" He got a variety of answers based on Baptist distinctives, but none satisfied him. He continued to push for the response he was hoping for, but nobody said, "Because we believe that Jesus is the Christ, the Son of the living God."

What makes one conservative church group different from another is almost never Christ. If that were so, they would likely be labeled a cult. Cults are considered such because what they teach about Jesus does not agree with the ecumenical councils. Rather, the church is divided over baptism, communion (or is it Eucharist? Mass?), sanctification, salvation, music, styles of worship, time of services, color of the walls, donuts vs. bagels, and so on, ad nauseam. The battle between individual wills has pushed aside God's will. Hostilities have separated brothers and sisters, and intellectual arrogance rules the day. The need to be "right" has supplanted the need to be holy, loving, gracious, kind, and forgiving.

I have participated in higher Christian education for years, both as a student for 25 years and as a seminary professor for 10 years. I was on the intellectual path of academia. I had five earned degrees, two of which are doctorates. I wanted to be near the center of the bell-shaped curve, an esteemed member of the Evangelical Theological Society. That would help ensure job security and acceptance by my colleagues. Then God brought me to a fork in the road. I could continue on the path toward intellectual prominence (arrogance?), or I could take the path of humility and seek Him even if it meant the loss of status. I wish I could say that I was smart enough to choose the path of humility, but I wasn't. (Neither was the apostle Paul.) I will share how God got me on the other path in chapter 12.

Choosing whether we respond in pride or humility is a fork in everyone's road, and we have many opportunities during our lifetime to make the right or wrong choice. I would rather be known for my love than my intellect. Of course I want to be right, but even more, I want to be rightly related to God and His children. Don't you?

## Discussion Questions

1. What is the basis for our unity in Christ?

2. What is keeping you from being united to believers in other types of churches?

3. Have you come to believe something to be true that you sense would not be received in your present fellowship? How have you handled that?

4. Have you ever heard something about an author or another church and then come to find out later that what you heard wasn't true? Explain.

5. How did the early church strive for unity, and what does that suggest for today?

6. Are you on the rational or mystic side of the bell-shaped curve? Explain why.

7. Why do we need to be balanced in our thinking?

8. What defines your present church or denomination other than Christ?

9. What do you think would happen if you spoke the truth in love when you didn't fully embrace the teaching of your church, denomination, or school? What should you do?

10. Can you share a time when you had to make a choice between responding in pride or humility?

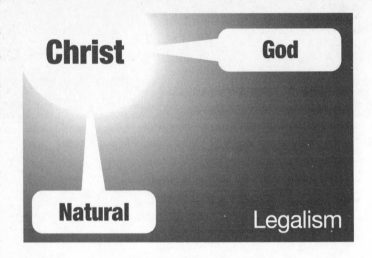

*Why the Law then? It was added because of transgressions, having been ordained through angels by the agency of a mediator, until the seed would come to whom the promise had been made. Now a mediator is not for one party only; whereas God is only One. Is the Law contrary to the promises of God? May it never be! For if a law had been given which was able to impart life, then righteousness would indeed have been based on the Law.*

GALATIANS 3:19-21

*Here arises a rather pertinent question: if faith justifies and even the former saints, who were justified before God, were justified through it, what need was there for the law to be given?...The law was given to a proud people, but the grace of love cannot be received by any but the humble. Without this grace the precepts of the law cannot possibly be fulfilled. Israel was rendered humble by transgression, so that it might seek grace and might not arrogantly suppose itself to be saved by its own merits; and so it would be righteous, not in its own power and might but by the hand of the Mediator who justifies the ungodly.[5]*

AUGUSTINE

# Chapter Two

# Overcoming Legalism

*As many as are of the works of the Law are under a curse; for it is written,*
"Cursed is everyone who does not abide by all things written in the
book of the Law, to perform them" *[Deuteronomy 27:26]. Now
that no one is justified by the Law before God is evident; for,* "The
righteous man shall live by faith" *[Habakkuk 2:4]. However, the
law is not of faith; on the contrary,* "He who practices them shall
live by them" *[Leviticus 18:5]. Christ redeemed us from the curse of
the law, having become a curse for us—for it is written,* "Cursed is
everyone who hangs on a tree" *[Deuteronomy 21:23] in order that
in Christ Jesus the blessing of Abraham might come to the Gentiles,
so that we would receive the promise of the Spirit through faith.*

GALATIANS 3:10-14

*It would not be right that the grace of the Spirit should come to one who
was graceless or full of offense. We're blessed first by the taking away of
the curse. Then, justified by faith, we receive the grace of the Holy Spirit.
So the cross has dissolved the curse, faith has brought righteousness, and
by God's own righteousness the grace of the Spirit has been given.[6]*

CHRYSOSTOM, "HOMILY ON GALATIANS 3:14"

In the above passage, Galatians 3:10-14, the apostle Paul instructs the
church that we are no longer under the Old Covenant by quoting four
times out of the Old Testament. What was only a shadow in the Old Testament is now revealed in the New Testament. The church is under the New
Covenant of grace, which Paul summarizes in the last sentence. We have
received the promise of the Spirit, which we appropriate by faith. It should
be evident that no one is justified by the Law, and I believe it *is* evident...
but why then do so many still struggle with legalism?

Several years ago, to gain some understanding as to how prevalent legalism still is, we asked George Barna's ministry to conduct some research for a book we were planning to write. Christians were asked to respond to statements that relate to legalism.[7]

1. "The Christian life is well summed-up as: Trying hard to do what God commands." The result: 57 percent strongly agreed and 25 percent somewhat agreed.

2. "I feel like I don't measure up to God's expectations of me." The result: 58 percent agreed (28 percent strongly, 30 percent somewhat).

3. We intentionally chose words in the next statement that Christians normally shy away from, like "rigid" and "strict." "Rigid rules and strict standards are an important part of the life and teaching of my church." The result: 39 percent strongly agreed and 27 percent somewhat agreed.

Apparently legalism is still functioning like a curse in many churches.

Rich Miller, the Director of Freedom in Christ Ministries for the United States, and staff member Paul Travis co-authored *Breaking the Bondage of Legalism* with me. Paul was our recovering legalist, and I was concerned that he might lose some of his support from churches that knew him in his former state. That didn't happen for an interesting reason, which is best explained by a question: Does a legalist know they are a legalist? No, they don't. Most would see themselves as the ultimate defenders of the faith.

Jesus waged war against the Pharisees. He called them "blind guides" and likened them to "whitewashed tombs which on the outside appear beautiful, but inside they are full of dead men's bones and all uncleanness" (Matthew 23:27). Such hypocrisy distorts the gospel and undermines our credibility.

Some people actually prefer to live under the law rather than under the grace of God. Having external standards appears to preserve traditional cultural values and provide structure to their lives. Rules and regulations are definable and may seem to be defensible from select passages in the Bible. The idea is, "Tell me what is right and what is wrong and I will try to do what is right." The problem is, we can't do what is right apart from the grace of God. The law could not connect us to God. It was intended by God to be a taskmaster that would lead us to Christ (Galatians 3:24). We are "servants of a new covenant, not of the letter but of the Spirit; for the letter [of the law] kills, but the Spirit gives life" (2 Corinthians 3:6).

How much do we do as believers that is based on a law or a principle that calls for us to respond in obedience? What we're doing in such cases is simply responding to a law or a principle. Contrast that question with the New Covenant, which promises new life in Christ and calls for us to live by faith according to what God says is true in the power of the Holy Spirit. Now we are responding to God, not a principle. The Old Covenant was conditioned upon our obedience to a law that had no power to give us life. The New Covenant is based on our union with God and His unconditional love and acceptance.

I once counseled a lady who asked, "What should I do?" I explained that the better question is, "Who should I be?" "What do you mean by that?" she asked. I explained her relationship with God, shared who she was in Christ, and that God's will for her life was her sanctification. Nobody could keep her from being the person God created her to be except herself. Then I explained how she could relate to her heavenly Father under the covenant of grace. She said, "Well, that is scary! Why won't you just tell me what I should *do*?"

## The Whole Gospel

There is another factor that prolongs the plague of legalism, and that is an inadequate understanding of the gospel. I have discovered all over the world that many are operating on the basis of just a third of the gospel. It sounds like this: "Jesus is the Messiah who died for our sins, and if we pray to receive Christ our sins will be forgiven, and when we die we will get to go to heaven." Does that sound okay to you? It doesn't to me. Let me explain.

God created Adam and Eve to be physically and spiritually alive. Physical life means that their souls were in union with their bodies. When believers die physically, they are absent from the body and present with the Lord. To be alive means to be in union with something, and to die means to separate from something.

Adam and Eve were also spiritually alive, which means that their souls were in union with God. He told them that if they ate of the tree of knowledge of good and evil, on that day they would surely die. They ate and they died—spiritually. Sin had separated them from God. Physical death would also be a consequence of sin, but for Adam that came over 900 years later.

As a result of the fall, every one of Adam and Eve's descendants has been born physically alive, but spiritually dead. The apostle Paul wrote,

> You were dead in your trespasses and sins, in which you formerly walked according to the course of this world, according to the prince of the power of the air, of the spirit that is now working in the sons of disobedience (Ephesians 2:1-2).

"The prince of the power of the air" is Satan, and he does work in the sons of disobedience.

What Adam and Eve lost in the fall was *life*—that is, eternal/spiritual life. What Jesus came to give us was *life*. If you wanted to save someone who had died from cancer, what would you do if you had the power to do it? Give them life? If you did, they would only die again. To save the dead person, you would have to not only give them life, but also cure the disease that caused them to die. For us, the cause of death was sin, because "the wages of sin is death" (Romans 6:23a). So Jesus went to the cross and died for our sins. But is that the whole gospel? No! Finish the verse: "But the free gift of God is eternal life in Christ Jesus our Lord" (Romans 6:23b).

Jesus said, "I am the resurrection and the life; he who believes in me will live [spiritually] even if he dies [physically], and everyone who lives and believes in Me will never die. Do you believe this?" (John 11:25-26). Jesus is the bread of *life*. He is the way, the truth, and the *life*. If you are born again, your name is written in the Lamb's book of *life*.

There was a time in my own Christian experience when I thought eternal life was something I got when I died. But that is not true. "He who has the Son has the life; he who does not have the Son of God does not have the life" (1 John 5:12). If you don't have eternal life before you physically die, all you can look forward to is eternal damnation.

### Raised to Life in Christ

I was having lunch with a prominent evangelical pastor and I asked him, "As Evangelicals, what have we emphasized the most—the cross or the resurrection?" He thought for a moment and said, "The cross," and I think he is right. Please don't get me wrong. I thank God for Good Friday and for the sacrificial death of Jesus who physically died for our sins. That removed the enmity that exists between us and God. However, what we celebrate every spring is the resurrection. The emphasis of the early church was clearly the resurrection and the primary focus of worship every Sunday. They defined salvation as union with God and focused their efforts on enhancing that relationship.

Over lunch a Reformed theologian asked me, "When did we take the resurrection out of our gospel presentation?" I didn't know, but I was sure he did—or he wouldn't have asked me the question. He said he thought the emphasis had moved from the resurrection to the cross during the time of the Puritans. Every Evangelical gospel presentation I have seen emphasizes the cross. It is the bridge in the diagram that spans the gap between sinful humanity and a holy God.

But when we cross that gap, who are we? Are we the same old creatures we were before, only forgiven—or are we new creations in Christ? Are we just natural children of our physical heritage? The apostle John thought otherwise: "As many as received Him, to them He gave the right to become children of God" (John 1:12). He also wrote,

> See how great a love the Father has bestowed on us, that we would be called children of God; and such we are...Beloved, now we are children of God...And everyone who has this hope fixed on Him purifies himself, just as He is pure (1 John 3:1-3).

Being spiritually alive is most often portrayed in the epistles as being "in Christ," or "in Him," or "in the beloved." There are 40 such prepositional phrases in the six chapters of Ephesians alone. Dear Christian, you are no longer "in Adam," you are alive "in Christ." You are no longer "in the flesh," you are "in the Spirit, if indeed the Spirit of God dwells in you" (Romans 8:9). You have been transferred out of the kingdom of darkness into the kingdom of God's beloved Son.

## We Don't Know Who We Are

Jesus Himself taught us to pray by addressing God as "Our Father, who is in heaven." That alone suggests that we are His children.

After attending my two-day conference on discipleship counseling a pastor in England shared that he has been doing seminars around the country on the subject of prayer using the Lord's prayer as the model. Then he said,

"This is the first time I have understood that when I say 'Our Father,' it also means that I am His child."

Every defeated Christian that I have had the privilege to help around the world had one thing in common: None of them knew who they were in Christ, nor understood what it means to be a child of God. If the Holy Spirit is testifying with our spirit that we are children of God, why weren't they sensing it?

### Ignorance of the Truth

There are two possible reasons. The first is ignorance. If you don't know the truth it can't set you free. The prophet Hosea said, "My people are destroyed for lack of knowledge" (Hosea 4:6). I have also encountered a lot of misunderstanding about the completeness of salvation. When applied to believers, salvation is presented in past, present, and future tenses in the Bible. We have been saved (Ephesians 2:5,8; 2 Timothy 1:8-9); we are presently being saved (1 Corinthians 1:18; 2 Corinthians 2:15), and someday we will be fully saved (Romans 5:9-10; 13:11). As believers our salvation experience is not yet complete, and it won't be until we physically die, receive a resurrected body, and reside in the presence of God. However, God does desire for us to presently have the assurance of salvation. There is a "coming wrath" (1 Thessalonians 1:10) of God, but we have the assurance that when that wrath comes, we will be saved from it. Having believed,

> You were sealed *in Him* with the Holy Spirit of promise, who is given as a pledge of our inheritance, with a view to the redemption of God's own possession, to the praise of His glory (Ephesians 1:13-14).

I heard a man boast that he was saved, sealed, and sanctified, implying that there was nothing more he needed to do. For him salvation and sanctification are both complete. He is not alone in that assessment. Many believers think they have been saved fully in the past, and that is all that has to happen. Such erroneous thinking doesn't provide very much motivation to press on in the pursuit of God, as the apostle Paul exhorted us to do in Philippians 3:13-14,

> Brethren, I do not regard myself as having laid hold of it yet; but one thing I do: forgetting what lies behind and reaching forward

to what lies ahead, I press on toward the goal for the prize of the upward call of God in Christ Jesus.

If you have been born again, you are indeed in the kingdom of God, but you will likely be stagnant in your growth if you fail to "work out your salvation with fear and trembling" (Philippians 2:12). Notice that you don't work for your salvation, which is a free gift of God appropriated by faith. But we all need to work out in our experience what God has worked in us. Beyond our initial salvation experience, God's will for our lives is our sanctification (1 Thessalonians 4:3), which also occurs in Scripture as past, present, and future tenses when applied to believers. In other words, believers *have* been sanctified (1 Corinthians 1:2; 6:11), they *are* being sanctified (2 Corinthians 7:1; 1 Thessalonians 4:3), and someday they *will* be fully sanctified (1 Thessalonians 3:12-13; 5:23-24). The sanctifying process begins at our new birth and ends in glorification. The author of Hebrews wrote, "Make every effort to live in peace with all men and to be holy; without holiness no one will see the Lord" (12:14 NIV). Holiness and sanctification are the same concept.

Past-tense sanctification is referred to by theologians as *positional* sanctification, and present-tense sanctification is referred to as *progressive* sanctification. Holiness churches (Pentecostal and Nazarene) have the tendency to focus on positional sanctification and see sanctification as a done deal, which can lead to serious errors. One man boasted that he hadn't sinned in 20 years. I asked him if his wife would agree with that assessment. The apostle John wrote, "If we say that we have no sin, we are deceiving ourselves and the truth is not in us" (1 John 1:8).

Reformed theology tends to focus on progressive sanctification, which makes sanctification synonymous with growth or maturity. Positional sanctification is often dismissed as just positional truth, as though it is irrelevant. Consequently many are trying to become someone they already are. However, positional sanctification (who we already are in Christ) is the basis for progressive sanctification (who we are becoming in Christ). Christians are not *trying* to become children of God, they *are* children of God who are in the process of becoming like Christ.

The apostle Paul explains that we should be firmly rooted "in Christ," in order to be built up "in Christ," so that we may live "in Christ" (Colossians 2:6-10).[8] It is a false assumption to think that all professing believers are firmly rooted in Christ, when most of them don't even know who they are in Christ. Paul wanted to give the Corinthian believers solid food, but he could only give them milk, because they "were not yet able to receive it" (1 Corinthians 3:2). They were not necessarily unwilling—they were unable. He explains why in the next verse: "You are still fleshly. For since there is jealousy and strife among you, are you not fleshly, and are you not walking like mere men?" (verse 3).

Many Christians today are walking like mere men. The difference between Christians and non-Christians seems to be getting more and more blurred. Applying a little logic to the above passage, one would have to conclude that we need some way to resolve those problems or we will have people sitting in our churches who are unable to receive the solid food of God's Word.

### Lack of Repentance

The lack of repentance is the second reason some Christians are ignorant of their true identity in Christ. In the United States there are many opportunities to grow in our faith. We have option overload with Christian material and programs, along with hourly messages on radio, television, and the Internet. But there are few opportunities to genuinely repent, and in many cases we are not even sure how to. We are saved by faith, but if we want to experience that new life in Christ and grow in the grace of God we have to repent. Jesus called us to repent and believe the gospel (Mark 1:15). Paul preached, "Having overlooked the times of ignorance, God is now declaring to men that all people everywhere should repent" (Acts 17:30).

Without genuine repentance most Christians come to church with a lot of baggage from the past. They enter the door, set their baggage down, hear a good message, pick up their baggage, and go back home…week after week. Helping people get rid of their baggage is variously understood in the church. Do such people need discipling, counseling, inner healing, or deliverance? Generally speaking the four quadrants of the church deal with this differently, as shown in the following illustration, with the major emphasis in each quadrant given at the top and the other three ministries following in descending order of emphasis:

## We Must Recognize the Spiritual Battle

The closer you get to Christ the more you realize the need for all four ministries mentioned above, which brings us to the final third of the gospel. According to the apostle John, "The Son of God appeared for this purpose, to destroy the works of the devil" (1 John 3:8). This aspect of the gospel was totally foreign to me in my youth and remained so for many years when I was a new believer. My initial seminary experience vaguely introduced me to the reality of the spiritual world, but didn't equip me to interact with it or help those who were being held captive by Satan to do his will (2 Timothy 2:26). I learned about the kingdom of God, but the kingdom of darkness was hardly mentioned.

I have since come to understand that there are two kingdoms mentioned in the Bible. From Genesis to Revelation the battle is between good and evil, between true prophets and false prophets, between the Spirit of truth and the father of lies, between the Christ and the Antichrist. We are all in that battle whether we like it or not. That's why Paul admonishes believers to

> be strong in the Lord and in the strength of His might. Put on the full armor of God, so that you will be able to stand firm against the schemes of the devil. For our struggle is not against flesh and

blood, but against the rulers, against the powers, against the world
forces of this darkness, against spiritual forces of wickedness in the
heavenly places (Ephesians 6:10-12).

Adam and Eve were created by God to have dominion over this world.
When they sinned they forfeited their position in Christ, and the devil
became the rebel holder of authority over this fallen world. Jesus referred
to him as the ruler of this world (John 12:31; 14:30; 16:11). John wrote that
"the whole world lies in the power of the evil one" (1 John 5:19). This third
leg of the gospel is what people in the third world are waiting to hear. They
*know* they live in a spiritual world. They make offerings to appease the dei-
ties and they contact shamans or quack doctors in order to manipulate the
spirits. (Most Christians in the United States are not aware that spiritism/
animism is the most prevalent religious orientation in the world.)

The church has the privilege and responsibility to announce that all
authority has been given to Jesus in heaven and upon this earth, that Satan
and his demons have been disarmed, and that the kingdom of God has
authority over the kingdom of darkness. That truth is just as much a part
of the gospel as the truth that our sins are forgiven. Paul shares all three
aspects of the gospel in Colossians 2:13-15:

> When you were dead in your transgressions and the uncircumci-
> sion of your flesh, He made you alive together with Him, having
> forgiven us all our transgressions, having canceled out the certifi-
> cate of debt consisting of decrees against us; and He has taken it
> out of the way, having nailed it to the cross. When he disarmed
> the rulers and authorities, He made a public display of them, hav-
> ing triumphed over them through Him.

### We Have Three Enemies

The tendency among Evangelicals is to see only the flesh and the world
as the enemies of our sanctification. Some may be tempted to think that
1 John 2:16 is a proof text for that conclusion: "All that is in the world, the
lust of the flesh and the lust of the eyes and the boastful pride of life, is not
from the Father, but is from the world."

There are two problems with that conclusion. First, the lust of the flesh,
the lust of the eyes, and the pride of life are the three channels that the devil
used to tempt Eve. They are also the same three channels that the devil

used to tempt Jesus. Satan works through those three channels to tempt us. He tempts us with thoughts like, *You know you want to do it. Everyone else is doing it. You will be on the inside track if you do it.* The moment we give into the temptation he then becomes the accuser. *How can you call yourself a Christian and do that? God doesn't love you. You are a hypocrite and a phony.* Satan deceives the whole world and accuses us day and night (Revelation 12:9-10).

Every Christian has been subjected to those temptations and accusations, but that isn't Satan's primary weapon. If he tempted you, you would know it. If he accused you, you would know it. But if he *deceived* you, you wouldn't know it. That has been the primary battle from the beginning. Eve was deceived and she believed a lie, and that happened before she had ever sinned. Good people can be deceived.

Second, believing that our enemies are only the flesh and the world ignores the previous context. John also identifies three levels of growth. We begin as "little children," progressing to "young men," and finally "fathers" of the faith (1 John 2:12-14). "Little children" have a knowledge of God and their sins are forgiven. In other words, they know who their heavenly Father is and they have overcome the penalty of sin. "Fathers" have known God from the beginning. This implies a deep reverential and experiential knowledge of God. "Young men" are identified as such because they have overcome the evil one, and the apostle repeats that characterization twice. You could say that "young men" in the faith have overcome the power of sin—that is, they have no uncontrollable appetites and can live a righteous life.

How are we going to help Evangelical believers come to full maturity if they haven't learned how to overcome the evil one? It's even more difficult when many try to live as though the evil one doesn't exist. I know of one Christian association that believes Christians can't have spiritual problems, and thus there's no need for the armor of God or the necessity of taking every thought captive to the obedience of Christ (2 Corinthians 10:5).

Such ignorance is in stark contrast to what Jesus is praying for in the high-priestly prayer in John 17:15-20:

> I do not ask You to take them out of the world, but to keep them
> from the evil one. They are not of the world, even as I am not of
> the world. Sanctify them in the truth; You word is truth. As You
> sent Me into the world, I also have sent them into the world. For

> their sakes I sanctify Myself, that they themselves also may be
> sanctified in truth. I do not ask on behalf of these alone, but for
> those also who believe in Me through their word.

The first concern of our Lord is that we be kept from the evil one. He is not asking that just for the 11 apostles who are still remaining. Recall that Jesus had already lost one of His disciples to the evil one: "During supper, the devil having already put into the heart of Judas Iscariot, the son of Simon, to betray Him" (John 13:2). Jesus is praying for all those who believe in Him through the teaching of the apostles and later the apostle Paul.

In the West we have all been influenced by Western rationalism and naturalism that tends to overlook the reality of the spiritual world. According to the Bible the spiritual world is just as real as the material world we see with our physical eyes. Paul wrote, "We look not at the things which are seen, but at the things which are not seen; for the things which are seen are temporal, but the things which are not seen are eternal" (2 Corinthians 4:18).

## Where Have We Gone Wrong?

Nobody reading this book is more committed to the authority of God and His Word than I am, and I preach and teach His Word to the best of my ability. I hope that is true of most Evangelical pastors. It isn't what we are doing that is necessarily wrong; it's what we're *not* doing. Visit a typical Bible-believing church any Sunday morning. In the better ones you will find a parking place reserved for visitors and be cheerfully greeted. You will be given a packet of material and invited to a reception room after the service to meet the pastor.

The service begins with some good (hopefully) contemporary music that's followed by a message from God's Word with practical advice for how you should live. Then perhaps some will attend Sunday-school classes to learn more. The larger churches take on the appearance of a school that has a large assembly hall, a gymnasium, and many classrooms. The focus is education, and that resonates with me since my education includes a master's in christian education and a doctorate of education.

### *"Christian Behavioralism"*

However, such activities can be just an intellectual exercise implying that Christianity is simply a better way to live. That, however, is Christian behavioralism, a.k.a. legalism. Being saved by faith but trying to be perfected by the law is the Galatians heresy. "You foolish Galatians, who has bewitched you, before whose eyes Jesus Christ was publicly portrayed as crucified? This is the only thing I want to find out from you: did you receive the Spirit by the works of the Law, or by hearing with faith" (Galatians 3:1-2)?

As evangelicals we are confident we have the right answer to Paul's question. We are saved by the grace of God through faith. Then how are we perfected? The apostle continues:

> Are you so foolish? Having begun by the Spirit, are you now being perfected by the flesh? Did you suffer so many things in vain—if indeed it was in vain? So then, does He who provides you with the Spirit and works miracles among you, do it by the works of the Law, or by hearing with faith? (verses 3-5).

If all we are doing is preaching and teaching God's Word, then we can be replaced by a book or CD. You can also hear much better Christian music in your own home played on your surround-sound system recorded by artists in professional sound studios. According to George Barna, approximately 20 million Evangelical believers in the United States have figured that out and are indeed staying home.[9] That may seem to work for them, but where will the church be in the next generation?

Having the wrong goal is a major problem in Christian education. If we make knowledge an end in itself we will distort the very purpose for which it was intended. Paul warned us that "knowledge makes arrogant, but love edifies" (1 Corinthians 8:1). "The goal of our instruction is love from a pure heart and a good conscience and a sincere faith" (1 Timothy 1:5). The apostle is talking about the character of God, for God is love (1 John 4:8). If our instruction is right, we should be able to say, "I am more loving this year than last, and more patient, kind, gentle," and all the other fruit of the Spirit. If we can't say that, we are not growing, no matter how knowledgeable we are in God's Word.

What are we doing to help people connect with God in a living and liberating way? I invited local pastors to a free lunch during one of our Discipleship Counseling conferences. I asked them why we aren't doing more to help people individually. One pastor said, "Well, that can be messy—working with people!" I said, "Welcome to the ministry." Then he said, "What about lawsuits?" I asked if anyone knew of a pastor who has been sued for trying to help someone. Nobody did, but the pastor didn't stop. He said, "The seminary I graduated from told me to just preach the Word, and let counselors deal with such problems."

I doubt if that is what they said at his seminary. At least I hope that is not what they are teaching. We are all in this mess because of the fall, and God has only one answer and that is to get back in a righteous relationship with Him. Sharing a gospel tract is not enough, nor is the initial conversion experience, if we want to see any lasting fruit.

### We Need to Help People Connect with God

When people had problems 60 years ago they went to see their pastor or priest. Pastors made house calls, and they relied on God and His Word to counsel people. Those who wanted to help hurting people got their master of divinity degree and became pastors.

Then came the 1960s with the Vietnam War and free sex and drugs, and it took a toll on our marriages and families. In response to the overwhelming needs, Bible schools and seminaries started offering degreed programs on marriage and family counseling. For the sake of accreditation the professors needed to have their doctoral degree or at least a master's degree, but where did they get their degrees from? Christian schools? There were no Christian schools offering doctoral degrees in psychology or counseling in those days. Consequently, the Christian community was introduced to secular psychology, which helps us understand the natural person, but doesn't take into account the authority of God's Word or the reality of the spiritual world, nor does it include God in the process of counseling.

Those who want to counsel people today are inclined to get a degree in psychology. Presently there are far more students working for a degree in psychology than a degree in theology. Many are looking for answers for themselves. Theology is not perceived by many to be an answer, even by some Christians. For instance, a one-page article appeared in a leading Christian publication about a pastor who had an affair. The article ended by saying, "When are pastors going to realize that they need psychological help?" Are they implying that God isn't enough? That psychologists know something God doesn't know? I don't know of any secular psychological programs that are freeing people from lust, sexual addictions, or sexual identity confusions. They are helping them live with their sins! Secular psychologists don't hold to our standards of sexual purity. On the other hand our ministry sees God set people free from sexual strongholds on a regular basis.

I believe the church has the answer, but if we are not helping people connect with God we will see more and more drift away. Just telling them that their sins are forgiven and instructing them how to live will not be enough.

## We Need to Deal with Spiritual Bondage

There are myriads of problems plaguing believers, but let's just look at two. First, consider the need to forgive others from our hearts. When I was conducting Living Free in Christ conferences, I shared a message on what forgiveness is, why we need to do it, and how to do it. I always asked for a commitment at the end. Not wishing to publicly embarrass anyone, I only asked them to stand. In doing so they were saying to God, "Yes, there is one or more persons I need to forgive, and I am standing to say I'm going to do that, but I need the grace of God to forgive as I have been forgiven." At least 95 percent of the audience stood every time.

I am thankful for the opportunity to help people resolve this critical issue, but let me ask a question: Will those people be able to grow in the grace of God if they don't forgive? Should they partake in communion if they hold on to their bitterness? Nothing will keep a Christian more bound to their past than unforgiveness. God Himself will turn them over to the tormentors if they won't forgive from their hearts, but not because He doesn't love them. He convicts and disciplines those He loves.

Second, consider how many Christians are in bondage to lust, sexual addiction, or abuse. On November 21, 2003, I was watching the Sunday evening program *60 Minutes*. One segment was on "adult entertainment," which I didn't particularly care to watch, but I ended up downloading a hard copy of their report, because I was so astonished by what they said. In summary:

- Ten billion is spent every year on adult entertainment. "Reputable" firms like General Motors, most hotels, and Time Warner are cashing in because the profit margin is so high.

- There are 800 million rentals of adult videotapes and DVDs in video stores.

- In 2002 the porn industry produced 11,000 titles.

- The porn industry employs 12,000 people in California alone.

- Fifty percent of the guests at major hotels will use pay-per-view porn, which accounts for 75 percent of the hotels' video profits.

- Type in the word *sex* in a search engine like Google and you will get 180 million sites. From 2003 to 2008 that number quadrupled!

A report from the Centers for Disease Control from the year 2000 informs us,

> In the United States, more than 65 million people are currently living with an incurable sexually transmitted disease (STD). An additional 15 million people become infected with one or more STDs each year, roughly half of whom contract life-long infections (Cates, 1999).

Dave Foster, the child of a Presbyterian pastor, gained some fame as an actor, but wasn't acting when he made extra money as a male prostitute. Life in the gutter finally drove him to Christ, and he has become a powerful witness for sexual freedom and healing through his organization, Mastering Life Ministries. According to Dave, if there are sixteen people sitting in one pew in any church, two of them will be struggling with sexual identity. He is not suggesting that one in eight is gay—he is saying that one in eight has some mental confusion about their sexual orientation. Four of the sixteen people are sexual abuse victims. The "official" estimate is one out of every four women and one out of every seven men, but that is based only on what is reported, which makes the more likely scenario to be one out of every three women and one out of every four men.

In the same pew of sixteen people, an additional four will struggle with some form of sexual addiction, and that is true of every pew in your church. Those numbers would also be true if every person sitting on the pew was a pastor. Pastors are human beings just like the rest of us. I surveyed the student body of a good conservative seminary and found out that 60 percent of the male student body was presently feeling some sexual guilt. Of that group, 50 percent said they would take an elective that would train and help students and others overcome sexual bondage for credit if it were offered. Would you care to guess what happened when I showed the results to the dean?[10]

Nothing happened at the seminary, and very little happens when I share these statistics with pastors. Why not? Can people grow in their relationship with God with such unresolved problems? No, they can't! What then can we do? Discipleship by itself may not be enough. Besides, with the phenomenal growth of psychology we have almost lost the art of discipleship. In many cases discipleship ministries have degenerated into such basic questions as: What curriculum are you using and what program are you following? Programs and curriculum can't set people free no matter how biblical they are. Only Christ can do that.

### The Need for True Discipleship

Discipleship is not building my life into yours or you building your life into mine. It is building the life of Christ into one another under the authority of God's Word. To make someone a disciple of Christ we have to connect them to the Source of life that sets them free to become the person God intended them to be. When that happens, the Ten Commandments become the ten promises. They will have no other gods before them. They will not take the name of the Lord their God in vain. They will not commit adultery, murder, or steal.

Jesus said, "If you love me, you will keep My commandments" (John 14:15). Legalism is trying to keep His commandments, thus showing that we love Him. Grace incorporates the whole gospel and liberates the true disciple to love the Lord their God. And those who do will keep His commandments, because the love of God is flowing through them.

Jesus said, "My Father is glorified by this, that you bear much fruit, and so prove to be my disciples" (John 15:8). Thinking that we have to bear fruit is the wrong conclusion. If we want to bear fruit, we have to abide in Christ. The fruit is just the evidence that we are abiding in Christ. Do you want to be a disciple of Jesus and disciple others? Then abide in Christ, because apart from Him "you can do nothing" (John 15:5).

## Discussion Questions

1. What has been your personal struggle with legalism, and how has it affected you?

2. Why would someone prefer to live under the law?

3. Christians are called to live a righteous life. Is that more related to what we do, or who we are? Explain your reasoning.

4. How would you explain the whole gospel?

5. Why don't some believers know who they are in Christ?

6. Are you saved? Explain your answer.

7. Are you sanctified? Explain your answer.

8. In helping others, should we disciple them, counsel them, do inner healing, or deliver them?

9. Why do you think many Evangelical churches shy away from teaching about the kingdom of darkness, or trying to help those who are being held captive by Satan to do his will (2 Timothy 2:26)?

10. Why isn't getting the right information out to our people enough?

11. Other than unforgiveness and sexual sins, what other problems are Christians facing?

12. What is discipleship?

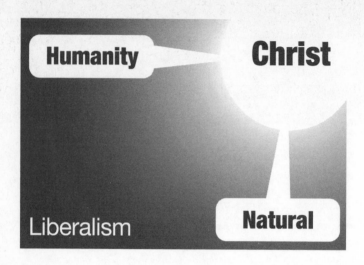

*See to it that no one takes you captive through philosophy and empty deception, according to the tradition of men, according to the elementary principles of the world, rather than according to Christ.*

Colossians 2:8

*He calls that philosophy worldly by which men who desire to be wise in earthly terms are seduced.[11]*

"Ambrosiaster's Commentary on the Letter to the Colossians"

*The enemy here is philosophy that believes that the power of God rises from natural things, that nothing can be made from nothing, that the soul cannot have a beginning or be mortal, that a virgin cannot conceive, or God be born of a man or die and rise again.[12]*

"Pelagius's Commentary on the Letter to the Colossians"

# Chapter Three

# Overcoming Liberalism

*A man has deprived himself of the best there is in the world who has deprived himself of this: a knowledge of the Bible...This book is the one supreme source of revelation, the revelation of the meaning in life, the nature of God, and the spiritual nature and need of men. It is a book which reveals every man to himself as a distinct moral agent, responsible not to men, not even to those men whom He has put over him in authority, but responsible through his own conscience to his Lord and Maker. Whenever a man sees this vision, he stands up a free man whatever may be the circumstances of his life.*

WOODROW WILSON

I was conducting a conference in Canada, when I got a message from a pastor's wife asking if I would spend some time with their 22-year-old son. I agreed to meet with him if they attended the conference with him. When we met for counseling, the young man said, "My mother is a Christian, but my father isn't." That turned out to be true. The father attended the whole conference and at the end made a decision for Christ. He later said, "I have been a pastor for over twenty-five years and I have five more years to go before retirement. In the end I will have five years of ministry!"

I always wondered why pastors stay in the church if they don't believe the Bible. Why don't they study psychology or sociology and find work in some kind of human services? So I asked him. He said, "Do you know who I have been counseling for the past twenty-five years? Castoffs from fundamental churches who have been beaten up spiritually. If that is the result of churches who translate the Bible literally, I wanted nothing to do with it." Sobering, isn't it?

I have heard people say they don't go to church because they don't need another guilt trip. But aren't we supposed to go to church to get *rid* of guilt? The emerging church, postmodernism, and liberalism are often reactionary movements to legalism. If we try to measure up to external standards by living under the law, we will become a driven person and fail miserably or be a hypocrite. Without the life of Christ to enable us to live a righteous life the alternative is to rebel against the law—because a rule without a relationship usually leads to rebellion.

If we can't live up to external standards we either do away with them ("I don't believe the Bible") or redefine biblical standards of conduct. In most cases liberal churches redefine marriage and sexuality, usually in the name of "love"—which is also redefined. The real issue isn't homosexuality, or what constitutes a marriage, or whether we should ordain a practicing homosexual. The real issue is the authority of God's Word. If we lose the Bible, we lose our way. There is nothing left, but "philosophy and empty deception…according to the elementary principles of the world, rather than according to Christ" (Colossians 2:8).

Mainline denominations were biblically conservative at one time, and they largely represented Protestantism in the West. Today their numbers are dropping precipitously. What led to their decline? Has academia replaced godliness? Has empirical research replaced divine revelation? Has the wisdom of this age usurped God's omniscience? Has our perspective replaced the divine perspective? Have we failed to make the gospel relevant to the needs of society? Many in the liberalism quadrant are not asking whether or not there is a God. The vast majority of Americans say they believe in God. They are asking, "So what?" Who wants to attend an irrelevant church that is bearing no fruit and then asks for ten percent of their income?

## Syncretism

Committed Christians working in cross-cultural ministries understand the problem of syncretism, which by definition means the combination of different forms of belief. For instance, missionaries in Third World countries lead people to Christ, but these new converts continue to see their quack doctors or shamans, thus combining spiritism with divine revelation. It's easier to see syncretism in other cultures than it is to see the problem in our own. Syncretism exists in the West when the church is married more to the world than it is to Christ.

The danger in this quadrant is to put more emphasis on empirical research (general revelation) than on special revelation (God's Word). There is an important place for general revelation and empirical research, because it helps us understand what is. Psalm 19:1 illustrates general revelation: "The heavens are telling of the glory of God; and their expanse is declaring the work of His hands."

There are four reasons why general revelation is not enough and why it must be subjected to special revelation. First, *special revelation (the Bible) is authoritative, whereas general revelation (nature) is illustrative.* Without special revelation to explain life and its meaning, we have no recourse but to fall back on philosophical speculation and scientific rationalism. Research may reveal what *is*, but it can't explain *why*.

Second, *empirical research leaves out the reality of the spiritual world by its very definition.* God does not submit to our methods of investigation or verification. We cannot scientifically prove the existence of God to the satisfaction of the skeptic. The Bible makes no attempt to prove itself. Those who come to God "must believe that He is and that He is a rewarder of those who seek Him" (Hebrews 11:6). Rest assured that Satan—the god of this world—is not going to cooperate with our research methods either. Satan operates under the cloak of deception and will not voluntarily reveal himself for our benefit.

Third, *the rational process of verification is always interpreted through the grid of our own cultural, educational, and personal experiences.* We naturally interpret what we observe from our own perspective, which we have a tendency to perpetuate even in Christian circles.

Finally, *God intended general revelation to be evaluated through the grid of special revelation.* A skeptic and a mature Christian can look at the same data, and draw different conclusions.

For instance, people all over the world hear "voices" in their head. This is not unknown to secular psychologists or psychiatrists. They interpret it as a chemical imbalance and medicate the "mentally ill."

A mature believer should respectfully ask more questions, such as "How can a chemical produce a personality or thought?" Or, "How can our neurotransmitters randomly create a thought that I am opposed to thinking? Is there a natural explanation for that? Are we dealing with mental illness? Or do such symptoms indicate a spiritual battle for the mind?" The apostle Paul speaks to this issue in 1 Timothy 4:1: "The Spirit explicitly says that in later times some will fall away from the faith, paying attention to deceitful spirits and doctrines of demons." Notice the strong linguistic emphasis. "The Spirit *explicitly* says." That is like saying, "Listen carefully. This is not Paul speaking. God is clearly telling you something you need to know, and He is not telling you by way of a parable. I am stating it plainly."

I have seen thousands set free in Christ from those demonic influences, and many of them experience for the first time the peace of God which surpasses all comprehension, guarding their hearts and their minds in Christ Jesus (Philippians 4:7). It is beyond my comprehension how God does that, but I know He does for those who will submit to Him and resist the devil. The following e-mail I received is a good example of one such victory.

> For years, ever since I was a teenager (I am now 36), I had these "voices" in my head. There were four in particular and sometimes what seemed loud choruses of them. When the subject of schizophrenia would come up on television or in a magazine I would think to myself, *I know I am not schizophrenic, but what is this in my head?* I was tortured, mocked, jeered—and every single thought I had was second-guessed. Consequently I had zero self-esteem. I often used to wish the voices would be quiet, and I always wondered if other people had this as well and if it was "common."

> When I started to learn from you about taking every thought captive to the obedience of Christ, and read about other people's experiences with these voices, I came to realize them for what they were, and I was able to make them leave. That was an amazing and beautiful thing, to be fully quiet in my mind after so many years of torment. I do not need to explain further all the wonderful things that come with this freedom of the mind—it is a blessing you seem to know well.

The secularist psychiatrist would likely respond by saying, "I gave my client antipsychotic medication and the voices receded." Did that actually cure the problem or narcotize it? Taking medication to quiet the voices is the same reason many people use drugs and drink alcohol. They have no mental peace so they drown out the thoughts with chemicals. I am certainly not against the proper use of medication. Taking a pill to cure our bodies is commendable, but taking a pill to cure our souls is deplorable—and may God give us the wisdom to know the difference.

If we fully understood natural law (what God has created) and divine revelation, they would not be incompatible academically, but our knowledge of both is incomplete. Science is mankind's attempt to understand natural law. (Those who have confidence in the ability of scientists to accurately explain nature should read a 50-year-old science book.) Theology is the Christian's attempt to systematize truth. The scientist and the theologian may be at odds with each other, but what God created and what God has revealed aren't. If you continue reading Psalm 19, notice what special revelation can accomplish in verses 7-9:

> The law of the LORD is perfect, *restoring the soul*: the testimony of the LORD is sure, *making wise the simple*. The precepts of the LORD are right, *rejoicing the heart*; the commandment of the LORD is pure, *enlightening the eyes*; the fear of the LORD is clean, enduring forever; the judgments of the LORD are true; they are righteous altogether.

## The Journey to Wholeness

Fernando Garzon's father came to the United States in order to attend medical school and later married a U.S. citizen. Fernando was brought up in a Christian home. Here is his story:

> I became a Christian when I was 16 years old and immediately got involved in various Bible studies and Christian fellowships. These were very good experiences for me, furnishing much love and support. In college I began encountering many friends who clearly needed some emotional healing. They went through deliverance, prayer sessions, and studied their Bibles, but they didn't seem to get better. That bothered me, because that was basically all I knew from a spiritual perspective about how they might get help. I was curious and began asking questions that most of my Christian friends couldn't answer.
>
> After college graduation, I began working at a psychiatric hospital to learn more about helping people. I thoroughly enjoyed the work and began considering a career as a psychologist. I eventually went to Fuller Seminary and received my doctorate in clinical psychology. While there, I learned a great deal more about what causes emotional stress and discovered strategies for helping people. Unfortunately, one thing I didn't learn was how to answer my initial questions about why spiritual interventions like deliverance,

Bible study, and prayer had been so limited in helpfulness with the people I'd known in college! Without clear answers, I began to de-emphasize the role of the spiritual in the healing process and to focus more on secular techniques. I might pray for my clients occasionally, but that was about the limit of my explicitly Christian interventions after graduate school.

The question of concrete, effective Christian interventions, however, continued to haunt me. I had plenty of excellent secular techniques at my disposal and some very good theology pertaining to integrating Christianity into my work, but the amount of concrete Christian intervention strategies I knew was dismal. Indeed, as I continued my clinical work, I started to ask myself serious questions as a Christian psychologist. If you're a Christian therapist, consider how the following scenario relates to you.

Suppose someone videotapes your work and that of a secular therapist who happens to be well-trained in how to sensitively handle religious issues in treatment. A born-again Christian walks into your office and wants Christianity actively integrated into treatment. Ten sessions are filmed. Let's say that same born-again Christian walks into the religiously sensitive therapist's office and ten sessions are also filmed. When someone watches both films, will they be able to tell who is the Christian therapist and who is the sensitively-trained secular therapist? Would there be enough concrete differences for an observer to say, "Yes, that's the Christian therapist, and that's the well-trained secular therapist."

I realized the only difference between us might be an opening prayer in which I asked God to guide the session or a closing prayer in which I summarized the issues the client brought in that day and asked God to help him. That was unsatisfactory for me. If those were the only overt Christian intervention strategies I used with Christian clients, then I hadn't learned very much that I didn't know before graduate school training! In short, if a Christian client wanted Jesus actively integrated into treatment, I had little to offer.

So I began asking the Lord to show me concrete Christian intervention strategies. Eventually I found Neil's first two books, *Victory Over the Darkness* and *The Bondage Breaker*. These books espoused approaches compatible with a well-researched clinical psychology called cognitive therapy, yet they were much broader in addressing a variety of areas consistent with a biblical worldview. Indeed, these books opened my eyes to an entirely different way of conceptualizing spiritual influences in therapy. They certainly were not the typical deliverance ministries I had been exposed to in my early Christian days. They had something more. Demons were not the major problem; rather, root issues and unresolved conflicts in our lives were the major problem. Based on my previous experiences (and now as a Christian psychologist), I could readily agree with that.

My journey was quite different from Fernando's. My ministry started with a good theological education, but I wasn't fully equipped to help people resolve their problems. I believed that Christ was the answer and that truth would set people free, but I didn't see the kind of results the Bible seemed to indicate. People had problems that I really didn't have answers for. When I was called to teach at Talbot School of Theology, I went there searching for answers.

I received permission to offer a master of theology elective and I felt like I was in the first grade in God's school, teaching kindergarten students. But the class grew from 18 the first year, to 23 the next year, then 35, then 65, then 150—and the last year it was offered, 250 students took a one-week intensive that included local pastors and Christian workers. I was seeing the lives of many students literally change as they discovered who they were in Christ and after they had resolved their personal and spiritual conflicts. That was when I first started to realize that defeated Christians simply didn't know who they were in Christ.

During those years God was bringing many wounded Christians with all kinds of problems to see me for personal counseling. Initially I would get stuck and not know where to go next. So I would stop and pray because God said that if we lacked wisdom we should ask for it. And I didn't do that privately. I told the inquirers that I didn't know what the answer was for their problem, but I believed God did. So I prayed out loud asking for guidance. I remember sitting in silence with one inquirer for about 15 minutes waiting upon the Lord.

Then one day the thought occurred to me that I was asking God to tell me the answer so I could tell them. That would make me a medium, and the apostle Paul wrote in 1 Timothy 2:5, "There is one God, and one mediator also between God and men, the man Christ Jesus." I could not find anywhere in the Bible that instructed me to function like a medium. So I thought, *Why don't I have them pray and ask the Lord?*

I can't think of one concept that has affected my understanding and method of doing ministry more than that simple concept. Keep in mind that every Christian is a child of God and we all have the same access to our heavenly Father. I believe in intercessory prayer, but that was never intended by God to replace the individual's responsibility to pray.

To illustrate, suppose you have two sons and the younger son is always going to his older brother with a request, "Would you go ask Dad if I can have $10 so I can go to the movies tonight?" Would you accept that as a parent—a secondhand relationship with one of your own children? Is that happening in our churches?

One afternoon I wrote out some simple petitions that the inquirer could pray and I tried it in counseling.[13] I was totally amazed at what happened. God showed them. I began to realize that whenever I attempted to help another individual there were always three of us present, and there is a role that God and only God can play in the other person's life.[14] I can't set a captive free and I can't mend broken hearts, but God can. And that is why Jesus came, according to Luke 4:17-19:

> The book of the prophet Isaiah was handed to Him. And He opened the book and found the place where it was written, "The Spirit of the Lord is upon Me, because He anointed Me to preach the Gospel to the poor. He sent Me to proclaim release to the captives, and recovery of sight to the blind, to set free those who are downtrodden, to proclaim the favorable year of the Lord."

## Having the Right Psychology

By definition, psychology is a study of the soul. I am certainly not speaking against psychology, but I am not in agreement with secular psychology, just like I am not in agreement with liberal theology. Secular psychology makes sense if all you are doing is studying fallen humanity and explaining its flesh patterns. The general theory of counseling is not complicated. The goal is to develop skills like empathy, congruence, concreteness, and so on—which are just good pastoral skills. The purpose is to gain the clients' confidence, draw out their life story, explain why they are not feeling and doing so well, offer better ways of thinking and living, and then help them cope with their situation. Many people won't submit to such an examination by another person unless they are somewhat desperate or their problems have already been exposed.

Secular psychologists can't accomplish any more than that, because they have no gospel and no God to lead them. The difference between secular and Christian psychology is not just a question of message, but also one of methodology. I can't fix your past, and neither does God. He sets you free from it. Most people are reticent to disclose themselves just to gain some understanding why they are screwed up, but almost everyone will self-disclose if God is convicting them for the purpose of resolving the problem.

## A Ministry of Reconciliation

God knows everything about us and He is the answer to our problems... so why aren't we including Him in the process? When I finally learned to do so, my ministry was transformed. It was no longer a question of learning better skills and counseling techniques. I began to see counseling as an encounter with God. Now I start my ministry with another by asking the inquirer what they are struggling with, and I listen to their story. I have learned over the years that the presenting problem is almost always a symptom of an underlying root issue, which God already knows. Then I ask, "Would you like to resolve this?" Nobody has ever said no. Then I say, "With your permission I would like to lead you through some steps to freedom in Christ." Again, nobody has ever said no.

The "Steps to Freedom in Christ" are mainly petitions that the inquirer prays, asking God to reveal to them issues that are critical in terms of their relationship with Him, including false guidance, deception, unforgiveness, rebellion, pride, sin, and issues handed down by parents.

Suppose someone comes to see his pastor, who ascertains that the primary origin of the person's problem was an abusive parent. So he explains what forgiveness is and how to forgive that parent from the heart, and the person chooses to do so. That will resolve a major conflict in the person's life, but is that enough? No, not in most cases. When they pray and ask God who they need to forgive, that parent will likely be the first person they mention, but chances are another 20 names will come out. How much have you helped them if they only forgive the one parent and not the others that need to be forgiven? Additionally, an abusive childhood can spin off a lot of other problems including a poor sense of worth (a symptom), rebelliousness, sexual promiscuity, and so on. God knows all that, and those issues will surface when the inquirer goes through the Steps.

I am always amazed as to what comes up when I take people through the Steps. I regularly hear people say, "I have never shared this with anyone ever before." That is not because I am a good counselor and they are not sharing the information with me to gain some understanding. They are sharing it with God to resolve their problem. You never have to point out the other person's sin. God will do that, and when the conviction comes from Him, it comes with the power to let the sin go and be absolved. The process helps people get in touch with the ugliest part of their lives, and they thank you for helping them do so. I have never seen anyone regret this encounter with God. That is what the apostle Paul alludes to in 2 Corinthians 7:9-10:

> I now rejoice, not that you were made sorrowful, but that you were made sorrowful to the point of repentance; for you were made sorrowful according to the will of God, so that you might not suffer loss in anything through us. For the sorrow that is according to the will of God produces a repentance *without regret*, leading to salvation, but the sorrow of the world produces death.

### The Effectiveness of Discipleship Counseling

Discipleship counseling is a ministry of reconciliation in which the counselor helps the person remove the barriers to their intimacy with God. How effective is this process? There have been several exploratory studies that have shown promising results regarding the effectiveness of the Steps to Freedom in Christ. Judith King, a Christian therapist, did three pilot studies in 1996. All three of these studies were performed on participants who attended a "Living Free in Christ" conference and were led through the Steps to Freedom in Christ during it.*

The first study involved 30 participants who took a ten-item questionnaire before completing the Steps. The questionnaire was re-administered three months after their participation. The questionnaire assessed for levels of depression, anxiety, inner conflict, tormenting thoughts, and addictive

---

* The "Living Free in Christ" conference is now available as a curriculum entitled *Freedom in Christ: A Small Group Bible Study* (Gospel Light Publications, 2008). It has a Leaders' Guide with all the messages written out, which the leaders can teach themselves, a Learner's Guide for each participant that includes the Steps to Freedom, and a DVD with 12 messages given by me, should the leader prefer the course to be taught that way.

behaviors. The second study involved 55 participants who took a 12-item questionnaire before completing the Steps, and it was then re-administered three months later. The third pilot study involved 21 participants who also took a 12-item questionnaire before receiving the Steps and then again three months afterward. The following table illustrates the percentage of improvement for each category.

|  | Depression | Anxiety | Inner conflict | Tormenting thoughts | Addictive behavior |
|---|---|---|---|---|---|
| Pilot study 1 | 64% | 58% | 63% | 82% | 52% |
| Pilot study 2 | 47% | 44% | 51% | 58% | 43% |
| Pilot study 3 | 52% | 47% | 48% | 57% | 39% |

Research was also conducted by the Board of the Ministry of Healing based in Tyler, Texas. The study completed at Tyler, Texas, was in cooperation with a doctoral student at Regent University under the supervision of Fernando Garzon, doctor of psychology.* Most people attending a "Living Free in Christ" conference can work through the repentance process on their own using the Steps to Freedom in Christ. In our experience about 15 percent can't, because of difficulties they have experienced. The people were offered a personal session with a trained encourager. They were given a pre-test before a Step session and a post-test three months later with the following results given in percentage of improvement:

|  | Oklahoma City, OK | Tyler, TX |
|---|---|---|
| Depression | 44% | 52% |
| Anxiety | 45% | 44% |
| Fear | 48% | 49% |
| Anger | 36% | 55% |
| Tormenting thoughts | 51% | 27% |
| Negative habits | 48% | 43% |
| Sense of self-worth | 52% | 40% |

The Steps to Freedom in Christ lead people to submit to God and resist

---

* The Board of the Ministry of Healing is chaired by Dr. George Hurst, who previously directed the University of Texas Health Center at Tyler, Texas. The Oklahoma and Texas data were combined together in a manuscript that was published by the *Southern Medical Journal*.

the devil (James 4:7). An encounter with God involves discipleship, coun-seling, inner healing, and deliverance from the evil one. We have learned how to do that without ever losing control in a session—even in the most severe cases. The process combines discipleship with counseling, which are the same ministries in the Bible. If you are a good discipler you are also a good counselor, and vice-versa. This is clearly the case when the counselor is doing cognitive therapy from a Christian perspective.

## Beyond Cognitive Therapy

Cognitive therapy is the most accepted method of counseling in the United States, both secular and sacred. The concept is not complicated. People are doing what they are doing and feeling what they are feeling because of what they have chosen to think or believe. Therefore, if you want to change what people are doing and feeling, what should you change? You should help them change what they believe or think. Isn't that repentance—which literally means a "change of mind?"

When I taught a doctor of ministry class at Regent University, Dr. Gar-zon asked if I would be willing to conduct research on the participating students. The class was a one-week intensive on discipleship counseling, lasting nine hours every day for five days. The students were led through the Steps near the end of the class. The class also included doctor of psy-chology students and master of divinity students—about forty in all. Keep in mind that these students did not represent the general population, since they were all committed Christians doing graduate work. Besides, most students take a class to fulfill a degree requirement and hopefully gain some insight to enhance their ministry, and not necessarily to have their life changed.

The students took pre-tests Monday morning at the beginning of the class, and Friday afternoon at the end of the class. They also took the same tests three weeks later. Every change in scale was statistically significant. Dr. Garzon reported the results in a paper that was published in the *Journal of Psychology and Theology*, which is published by Rosemead Graduate School of Psychology at Biola University. The school asked Dr. Garzon how I could explain such results. In other words, what was I doing beyond cognitive therapy? That is a good question. Their point was, I taught the students the truth, they believed the truth, and the truth set them free. End of story…or is it?

## *Limitations of Cognitive Therapy*

When Dr. Garzon relayed the question to me, I said that three issues come to mind. First, cognitive therapy is practiced by Christian and secular therapists, and when used effectively it does bring about brief changes in mood and behavior, but it doesn't change who the client is. Christians have the advantage because they have divinely inspired truth to work with. However, even if you use the words of Christ in cognitive therapy without the *life* of Christ, you will not be very effective in producing lasting change. As I mentioned in the previous chapter, correct information is not enough. When I say the life of Christ, I am not referring to the physical manifestation of God 2000 years ago—I am talking about the life of Christ that is in every believer.

The apostle Paul wrote, "I have been crucified with Christ; and it is no longer I who live, but Christ lives in Me; and the life which I now live in the flesh I live by faith in the Son of God, who loved me and gave Himself up for me" (Galatians 2:20). "Set your mind on the things above, not on the things that are on earth. For you have died and your life is hidden with Christ in God" (Colossians 3:2-3). Jesus is not just our helper. He is our *life*.

Second, you will not see the kind of results mentioned above using cognitive therapy if you don't take into account the reality of the spiritual world. If people are paying attention to deceiving spirits, you cannot resolve that by just submitting to God, without resisting the devil. I have often been asked how one can discern whether a problem is spiritual or psychological. Such a question presupposes a false dichotomy. Every problem includes the psychological because every problem includes our minds, emotions, and will. Every problem is also spiritual. There is no time or place when God is not present. In fact God "upholds all things by the word of His power" (Hebrews 1:3). God is the ultimate reality, and if He somehow disappeared, so would everything else. In addition, there is no time when it is safe to take off the armor of God, because there is no place or time where one is spiritually safe. The only sanctuary we have is our spiritual position in Christ.

There is always the possibility of being tempted, accused, and deceived, and that happens even in church buildings. If we accept that, then we will stop polarizing into psycho-therapeutic ministries that ignore the reality of the spiritual world, or into some kind of narrowly focused deliverance ministry that overlooks the individual's responsibility to submit to God and resist the devil.

Think of a person being a house where the garbage hasn't been taken out in months. That will attract a lot of flies. The answer is not to study the flight patterns of the flies, determine their names and rank, and cast them out. The answer is to get rid of the garbage, which is the responsibility of those we are trying to help. Repentance and faith in God have always been the answers, and they will remain the only answers until Christ comes back.

A Christian counselor shared with me why he was attending my class. He said, "I have been counseling for 15 years, and have never seen any evidence of the demonic in my counseling practise. But I have been reading about the New Age and I suspect that I will have to deal with it sometime in the future and I want to be prepared." A month later he wrote me a letter. "After the conference I returned to my practice and found that almost every one of my clients was being deceived and so was I."

Why didn't he see it before? The same reason I didn't see it the first few years of my ministry. If counselors are only seeking to understand, explain, and help people cope by caring for them, they will likely never see any demonic opposition. If a pastor is only teaching and preaching to people, it is also unlikely that they will ever see any opposition. Only when you seek resolution do you start to see the opposition.

Third, I am not the Wonderful Counselor. I didn't set that class free, neither did the Steps to Freedom in Christ. Who set them free was God. What set them free was their choice to repent and believe.

Suppose you were lost in a maze? Would you want a mazeologist to explain to you the intricacies of the maze and give you coping skills in order to survive? Would you want a legalistic preacher to scold you for getting lost in the first place? I think you would want to know the way, the truth, and the life.

I have a theory. I believe God made some people smart and others not so smart. As for those of us who may think we are smart, don't we have an obligation to make the plan of Christian living so simple that the simplest of God's creatures can enter into it? I think we do, but we dare not be simplistic. Salvation and the path back to God is not reserved for the intelligent only. "Believe in the Lord Jesus Christ and you will be saved" is not that complicated.

There are a million ways you could have sinned, but the answer is the same. There are a million ways you could have been abused. You can forgive your offender as Christ has forgiven you, accept His provision to be a new creation in Christ, and be free from your past. We are all in this mess because of the fall. You just have to be convinced that reconciliation with God is the answer. Many people have given up on God because they have never been fully reconciled to Him through faith and genuine repentance. Consequently, liberal churches have turned to natural and social sciences for enlightenment and to the government to be the provider.

## Recovery in Christ

Another way to illustrate how much we have been influenced by the world can be seen by taking a closer look at recovery programs for addicts and alcoholics. The popular 12-Step program began with the Oxford group, which originally had six steps. It was a Christ-centered Presbyterian program that bore fruit. Others took note and wanted to use the program, but didn't want to embrace Christ. Six more steps were added, the concept of God was replaced by a "higher power," and it ceased being a Christian ministry. The "Big Book" replaced the Bible.

The turbulent 1960s brought to the surface a number of Christians needing help to overcome addictive behaviors, and the church responded. Just like we tried to "Christianize" secular psychology, we tried to "Christianize" secular recovery programs, and with the programs came a lot of beliefs that aren't consistent with Scripture. Let me name a few:

1. *They instruct participants to work the program, because the program works.* That is not true. There is no program that can set anyone free. The reason the original six steps worked was because of Christ, not because of the program.

2. *They share that alcoholism is a disease and incurable.* Once you are an addict, you will always be an addict. That is bad theology that sounds like once a sinner, always a sinner. That is not true either. Once we were sinners, but now we are saints who sin. You can't expect to live a righteous life if your core identity is still that of a sinner. Blaming addictions on a disease is supposed to make people feel better about themselves, but for many it merely absolves them from assuming their responsibility to live a righteous life. Sin is *not* a disease. Sin is what separates us from God when we are sinners, and sin is what keeps us from an intimate relationship with Him when we become His children.

3. *They introduce themselves as addicts, alcoholics, co-addicts, and co-alcoholics.* Instead, shouldn't the Christian say, "Hi, I'm Neil— I'm a child of God who is struggling with a certain flesh pattern, but I am learning how to overcome my addiction by the grace of God." Reinforcing a failure identity is counterproductive to becoming complete in Christ.

4. *Their goal is sobriety.* If abstinence were the goal of Christianity, then Ephesians 5:18 would read, "Be not drunk with wine, therefore stop drinking." The apostle Paul has a different alternative: "Be filled with the Spirit." "I say, walk by the Spirit, and you will not carry out the desire of the flesh" (Galatians 5:16). What happens if you take alcohol away from someone addicted to it? You have a dry drunk, and the person will likely be more miserable than they were before. You just took away their means of coping without giving them a better option. Have you ever tried to take an old bone away from a dog? You will have a dogfight. Try throwing them a steak, and they will voluntarily spit out the old bone.

5. *They talk about dual diagnosis, but in reality there is a multiple diagnosis.* Show me anyone who is addicted to anything and I will show you someone who has a poor sense of worth, who is depressed, anxious, fearful, ashamed, angry, and bitter. Do you think you can resolve all that plus their relational problems at home by simply taking away their chemical of choice? Additionally, most people who are seeking treatment for chemical addiction are also sexually addicted, and in many cases that is not even addressed.

6. *Finally, if you attend one of these self-help groups you will hear phrases like "You have to get rid of that stinking thinking" or, "Don't pay attention to that 'committee' in your head."* Most recovery programs are not taking into account the reality of the spiritual world, and they don't acknowledge or understand the spiritual battle going on for minds. (Have you ever tried to not think sexual thoughts or tempting thoughts? Did that work?)

## "Wholistic" Health

The point I am trying to make is that we have a *whole* God who deals with the *whole* person, and He takes into account all reality all the time. As Christian doctors, psychologists, nutritionists, and pastors we should think "wholistically" from a biblical perspective. Western medicine has focused primarily on the cure of illnesses and the patching up of physical wounds. Good science is the guiding principle. Curing an illness, however, does not necessarily promote good health, just like trying not to think bad thoughts doesn't produce mental health. Doctors are telling us that most of their clients are sick for psychosomatic reasons, that can be resolved through genuine repentance and faith in God.

Consider Nancy, who is 50 years old and exhibits many maladaptive psychological, physical, and spiritual symptoms. She feels lethargic about life, struggles with interpersonal relationships at home, and doesn't seem to connect at church. She makes an appointment to see her doctor, who discovers that her blood-sugar levels are high. In spite of the fact that Nancy is more than 50 pounds overweight, the doctor doesn't question her about her eating habits or lack of exercise. Her spiritual condition isn't considered as an option for treatment, so the doctor gives Nancy a written prescription for an oral diabetes medication to treat her pre-diabetic symptoms.

Nancy dutifully takes her medication and makes an appointment to see her pastor. He listens patiently to her struggle with depression and family problems. He asks about her prayer and devotional life, which are virtually nonexistent. He suggests that she spend more time with God on a daily basis and recommends a good book to partially replace her television "addiction." Meanwhile she continues her same eating habits and tries to improve her spiritual disciplines.

The medication for her pre-diabetic condition gives her chronic indigestion, so she starts taking an H2 blocker that reduces her digestive symptoms, but now her stomach acid, which was low to begin with, is practically nonexistent. Consequently, she's not digesting food as well, which reduces her nutritional input. The medication also puts more stress on her kidneys and, with her low estrogen level, she gets a urinary tract infection.

Her doctor puts Nancy on antibiotics for her infection, but that lowers her immune system and kills all the beneficial bacteria in her colon. The result is a bad case of the flu that she can't seem to overcome and constant gas from a colon imbalance.

She starts taking antihistamines for a sinus infection and her doctor recommends a hysterectomy to solve her urinary tract problem. The advice seems logical, so Nancy has the surgery and starts taking synthetic hormones, which make her feel depressed and weepy. She sees a psychiatrist who writes out a prescription for Prozac to treat her depression. Nancy is now taking a diabetic medicine, an H2 blocker, antihistamines, synthetic hormones, and Prozac. She's exhausted all the time, mentally flaky, emotionally withdrawn, and waiting for the next health problem to hit—which it will!

Let's start over again. Instead of seeing her doctor, Nancy decides to confide in a good friend at church. Her friend asks Nancy about her past and present lifestyle. The encourager senses that Nancy has some unresolved personal and spiritual issues and invites her to attend a small group that is going to start a Freedom in Christ class. Nancy's inclination is to decline the offer, because another night out sounds like too much work for someone so exhausted. Her friend reminds her that it would be good to get away from family responsibilities once a week and do something for herself for a change.

Reluctantly, she agrees to come to the Bible study. Her friend also recognizes that Nancy needs a lifestyle change, and invites her to come with her to Curves and start an exercise program that isn't too extreme. She meets a new friend at the Freedom in Christ class, who shares how she lost several pounds just by eating smarter. They agree to meet and discuss proper nutrition.

Several months later, Nancy has found her freedom in Christ and discovered what it means to be a child of God. With the encouragement of her friend, she has stuck it out at Curves and her energy level has increased significantly, due partly to her new eating habits. She has lost 20 pounds and her blood sugar level is normal. She has made some new friends at Curves and at the small-group Bible study.

There is no one-dimensional answer for life. The right prescription calls for proper rest, exercise, diet, and righteous living with God. The tragedy is that one can faithfully attend a dead church for years and never hear the good news and encounter the real Christ. The liberal church may have failed you, but Christ hasn't. The invitation is always open. Come to Me, He says, "all who are weary and heavy-laden, and I will give you rest." (Matthew 11:28).

## Discussion Questions

1. Liberalism seldom starts in the pew. It usually begins in higher education and seminaries. Why do you think that is the case?

2. What is syncretism? Can you give illustrations from your own culture, besides those in the book?

3. Why shouldn't we give equal prominence to general revelation (what we observe in nature) in comparison to special revelation (God's Word)?

4. Is there conflict between science and divine revelation? Should there be?

5. How has your journey to wholeness been different or similar to Dr. Garzon's and the author's journeys?

6. What, if anything, is potentially wrong with secular psychology?

7. What stood out the most to you when reading about the method of discipleship counseling and the results?

8. According to the author, why isn't cognitive therapy as presently understood enough?

9. What is missing in secular recovery programs?

10. Why do you think we are seldom given a wholistic answer? Why do we need one?

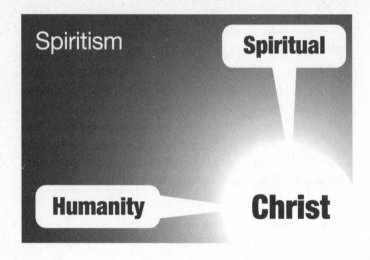

*The Spirit explicitly says that in later times some will fall away from the faith, paying attention to deceitful spirits and doctrines of demons.*

1 TIMOTHY 4:1

*There were prophets a very long time ago more ancient than these who are reputed to be philosophers, blessed and righteous and dear to God. They spoke by a divine Spirit, and they oracularly predicted future events which are now taking place. They are truly called prophets…Past events and events now taking place compel us to agree with what was spoken by them. Furthermore they deserved to be believed because of the miracles which they performed, since they were glorifying God the Creator and Father of the universe and they were announcing the Christ coming from Him, His Son. The false prophets who were filled with the deceitful and filthy spirit never did nor now do this. They dare to work various supposed miracles in order to impress men, and they glorify the spirits and demons of deceit.*[15]

JUSTIN MARTYR, "DIALOGUE WITH TRYPHO"

# Chapter Four

# Overcoming Spiritism

*The devil, however, as he is the apostate angel, can only go to this length, as he did at the beginning, to deceive and lead astray the mind of man into disobeying the commandments of God, and gradually to darken the hearts.*

IRENAEUS, *AGAINST HERESIES* V.24.3

As we consider the next two quadrants that make up the church, keep in mind there are many godly and fruitful expressions of Christianity that place more emphasis on the reality of the spiritual world than those in the previous quadrants we examined. Part of the church needs to be sensitized to the reality of the spiritual world and part of the church needs to be *de*sensitized to it.

I mentioned earlier that John Wimber was a good representative of this quadrant. John was an adjunct professor at Fuller Seminary and co-taught, with Peter Wagner, a class on signs and wonders. John was the founder of the Vineyard Movement and wrote two popular books, entitled *Power Evangelism* and *Power Healing*. He began his ministry as an Evangelical and later sought the fullness of the Spirit.

John and I were both making presentations at a conference and I mentioned to him my appreciation for his two books. But I had a couple of questions I hoped he would help me with. First, I thought it was one thing for him to move into a greater understanding of the Holy Spirit's work, and another for young converts who were not theologically grounded as he was. John responded, "That's the biggest problem we have as a movement. Everybody wants the power, but not enough want to study God's Word and become disciplined in their spiritual walk." John Wimber was an honest man, and in the latter years of his ministry he focused more on personal holiness.

Second, I used an exhaustive concordance to find every use of the words *signs* and *wonders* either by themselves or together with each other in the New Testament. When the context was referring to the latter days of the church, every usage of these two words was assigned to a false teacher or prophet. I asked John if he was aware of that. He was surprised to hear it, but sobered as well, and he invited me to speak at their annual convention, which I did.

### Evaluating Signs and Wonders

God has made His presence known through signs and wonders, and He may still do so. Consider the early church's experience in Acts 2:43, "Everyone kept feeling a sense of awe; and many wonders and signs were taking place through the apostles." However, we have an obligation to teach that the devil may also use signs and wonders, and we need to exercise discernment as to the source. Jesus warned us about this possibility in Matthew 7:21-23:

> Not everyone who says to me, "Lord, Lord," will enter the kingdom of heaven, but he who does the will of My Father who is in heaven will enter. Many will say to Me on that day, "Lord, Lord, did we not prophesy in Your name, and in Your name cast out demons, and in Your name perform many miracles?" And then I will declare to them, "I never knew you; Depart from Me, you who practice lawlessness."

Jesus also said to the Pharisees and Sadducees, "An evil and adulterous generation seeks after a sign" (Matthew 16:4). A sign only points to something and should never be considered an end in itself, just like knowledge is not an end in itself (which is the problem of legalism). Righteousness is the ultimate test of orthodoxy. Just be apprised that the devil can and does perform signs and wonders. To illustrate, I received the following e-mail from a former psychic:

> I just finished your DVD based on *The Bondage Breaker*, in which you discuss deception and the lure of knowledge and power. As a former channeler let me share how psychics work. They only know what they are told by demons, and demons only know that which they have observed or what has been spoken out. For example, if my husband and I were talking about going to Hawaii for a vacation and I went to see a psychic, they might say something like, "I see

you on vacation somewhere warm. There is a beach and sand. You're with a tall dark man—your husband. I believe it is Hawaii."

Of course anyone would be impressed (deceived) by that apparent knowledge of the unknown. I worked as a psychic and ran in circles with those who were very "gifted" in that area. I got hooked at an early age. They were always able to tell me what had been spoken out and even some things that looked like they might happen. For example, I have always been a writer (and musician) and they would tell me that I was talented and would succeed in both areas, but everyone (even non-channelers) told me that because of my passion for writing. It was an obvious gift, and I was persistent. So of course I would find ways to get published, and eventually that happened. It did not happen in the time frame they predicted, because that was unknown to them—so they bluffed their way through. Some of their future predictions happened and some of them didn't. What I did notice was that a psychic could give intimate details about a person's past, but not their future. That was always vague and often untrue in the unfolding events.

The key to becoming a good psychic is submitting to "the spirit," which I was constantly told. I had the "gift," but it would be stronger/better if I'd only submit more. I was told I was rebelling from my "gift" when I resisted. God is gracious and merciful. There was always something (the Lord, no doubt) that held me back to fully committing, and even though I was not a believer I eventually saw the inconsistency and deception, and slowly stepped away. After becoming a believer and going through your Steps to Freedom I was set free from my involvement in these areas and saw the entire deception clearly.

## False Guidance

I pray that every believer could see the deception clearly, but that is not the case. A seminary student stopped by my office to tell me he was having difficulty getting to school on time. What should have been a 5-minute drive had lengthened to 45 minutes because a voice in his mind kept telling him to turn at various intersections. Not wanting to disobey what he perceived to be the "still, small voice of God," he was treated to a tour of the city almost every morning.

A pastor's wife, desperately needing the comfort of the Holy Spirit and desiring His leading, passively believed that whatever entered her mind was from God. She soon found herself bound by fear and plagued by condemning thoughts.

A seminary professor's wife confided in me that she wasn't sure she was a Christian. I was shocked by her assessment since she was a lovely Christian woman. I said, "If you aren't a Christian, I'm in deep trouble. Why would you believe that?" She replied, "When I start to read my Bible I have these foul thoughts go through my mind and I struggle with blasphemous mental thoughts when I go to church. How could I be a Christian and have those thoughts?"

"Those are not your thoughts," I responded. "According to Romans 7:22, your inner person (the real you) joyfully concurs with the law of God. Did you personally choose to think those thoughts?" I asked.

"Of course not," she said.

"Then why do you believe those are your thoughts?" I asked.

If those were her thoughts, then what would she conclude about herself? That she was probably not a Christian, because how can a real Christian have thoughts like that? Thinking herself to be evil, she subsequently questioned her salvation.

Many Christians struggle with thoughts that aren't their own. John Wesley wrote,

> Do not hastily ascribe things to God. Do not easily suppose dreams, voices, impressions, visions or revelations to be from God. They may be from Him. They may be from nature. They may be from the devil. Therefore, do not believe every spirit, but try the spirits, whether they are from God.[16]

## The Father of Lies vs. the Spirit of Truth

Martin Wells Knapp, cofounder of the Wesleyan Church, wrote the book *Impressions: From God or Satan, How to Know the Difference.*[17] Writing at the end of the nineteenth century, Knapp attempts to distinguish between the lies of Satan and the leading of the Holy Spirit. Quoting Hannah Whitall Smith, he offers this insight:

> There are the voices of evil and deceiving spirits who lie in wait to entrap every traveler entering the higher regions of spiritual life. In the same epistle that tells us we are seated in heavenly places

in Christ, we are also told that we will have to fight with spiritual enemies. These spiritual enemies, whoever or whatever they may be, must necessarily communicate with us by means of our spiritual faculties. And their voices, as the voice of God, are an inward impression made upon our spirit. Therefore, just as the Holy Spirit may tell us by impressions what the will of God is concerning us, so also will these spiritual enemies tell us by impression what is their will concerning us, though not of course giving it their name.[18]

In the same book, Knapp wrote, "Oh, that I could write one message with the point of a diamond upon the heart of every Christian. It should be this: Be sure that the slightest impression upon your heart disposing you to do Christian work has a divine stamp. And then obey it at whatever cost."

I have shared with many tormented people who fear they're going crazy, that what they are really experiencing is a battle for their minds. They often respond, "Praise the Lord—someone understands." It's liberating to know the truth, because if people are mentally ill for some neurological reason, the prognosis is not very good. But if there is a battle going on for their minds, they can win that war.

## Satan's Strategies

One of Satan's obvious strategies is temptation. Don't confuse the process of temptation with the objects he may use. Satan used a piece of fruit to tempt Eve, but it was his deceptive words that led to her downfall. Every tempting thought is an attempt to get us to live our lives independently of God, and we are most vulnerable when the temptation is associated with legitimate needs. The question is, will these needs be met by living independently of God or by living dependently upon our heavenly Father who "will supply all your needs according to His riches in glory in Christ Jesus" (Philippians 4:19)? Satan wants to destroy the lifestyle of Christ-dependency and rob us of our victory. Self-sufficiency is the greatest threat to our sufficiency in Christ (see 2 Corinthians 3:5-6).

Satan is also the *accuser of the brethren*. His initial thrust is to tempt us, and then when we give in to the temptation, he accuses us. Satan can't do anything about our identity or position in Christ, but if he can get us to believe it isn't true, we will live as though it isn't true. The father of lies keeps many Christians from experiencing the joy of their salvation. Entertaining thoughts like *I'm stupid, I can't, I'm no good, God doesn't love me,* or *I'm different from others* will keep many people in bondage or questioning their sanity if they believe his lies. The apostle John writes in Revelation 12:10-11,

> Now the salvation, and the power, and the kingdom of our God and the authority of His Christ have come, and the accuser of our brethren has been thrown down, who accuses them before our God day and night. And they overcame him because of the blood of the lamb and because of the word of their testimony, and they did not love their life even to death.

## Deception

The most insidious strategy of Satan is *deception*: "[He] does not stand in the truth, because there is no truth in him. Whenever he speaks a lie, he speaks from his own nature; for he is a liar, and the father of lies" (John 8:44). Satan is determined to undermine the work of the Holy Spirit, who was sent to lead us into all truth.

The only thing a Christian ever has to admit to is the truth, which is never our enemy. Scripture teaches that truth is the liberating agent:

> If you continue in My word, then you are truly disciples of Mine; and you will know the truth, and the truth will make you free (John 8:31-32).

> I am the way, and the truth, and the life; no one comes to the Father but through Me (John 14:6).

> I do not ask You to take them out of the world, but to keep them from the evil one. They are not of the world, even as I am not of the world. Sanctify them in the truth; Your word is truth (John 17:15-17).

When we put on the armor of God, the first thing we do is gird our loins with truth (Ephesians 6:14). Truth is our first line of defense against deception. This was dramatically illustrated when God struck down Ananias and Sapphira. Why the severity of the discipline? Because they were living a lie. Peter exposed the source of the lie when he asked, "Why has Satan filled your heart to lie to the Holy Spirit?" (Acts 5:3).

God knows Satan's primary strategy. He knows that if Satan can operate undetected in any home, church, family, committee, or person, and get people to believe a lie, he can exert some control over their lives. We must win the battle for our minds if we are going to be led by God. Paul wrote, "We are destroying speculations and every lofty thing raised up against the knowledge of God, and we are taking every thought [*noema*] captive to the obedience of Christ" (2 Corinthians 10:5).

## Taking Thoughts Captive

An unwillingness to forgive others may afford Satan his greatest access to the church. Paul wrote,

> One whom you forgive anything, I forgive also; for indeed what I have forgiven, if I have forgiven anything, I did it for your sakes in the presence of Christ, so that no advantage would be taken of us by Satan, for we are not ignorant of his schemes [*noema*] (2 Corinthians 2:10-11).

Jesus admonished us to forgive from our heart—else He has no recourse but to hand us over to the torturers (Matthew 18:34). The word for *torturer* is used throughout the New Testament for "spiritual torment." Bitter people set themselves up for personal torment and spiritual defeat. Jesus urged us to forgive others as He has forgiven us in order to be free from our past and free from demonic attack.

Satan, the architect of torment, is also battling for the mind of the unbeliever:

> Their minds [*noema*] were hardened; for until this very day at the reading of the old covenant the same veil remains unlifted, because it is removed in Christ…Even if our gospel is veiled, it is veiled to those who are perishing, in whose case the god of this world has blinded the minds [*noema*] of the unbelieving so that they might not see the light of the gospel of the glory of Christ, who is the image of God (2 Corinthians 3:14, 4:3-4).

As I was counseling a deeply troubled young man, I asked him about his personal relationship with God. Realizing he had none, I shared God's plan of salvation. I asked him if he'd like to make a decision for Christ, and he said he would.

When he started to pray, his mind blanked out and I could sense the presence of evil in the room. I said, "There's a battle going on for your mind.

I'm going to pray and read Scripture. As soon as you can, call upon the name of the Lord." After about five minutes, one word at a time came out, "Lord…Jesus…I…need…you." The moment he said it, he collapsed in his chair. Then he looked up with tears in his eyes and said, "I'm free."

Did you notice in several of the above Scripture verses the word *noema* was in parentheses? The English words, *schemes, thoughts*, and *mind* are all translated from that same Greek word, *noema*. Other than 2 Corinthians, the only other place the word is used is in Philippians 4:7, "The peace of God, which surpasses all comprehension, will guard your hearts and your minds [*noema*] in Christ Jesus."

We must learn to take every thought (*noema*) captive to the obedience of Christ. If what we're thinking isn't true, then let's not believe it. We don't win this battle by rebuking negative thoughts; we win the battle by choosing the truth. We are not called to dispel the darkness; we are called to turn on the light. We also need to fix our eyes on Jesus, the author and perfecter of faith (Hebrews 12:2). We are deceived when our thoughts are led astray from the only legitimate object of our faith.

Paul wrote in 2 Corinthians 11:3-4,

> I am afraid that, as the serpent deceived Eve by his craftiness, your minds [*noema*] will be led astray from the simplicity and purity of devotion to Christ. For if one comes and preaches another Jesus whom we have not preached, or you receive a different spirit which you have not received, or a different gospel which you have not accepted, you bear this beautifully.

Cults talk and write about the same historical Jesus as we do, but they preach Him another way. According to their understanding, He is not the eternal Son of God; He's just a good person who gave us a good example to follow. Consequently they have a completely different gospel—one of works rather than grace—and they receive a totally different spirit, which is not the Holy Spirit.

## Choosing Truth

It is our responsibility to actively use our minds and to know and choose to believe the truth. Scripture never teaches us to use our minds passively or direct our thoughts inwardly. God never bypasses our minds. He works through them. We are transformed by the renewing of our minds (Romans

12:2). We are, "to think so as to have sound judgment" (Romans 12:3). "Do not be children in your thinking; yet in evil be infants, but in your thinking be mature" (1 Corinthians 14:20). We must also gird up our minds for action (1 Peter 1:13). That means that we don't play fantasy games or use visualization techniques that are not based on truth. Nor do we live in an imaginary world. It's okay and helpful to visualize yourself doing something as long as you actually do it and it's consistent with God's Word. That is how we gird up our minds for action.

Passively putting your mind in neutral invites spiritual disaster. We are to think actively and continuously choose to believe the truth, as Paul directs us in Philippians 4:8-9:

> Whatever is true, whatever is honorable, whatever is right, whatever is pure, whatever is lovely, whatever is of good repute, if there is any excellence and if anything worthy of praise, dwell on those things. The things you have learned and received and heard and seen in me, practice these things; and the God of peace shall be with you.

Paul warned us not to pay attention to deceiving spirits. If a thought comes to your mind, compare it with the list in Philippians 4:8 above. Don't entertain thoughts contrary to it. Then follow the admonition of the next verse (verse 9), and put into practice what you know to be true. If we really believe the truth, we will do what we know to be right.

When I counsel people experiencing personal and spiritual conflicts, I have two goals. First, I want them to know who they are as children of God. Second, I want them to experience the peace of God in their hearts and minds. How are they going to be led by the Holy Spirit if they are paying attention to deceiving spirits?

I had the privilege to help a struggling missionary. She was seeing her pastor, psychologist, and psychiatrist once a week just to hold her life together. After she had resolved her personal and spiritual conflicts and found her freedom in Christ, she sent me this letter:

> The edge of tension and irritation is gone. I feel so free. The Bible has been really exciting, stimulating and more understandable than ever before. I am no longer bound by accusations, doubts, and thoughts of suicide, murder or other harm that comes straight from hell into my head. There is serenity in my mind and spirit, a clarity of consciousness that is profound. I've been set free. My

ability to process things has increased manyfold. Not only is my spirit more serene, my head is actually clearer. It's easier to make connections and integrate things now. It seems like everything is easier to understand now.

My relationship with God has changed significantly. For eight years, I felt He was distant from me. I was desperately crying out to Him to set me free, to release me from the bondage I was in. I wanted so badly to meet with Him, to know His presence with me again. I needed to know Him as a friend and companion, not as the distant authority figure He had become in my mind and experience.

Now that I am free in Christ, I have seen my ability to trust grow and my ability to be honest with Him increase greatly. I really am experiencing the spiritual growth I had been praying for.

## Inner Healing

The missionary above was set free from the lies of the evil one through the process of discipleship counseling mentioned in the last chapter and she experienced inner healing. Many "inner healing" ministries have become popular around the world, and they vary considerably in theory and practice. Some practices look suspiciously similar to the testimony of the former psychic mentioned earlier. In such cases the practitioner functions like a medium. They receive information from what they believe is from God and share it with the inquirer. Some would explain this as a prophetic ministry, with the practitioner using their God-given gift.

Such movements either mature and become biblically balanced or gradually fade away. If you're not familiar with such approaches to ministry, let me suggest a book by Andy Reese, who offers a more balanced approach to inner healing entitled *Freedom Tools* (Chosen, 2008). Andy espouses the prophetic movement, deliverance from demons, and inner healing, but with some proper restraints. Let me share what we have in common and what my concerns are.

Legitimate inner healing ministries recognize the reality of the spiritual world and incorporate God in the process of ministry. This requires discernment and caution about sharing whatever thoughts come to one's mind. Every Christian should be aware of the possibility that such "insights" could be coming from the wrong spirit. Again, I make the appeal for balance as Paul does in 1 Thessalonians 5:19-21:

Do not quench the Spirit; do not despise prophetic utterances.
But examine everything carefully; hold fast to that which is good;
abstain from every form of evil.

Many Christians in the first two quadrants (previous two chapters) are despising prophetic utterances and many in the quadrant we're now discussing and in the final quadrant (next chapter) are failing to "examine everything carefully." All ministry practices should be evaluated through the grid of Scripture and strive to be wholistic and balanced.

Someone once said to me, "Face it, Anderson, God has given you 'the word of knowledge'!" That is a possible manifestation of the Holy Spirit (1 Corinthians 12:8), but one does not develop a ministry or theology from half a verse in the Bible.

Suppose I'm trying to help an individual and sense that something in his story is missing. Then I have the thought that the person is struggling with homosexuality. Advocates of inner healing would say that is a word of knowledge or a prophecy that needs to be shared. They may be right, but I have an obligation to test that impression. This may be the leading of God to get at the heart of the issue. I would test that by asking a probing question at the proper time, such as, "Have you ever struggled with homosexual thoughts or tendencies?" This accomplishes three goals. First, if that impression wasn't from God they would simply say no. In the process I haven't falsely accused them of anything and it does no damage to the relationship.

Second, if they are struggling with homosexual issues I'm giving them an opportunity to share without condemnation. In my experience that's usually what happens. Third, if they are struggling with those issues, but don't want to share them with me or at that time, I respect that choice. It's very likely they will want to share with me or someone else at a more convenient time. Some are just not ready to be helped, and this approach will pave the way for future ministry in God's timing.

Inner healing ministries should be concerned about who the responsible party is and what they are responsible for. We should never usurp the role that God has with His children. That means we don't play the role of a mediator, which only Christ can properly do. We assume the role of reconciler, which means we help remove the barriers to their intimacy with God through genuine repentance and faith. We don't deliver them or heal them. God does that. We pray for them, but we don't do their praying for them.

We help them assume responsibility for their own attitudes and actions. We use our gifts to build up the body of Christ in order to obtain faith, hope, and love (1 Corinthians 13:13). Gifts are a means to an end, and never an end in themselves. Spiritual gifts are dispersed by God to whom He sees fit, and the use of gifts works in conjunction with the Holy Spirit, but never usurps His role in an individual's life.

## Prosperity and Power

The pursuit of power and material prosperity is outside the tolerance boundary, and pursuing such will hinder your walk with God. There are no verses in the Bible instructing us to seek more power, because we already have all that we need. Our pursuit is truth, and Jesus is the Truth. The power of the devil is in the lie, and you break his power by exposing the lie. The power of the believer is in the Truth. God obviously knew we would struggle with this, which is why He inspired Paul to pray in Ephesians 1:16-20:

> I...do not cease giving thanks for you, while making mention of you in my prayer; that the God of our Lord Jesus Christ, the Father of glory, may give to you a spirit of wisdom and of revelation in the knowledge of Him. I pray that the eyes of your heart may be enlightened, so that you will know what is the hope of His calling, what are the riches of the glory of His inheritance in the saints, and what is the surpassing greatness of His power toward us who believe. These are in accordance with the working of the strength of His might.

Pursuing something you already have (power) can't help but lead you down the wrong path. God wants you to know who you are in Christ and the power you already have to live the Christian life. God does want His children to prosper according to 3 John 2: "Beloved, I pray that in all respects you may prosper and be in good health, just as your soul prospers." However, what is your definition of prosperity? Is it materialism, which is nothing but a love of this world? Those who pedal the "prosperity gospel" are the ones who usually end up with most of the money (*your* money), and they pay little attention to restoring the soul.

Psalm 37:4 reads, "Delight yourself in the LORD; and He will give you the desires of your heart." What do you think would happen if you first delighted yourself in the Lord? Your desires would change. If you don't first delight yourself in the Lord, your desires will be of the flesh—and your flesh cannot be satisfied. But if you delight yourself in the Lord, your desires will be of the Spirit—love, joy, peace, patience, kindness, goodness, faithfulness, gentleness, and self-control. What would you exchange for the fruit of the Spirit? A new car? A bigger house? Delighting yourself in the Lord will heal your soul. Greed and counterfeit power will corrupt your soul.

The name-it-and-claim-it "prophets" sound a lot more like New Age practitioners than gospel preachers. They say, "It will be true if you believe hard enough." Christianity says, "God and His word are true, therefore we believe Him." Believing God's Word does not make it true, and not believing it doesn't make it false. We don't create reality with our minds. We are mentally healthy when we are in touch with reality, and the ultimate reality is God.

## New Age

Eastern religions and philosophies have spawned New Age beliefs in the Western world, and some Christians actually think those beliefs are compatible with Christianity. For instance, the number-one spokesperson for wholistic health in the United States is a medical doctor named Deepak Chopra, who is a Hindu. When I mentioned that to my personal physician she said, "Isn't he wonderful!" I said, "No, he isn't wonderful." She was surprised by my response. So I said, "What would you think as a medical doctor if I said any medicine will do as long as some doctor prescribed it and the one taking it is sincere?" She said that would be sheer nonsense. So I said, "Any spirituality will do as long as the believer is sincere!" "Oh," she said, "I think I see where you are coming from." I sure hope so.

God has natural laws governing the natural world He created. God has spiritual laws that govern the spiritual world as well. Eastern religions are not compatible with divine revelation. Some Eastern mystics see the mind as man's problem. According to Guru Maharaj-Ji the mind must thus be bypassed:

> Ignorance is only created by the mind, and the mind keeps the secret that you are something divine away from you. This is why you have to tame the mind first. The mind is a snake, and the treasure is behind it. The snake lies over the treasure, so if you want that treasure, you will have to kill the snake. And killing the snake is not an easy job.

Mystic sects talk of a "new organ of perception" in man, another way of "knowing." Yoga refers to the development of a third eye, which gives spiritual sight to the advanced yogi.

Other sects refer to "intuition," the "psychic self" or the "unconscious mind" as the means of perception. They say that the first step toward spiritual growth is to train oneself to ignore all messages from the mind. Next comes the tuning of one's "second organ of perception" to the "universal mind" or the impersonal "god of mysticism." Once attuned, the psychic self can bypass the mind and thus perceive reality directly. Practical attempts to erase the mind include a range of beliefs, from transcendental meditation to Silva Mind Control.

Most Westerners, however, are uncomfortable throwing their minds into neutral, and Hinduism is too ascetic for the materialistic Westerner. The New Age, however, has made unpalatable Eastern religions appealing to Westerners.

The New Age movement modifies this mindless approach by claiming that the mind is not being bypassed; it is actually the mind that is achieving "cosmic consciousness." They believe they can actually create reality with their minds. This is similar to the teachings of the Church of Religious Science. Ernest Holmes and other proponents of Science of Mind teaching believe that the supreme, creative power of the universe is a cosmic principle, which is present throughout the universe and in every one of us. Science of Mind teaches that we are creating our own day-to-day experiences through the form and procession of our thoughts. They believe that anybody, by the way they think, can bring whatever they desire into their experience.

## New Age Beliefs

In preparation for a conference designed to reach New Agers I was reading several books in that genre and was struck by the fact that differing religious and philosophical groups that previously had very little in common were finding unity under the banner of New Age.

The New Age movement is not seen as a religion but a new way to think and understand reality. That's why it's so dangerous. It's very attractive to the natural man who has become disillusioned with organized religion and Western rationalism. He desires spiritual reality but doesn't want to give up materialism, deal with his moral problems, or come under authority.

The mind is not a snake, but there was a snake in the Garden—and all false religions are nothing more than different humps of that same snake. It would only make sense that they would hold some things in common. Push down one hump of the snake and another arises. New Age practitioners can be very diverse in their beliefs. However, there are six unifying factors in New Age thinking.

The first is *monism*—the belief that all is one and one is all. It says we all swim in one great cosmic ocean. All human ills stem from an inability to perceive this unity. History is not the story of humanity's fall into sin and its restoration by God's saving grace. Rather, it is humanity's fall into ignorance and the gradual ascent into enlightenment.

Clearly, this is not the case. There is a definite boundary between the finite and the infinite. Monism is a counterfeit to the unity Jesus prayed for in John 17:21. That unity is possible only as we are united together in Christian fellowship. New Agers seek unity without the Holy Spirit.

Second, *all is God*. If all is one, including God, then one must conclude that all is God. Pantheism would have us believe that trees, snails, birds, and people are all of one divine essence. A personal God is abandoned in favor of an impersonal energy force or consciousness, and if God is no longer personal, He doesn't have to be served.

Hinduism says, "Atman is Brahman" (The individual self is really the universal self). Occultists say, "As above, so below" (God and humanity are one). That sounds remarkably like Satan who said, "You will be like God" (Genesis 3:5).

Many New Age proponents believe, "We are gods, and we might as well get good at it." Progress for them is to say, "When I was a little child, I believed in God. When I began to mature, I stopped believing in God. Then I grew up and realized I was God." That's like me saying, "When I was a boy I believed in Santa Claus. Then I grew up and didn't believe in Santa Claus. Then I grew up some more and I discovered that I was Santa Claus!"

A third unifying factor is belief in a *change in consciousness*. If we are God, then we need to know we are God. We must become cosmically conscious, also called "at-one-ment" (a counterfeit of atonement), or self-realization, or god-realization, or enlightenment or attune-ment. Some who reach this enlightened status will claim to be "born again." This is a counterfeit conversion. Their faith has no object, neither does their meditation, so it becomes an inward subjective journey. To us, the essential issue is not whether we believe or meditate, but whom we believe in and what we meditate upon. Christians believe God and meditate upon His Word.

The fourth unifying factor is a *cosmic evolutionary optimism*. They believe that there is a New Age coming. There will be a new world order with a one-world government. New Agers believe in a progressive unification of world consciousness eventually reaching the "omega point." This is a counterfeit kingdom and we know who their king is. It's not hard to identify the head when it is attached to the humps of this snake.

Fifth, New Agers *create their own reality*. They believe they can determine reality by what they believe, so by changing what they believe, they can change reality. The metaphysical influences of Taoism's yin and yang, the ebb and flow of competing and complementary forces, have erased all moral boundaries. There are no moral absolutes because there is no distinction between good and evil.

Sixth, New Agers *make contact with the kingdom of darkness*. Calling a medium a "channeler," and a demon a "spirit guide" does not change the reality of what they are. They have connected with the god of this world instead of the God of Abraham, Isaac, and Jacob and they don't know it.

I received a call from a lady who was concerned about the turn of events in a small church Bible study she was attending. It had started out as a "rebirthing" class attended by a group of supposedly Christian women. A woman in the group began to function as a medium, and they thought they were hearing from God through her. They recorded six hours of videotape and made a hundred page manuscript. In the six hours of taping, five different personalities could be identified in the medium. The group was convinced they were hearing from God, Jesus, the Holy Spirit, and two angels.

The lady functioning as a medium was later identified as not being a Christian. In the tape her eyes rolled back in a trancelike state. At one point a voice says through her, "It's going to snow here tomorrow." I'm surprised that, when it didn't snow the next day, they couldn't see the "snow job" being done on them! How can a thinking person who professes to be a Christian consider this as anything other than demonization?

## Discussion Questions

1. What place do signs and wonders have or don't have in God's plan?

2. Where do psychics get their information, and what are the limits of their "insights"?

3. How can a Christian keep from being deceived?

4. What are Satan's strategies, and which is most devious? Why?

5. How can we overcome Satan's strategies?

6. What is inner healing?

7. How can someone practicing inner healing be deceived or be out of balance?

8. What is the proper way to respond to "words of knowledge"?

9. Why is it important in ministry to keep in mind who is responsible and what they are responsible for?

10. Why doesn't the believer need more power?

11. What is wrong with the prosperity gospel?

12. What is the New Age, and how has it crept into the Western world?

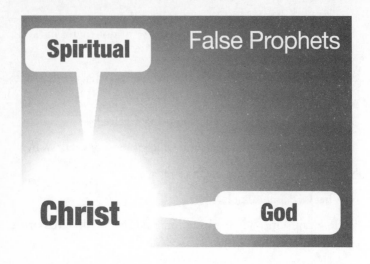

*Such men are false apostles, deceitful workers, disguising themselves as apostles of Christ. No wonder, for even Satan disguises himself as an angel of light. Therefore it is not surprising if his servants also disguise themselves as servants of righteousness, whose end will be according to their deeds.*

2 CORINTHIANS 11:13-15

*The false apostles looked good on the surface, but underneath they robbed the soul. Indeed, they took money as well, though they were careful to conceal that as much as possible…An angel of light is one who is free to speak because he stands close to God. This is what the devil pretends to be.*[19]

CHRYSOSTOM, "HOMILIES ON THE EPISTLES OF PAUL TO THE CORINTHIANS"

*These illusions are apparitions of that spirit who seeks to ensnare unhappy souls in the deceptive rites of a multitude of false gods and to turn them aside from true worship of the true God, by whom alone they can be purified and healed.*[20]

AUGUSTINE, *CITY OF GOD* 10.10

# Chapter Five

# Overcoming False Prophets and Teachers

*It appears probable enough that this man [Marcus, a heretic] possesses*
*a demon as a familiar spirit. By means of this spirit, he seems to*
*be able to prophesy. He also enables others to prophesy—as many*
*as he counts worthy to be partakers of his charis…However, the*
*gift of prophecy is not conferred on men by Marcus, the magician.*
*Rather, only those to whom God sends His grace from above possess*
*the divinely-bestowed power of prophesying. And they speak where*
*and when God wishes, not when Marcus orders them to do so.*[21]

IRENAEUS (C. 180)

During dinner conversation with a fine church staff in Venezuela, the pastor rather sheepishly commented to me, "I guess I'm now considered to be an apostle." Some international figure had appointed him as such, and he seemed to be somewhat embarrassed about it. An identical experience happened in Colombia, South America. Both these pastors were credible leaders with fruitful ministries. In no way would I ever consider these two men to be false prophets, but does the label *apostle* aptly fit them? They were in a position of leadership over their denominational churches. Throughout church history they would have been considered bishops, who oversee other pastors.

In Latin America I have been given many business cards by pastors who identify themselves as "prophet so and so" or "apostle so and so." It is so common in Latin America and some Third World countries that the more "successful" ones are being called "superapostles," and "superprophets." There are also a growing number of pastors in America who identify themselves in a similar way. The trend has been labeled the "new apostolic reformation" by those within the movement.

Understanding the term *apostle* and distinguishing the gift of prophecy from the role of a prophet is going to be a challenge for the church in the twenty-first century. Certainly we don't want to limit the Lord from speaking to His people in these critical days. But if we don't ask important questions, some believers may come under the influence of false prophets and teachers at worst, or to a lesser degree face more unnecessary division within the body of Christ. Keep in mind that a true apostle or prophet of God would never be sent to only one segment of His body. On the other hand, a bishop does provide leadership and oversees a segment of the church. How can we tell the difference between the counterfeit and the real?

## Differences of Opinion

Some Evangelical Christians believe that the miraculous presence of God is no longer evident through prophetic gifts. God speaks to His church only through the written Word as understood by trained theologians and pastors. Others seek to glorify God by manifesting His presence in public worship through miraculous gifts and prophetic utterances. They strive to enter into the "holy of holies" in worship and allow the Lord to minister to them through prophecies, words of knowledge, healings, tongues, and every other manifestation hinted at or alluded to in the Bible.

Miraculous interventions of God have been reported in every century of the church's existence. However, the current terminology for apostles and prophets has been altered in the past hundred years in some Pentecostal groups. That is in sharp contrast to the Roman Catholic Church's belief in the apostolic succession:

> The Church is apostolic because she is founded on the apostles, in three ways:
>
> - she was and remains built on "the foundation of the Apostles, the witnesses chosen and sent on mission by Christ himself";
>
> - with the help of the Spirit dwelling in her, the Church keeps and hands on the teaching, the "good deposit," the salutary words she has heard from the apostles;
>
> - she continues to be taught, sanctified, and guided by the apostles until Christ's return, through their successors in pastoral office: the college of bishops, "assisted by priests, in union with the successor of Peter, the Church's supreme pastor."[22]

The Orthodox Church holds to the same apostolic succession but doesn't acknowledge the Pope as the supreme (singular) pastor. I'm sure most readers of this book are neither Catholic nor Orthodox, but I share the above quote for a reason. The church has *not* historically taught that there would be more apostles than the ones selected by Christ during His earthly ministry or, later, the apostle Paul. To my knowledge that was the position of the Reformers as well. While we may not agree on ecclesiastical titles and positions, I think we can agree on some concepts drawn from the warnings of Scripture. Let's start with a broad look at biblical history.

## The Prophetic Purpose

God created mankind to rule over the birds of the sky, the beasts of the fields, and the fish of the sea. His dominion extended over the earth. When Adam sinned, he lost his relationship with God and forfeited his dominion. Satan became the rebel ruler of this world. God's redemptive plan is to defeat the god of this world and restore a fallen humanity, establishing His kingdom so that His will will be done on earth as it is in heaven.

The Bible reveals God's plan. It includes historical accounts of the progress of His unfolding revelation, the establishment and commissioning of the church, and the assurance that His plan for the future will be accomplished. The place of the church in His unfolding plan is summarized in Ephesians 2:19-22:

> You are no longer strangers and aliens, but you are fellow citizens with the saints, and are of God's household, having been built upon the foundation of the apostles and prophets, Christ Jesus Himself being the corner stone, in whom the whole building, being fitted together, is growing into a holy temple in the Lord, in whom you also are being built together into a dwelling of God in the Spirit.

Christians are children of God who are seated with Christ in the heavenlies. Based on the foundation that has been laid by the apostles and prophets, we are being built up into a holy temple. The church has been established as "a dwelling of God in the Spirit."

The means by which God has communicated this redemptive plan is revealed in the Bible through the prophets and the apostles. The ultimate revelation of God is Jesus Himself, who is the cornerstone of the church:

> God, after he spoke long ago to the fathers in prophets in many
> portions and in many ways, in these last days has spoken to us in
> His Son, whom He appointed heir of all things, through whom
> also He made the world (Hebrews 1:1-2).

This passage doesn't say that there would not be prophets after Christ, but it certainly indicates that, though prophets were necessary before Christ, a more complete revelation has been accomplished in Him.

Old Testament prophets were messengers of God, and they never spoke presumptuously. God said to Moses, "Go, and I, even I, will be with your mouth, and teach you what you are to say" (Exodus 4:12). "I will raise up a prophet from among their countrymen like you, and I will put My words in his mouth, and he shall speak to them all that I command him" (Deuteronomy 18:18). God said to Jeremiah, "Behold, I have put My words in your mouth" (Jeremiah 1:9). And Ezekiel received this instruction: "You shall speak My words to them whether they listen or not, for they are rebellious" (Ezekiel 2:7).

When Old Testament prophets spoke, they spoke with authority: "Thus saith the Lord." It was God's message, not a message from a man. One test of a true prophet was that he was never wrong (Deuteronomy 18:20-22). People needed to discern whether a person was a true or false prophet, but they were not left with the responsibility of deciding what part of a prophecy was right and what part was wrong. If any part was wrong, the prophet was false. Unfortunately, they listened to a lot of false prophets and stoned a lot of true prophets because they didn't want to change their unrighteous ways of living. The Old Testament records one account after another of rebellious kings, Baal worshippers, and false prophets.

Old Testament history closes with the ushering in of 400 years of silence, during which the world was without a prophetic voice. Then the Word became flesh and dwelt among us (John 1:14). Planet Earth was about to hear from God again, but this time through His Son. What Jesus modeled was a life totally dependent upon His Father. "I did not speak on My own initiative, but the Father Himself who sent Me has given Me a commandment as to what to say and what to speak" (John 12:49). After a year of public ministry, Jesus appointed 12 disciples, who were identified as apostles. They proclaimed God's message in the early days of the church. They were not called prophets because the word *prophet* had commonly come to mean *any* messenger, secular or sacred.

## Does God Use Prophets Today?

Most conservative biblical scholars believe there are no longer any prophets and apostles who speak with the absolute authority of "Thus saith the Lord." Some have suggested that there are two prophets in Revelation 11:3, but the passage says they are "witnesses" who prophesy. What's the difference? They are identified as witnesses, but what they *do* is prophesy. In a similar fashion, I have been called a seminary professor who exhorts. A seminary professor is a person occupying a position; exhortation is a gift. The first describes my position at a seminary, the latter my gift. The same distinction applies to a prophet and the gift of prophecy.

Why are some Christians identifying their leaders as "apostles" and "prophets"? Some "apostles" and "prophets" are even self-appointed. It would be terribly unfortunate if they thought they were enhancing their status by giving themselves a lofty title. Is the whole church supposed to accept what these "apostles" and "prophets" say as authoritative in the same way we understand Scripture to be? This is not a new problem, as revealed by Irenaeus in the second century:

> He will judge false prophets, who have not received the gift of prophecy from God. They are not possessed of the fear of God. Instead, either for the sake of vainglory, or with a view to some personal advantage (or acting in some other way under the influence of a wicked spirit), they pretend to utter prophecies, while at the same time they lie against God.[23]

Some Pentecostal groups understand Ephesians 4:11 to be teaching a fivefold ministry of apostles, prophets, evangelists, pastors, and teachers. However, their definition of an apostle varies. Moderate Pentecostals see an apostle as someone who has been sent by God to offer leadership, while others see the title as more authoritative. They are the ones who would argue for a "new apostolic reformation." They see the church as dead or apostate and God as establishing a new apostolic succession. Obviously the rest of the church is not going to accept this.

The historical church has declared the canon of Scripture closed. The Old and New Testaments books are the authoritative sources for faith and practice. Scripture teaches that the foundation has already been laid (past tense) by the apostles and prophets. Of course God can reveal Himself and

His Word anytime He wants to. However, we have been clearly warned not to add to or take away from anything God has said (Revelation 22:18-19). God is still working today as He has in the past, through people called into ministry.

Prophets like Isaiah and apostles like Paul were people who had a God-ordained appointment to their office. The church has gifted people, and the gift of prophecy functions like other gifts within the church. However, the New Testament gift of prophecy is not the same as the Old Testament office of prophet. Having the gift of prophecy does not make anyone a prophet. Christians are children of God, supernaturally gifted to help build up one another in order to live righteously.

"God has appointed in the church, first apostles, second prophets, third teachers, then miracles, then gifts of healings, helps" (1 Corinthians 12:28). Notice that God appointed apostles, prophets, teachers, and miracles, and then he introduces the various sorts of gifts. God builds upon the foundation that has already been laid by the apostles and prophets by giving us evangelists and pastor/teachers (Ephesians 4:11-12). Evangelists and pastor/teachers are people ordained by God to equip the saints so they (the saints) can do the work of ministry.

Although Satan is disarmed, the kingdom of darkness is still operating during the church age. Along with true evangelists, pastors, teachers, and others gifted by God for ministry, we can expect Satan to have his false prophets, teachers, and messiahs. Whenever God sows a seed, the devil sows a counterfeit. Therefore, let's examine how to identify false prophets and teachers, first from the Old Testament and then from the New Testament. Before we do that, please keep in mind that many good Pentecostal leaders that have been given the title "apostle" or "prophet" are not false apostles or prophets...unless they fail the tests given below.

I appeal to this segment of the church to reconsider those titles for the sake of unity. Such titles do not enhance their status with the majority of the church. In fact, they close the door for inclusion in Christian circles other than their own, and many good leaders will be limited in their potential. (For instance, I know that many pastors of the Four Square denomination consider Jack Hayford an apostle, but I have never heard him present himself that way to the church at large. We need more humble servants like that who minister beyond their segment of the church.)

## Identifying False Prophets in the Old Testament

The standard way of identifying an Old Testament prophet has already been mentioned. Deuteronomy 18:20-22 explains that if an alleged prophet spoke presumptuously (that is, his own thoughts, not God's), the prophet was to die. If what he said didn't come true, he was a false prophet. That test works only when the words of the prophet predict some future event. But predicting the future was not the primary purpose of a true prophet. A prophet was more like an Old Testament preacher who proclaimed the truth calling for people to repent.

Prophecy literally means "to tell forth." It can mean to tell *before time*, or it can mean to tell *before people*. For instance, the Jewish arrangement of the Old Testament did not include Daniel among the prophets because he didn't preach, even though the book of Daniel has many prophetic messages concerning the future.

Deuteronomy 13:1-3 identifies an even more insidious characteristic of false prophets:

> If a prophet or a dreamer of dreams arises among you and gives you a sign or a wonder, and the sign or the wonder comes true, concerning which he spoke to you, saying, "Let us go after other gods (whom you have not known) and let us serve them," you shall not listen to the words of that prophet or that dreamer of dreams; for the LORD your God is testing you to find out if you love the LORD your God with all your heart and with all your soul.

In this case the signs and wonders come true, but their purpose is to lead people away from God to serve other gods. These dreamers of dreams are rebellious at heart (Deuteronomy 13:5). They use signs and wonders to lure people off the true path, and the gullible follow blindly because they accept anything supernatural as being from God. The intention is to draw us away from the Word of God. In Old Testament times God considered their evil so great that He required their life be taken by the hands of their own family members (Deuteronomy 13:4-10).

Back in the 1970s I had a college ministry near Long Beach, California. A nearby "ministry" created quite a controversy. Everybody was hearing about the great signs and wonders coming true at the hands of a young "prophet." Several students under my ministry went to their Friday evening services, which were held in a rented theater in downtown Long Beach. I personally struggled with this, since God seemed to be blessing his efforts more than mine. Several of my students were questioning why we weren't seeing the miracles in our ministry that they were seeing in his. The so-called "prophet" eventually moved his ministry, and within a few years he died of AIDS due to his decadent lifestyle. A lot of people had been led down the wrong path.

How can we identify a false prophet like that? Jeremiah 23:21-32 contains the most extensive analysis of false prophets in the Old Testament:

> I did not send these prophets, but they ran. I did not speak to them, but they prophesied. But if they had stood in My council, then they would have announced My words to My people, and would have turned them back from their evil way and from the evil of their deeds (verses 21-22).

### Errors of False Prophets

Notice two errors of these prophets. They were not sharing God's words, and what they were sharing did not turn the people away from their evil deeds. True prophets announced only God's words, and their primary purpose was to disclose unrighteousness. They called people back to the moral standards of the Law and declared the way of the Lord.

The false prophets would relay their dreams (Jeremiah 23:25), but Jeremiah explains the relative value of those dreams (verses 28-29):

> "The prophet who has a dream may relate his dream, but let him who has My word speak My word in truth. What does straw have in common with grain?" declares the LORD. "Is not My word like fire?" declares the LORD, "and like a hammer which shatters a rock?"

Being an old farm boy, I know the relative value of straw. If you try to feed straw to cattle, they won't eat it, because it has no nutritional value. It makes good bedding, but only grain has nutritional value. God says these prophets' dreams were like straw, but His Word is like wheat. We will grow only when we devour Gods' Word. When we substitute the chaff of dreams for the wheat of biblical truth, we will starve spiritually.

God is also against prophets who "steal [His] words from each other" (Jeremiah 23:30). Notice they are God's words, but false prophets have stolen them from others, and share them as though God has given the words to them. In today's language, that's called plagiarism.

In addition, God is against prophets "who use their tongues and declare, 'The Lord declares'" (Jeremiah 23:31). Tragically this is happening in some churches today. As one example, a pulpit committee stopped by my office for advice. The grandson of the former pastor had called the church and told them that God had revealed to him that he was to be the new pastor. Some on the committee believed the message the grandson had received was from God and therefore he should be called to be the pastor, but others were doubtful.

Some reasoned that if God had spoken to this man, they better extend him an invitation or they would be disobeying God. I asked them what the young man was like. They said he seemed legitimate, but he lacked any formal education. They were also troubled by his request for absolute authority to carry out the plan God had given him for the church. He didn't want to work through the elders.

I asked, "Don't you think God would work through the committee that was chosen by the congregation?" If I sensed that God was leading me to pastor a church, I hope that God would also give the responsible people in the church the same sense of my calling. If God wasn't leading them in the same way, I would understand my "leading" to be from my own flesh or from the pit rather than from God.

Using God's name to persuade others is another ploy that God detests. I have counseled several people who have been led astray because they have complied with other people's wishes who said they had heard from God. One young lady married a man because God told him they were to get married. She didn't want to disobey God. (Any man who would ask for my daughter's hand had better come with a proposal and not a mandate.) My wife calls this "pulling spiritual rank." I call it spiritual abuse. Those who use God's name to get leverage for what they want can only expect disaster down the road.

Finally, God says, "I am against those who have prophesied false dreams... and related them and led My people astray by their falsehoods and reckless boasting" (Jeremiah 23:32). I am troubled by those who keep promising great things in order to motivate people and keep the money coming in. They proclaim, "God is going to do a great work, a mighty work"—or worse—"a new thing!" Such spiritual hype is not of God.

## Identifying False Prophets and Teachers in the New Testament

The purpose for the gift of prophecy is to turn people's hearts back to God, according to 1 Corinthians 14:24-25:

> If all prophesy, and an unbeliever or an ungifted man enters, he is convicted by all, he is called to account by all; the secrets of his heart are disclosed; and so he will fall on his face and worship God, declaring that God is certainly among you.

God's Word is like fire; it purifies the church: "It is time for judgment to begin with the household of God" (1 Peter 4:17). God is far more concerned about church purity than church growth, because church purity is an essential prerequisite for church growth. Only the pure church can grow and bear fruit. Satan will use signs and wonders to lead people off the path of sanctification. He will divert our interest away from the eternal onto the temporal, and he will entice us to think of our physical needs rather than our spiritual needs.

God's Word is like a hammer that breaks up the hard ground and softens the heart. If church people were living in immorality and a word of prophecy came from the Lord, rest assured it would not be some generic word of comfort. It would reveal unrighteousness for the purpose of cleansing. That is what God's Word does. It cleanses the soul and draws us closer to Him in righteousness. Paul wrote in 2 Timothy 3:16-17,

> All Scripture is inspired by God and profitable for teaching, for reproof, for correction, for training in righteousness; so that the man of God may be adequate, equipped for every good work.

In my seminary experience, we went from teaching (doctrine) to training in *competence*. We bypassed the reproof and correction, which is necessary for repentance. We should be competent, but what is needed is training in righteousness. One Church Father said, "Test the man who says he is inspired—by his deeds and his life" (Hermas, c. 150). [24] The warnings against false prophets are numerous in the New Testament:

> Beloved, do not believe every spirit, but test the spirits to see whether they are from God; because many false prophets have gone out into the world (1 John 4:1).

The warnings intensify as the Lord prepares to return. In the Olivet discourse, Jesus said,

Many false prophets will arise, and will mislead many...for false Christs and false prophets will arise and will show great signs and wonders, so as to mislead, if possible, even the elect (Matthew 24:11,24).

### Characteristics of False Messengers

A righteous life is the first sign of a true messenger of God. Jesus said, "You will know them by their fruits" (Matthew 7:20). In the following three verses Jesus exposes the counterfeit prophet. False prophets and teachers may say, "Lord, Lord!" They may prophesy, cast out demons, and even perform miracles in the name of the Lord. But Jesus said, "Then I will declare to them, 'I never knew you; depart from Me, you who practice lawlessness'" (Matthew 7:23). Satan has only limited supernatural power to perform miracles, but he can get his demons to leave those they afflict, making it look like one of his workers has just cast them out. False teachers will live a secret life of sin, but eventually their deeds will find them out. Paul reveals this in 2 Corinthians 11:13-15:

> Such men are false apostles, deceitful workers, disguising themselves as apostles of Christ. No wonder, for even Satan disguises himself as an angel of light. Therefore it is not surprising if his servants also disguise themselves as servants of righteousness, whose end will be according to their deeds.

The above passage reveals a second characteristic of some false prophets and teachers. *They work within the church.* Most false religions and cults can be identified by their doctrine, which they make no attempt to hide. The most insidious deception is pulled off by false prophets and teachers who identify themselves as Christians and work within the church.

> False prophets also arose among the people, just as there will also be false teachers among you, who will secretly introduce destructive heresies, even denying the Master who bought them, bringing swift destruction upon themselves. Many will follow their sensuality, and because of them the way of the truth will be maligned; and in their greed they will exploit you with false words; their judgment from long ago is not idle, and their destruction is not asleep (2 Peter 2:1-3).

False teachers disguise themselves as ministers of righteousness. What we *see* seldom threatens the church. External and visible opposition can have a purging effect on the church that leaves the body stronger. False teachers are infiltrators whose purpose is to influence the church in a negative way. These "tares are the sons of the evil one; and the enemy who sowed them is the devil" (Matthew 13:38). Their purpose is to secretly introduce destructive heresies. Heretics are people who cause schisms. If we were spiritually alert we would "reject a factious man after a first and second warning" (Titus 3:10).

Heretics seek to discredit righteous workers and sow disunity. They seduce people by their "sensuality." The result is that many people will be mesmerized and follow their destructive ways.

A third characteristic of false prophets and teachers is their *rebellious heart*. They despise authority (2 Peter 2:10). This may be the easiest way to spot them. They won't answer to anyone. They have independent spirits and are not compatible with those who desire to live righteously. True Christian leaders have a servant's heart. True leaders don't seek to lord it over others. They prove to be an example. True leaders don't appeal to their title or position to enhance their status or demand allegiance. The only position they need is the one they have in Christ, and the only title or identity they rely on is being children of God. The authority of true leaders is derived from their godly character and based on their position in Christ, not on some title bestowed upon them by themselves or others.

### Cautions Are in Order

As you guard against false prophets, I caution you not to go on a witch hunt. Some "heresy hunters" are self-righteous, arrogant, and judgmental. They become as divisive as the heretics they try to expose. You can't focus on what is wrong for too long. It will have a negative effect on your life. We shouldn't be known for what we don't believe, but rather for what we do believe. Growing Christians are proclaimers, not disclaimers. Commit yourself to know the truth and that will expose the lies. Just knowing the lies by itself does not reveal the truth.

True Christian fellowship is enhanced when and where truth is proclaimed in a balanced way. Remember that good people can be deceived. If you come across someone who is a victim of bad counsel, show him the light, not the exit.

Be careful not to throw somebody out because of one moral indiscretion. The concern is for "those who *practice* lawlessness." Even then be careful, because there are many who have accepted God's standards and desire to live a righteous life, but are in bondage to sinful habits. They aren't false teachers if they aren't trying to teach anybody. Our hearts need to go out to such people, because they are enslaved to sinful habits and are being held captive by Satan to do his will (2 Timothy 2:26).

## The Gift of Prophecy

The apostle Paul was concerned that the church has a balanced and biblical perspective on the proper use of prophecy, tongues, and words of knowledge. Perspective is the value of distance, so let's stand back and consider the larger context of 1 Corinthians 12–14. There are a variety of spiritual gifts and manifestations of the spirit. In the midst of this diversity, there is unity, because there is only one Spirit and one Lord. God gives the gifts as He wills. Gifts and manifestations come and go and come again for the purpose of accomplishing God's will. The consistent work of the church is to establish faith, hope, and love. These are the lasting and continuous standards by which we evaluate our ministry and lives.

Paul says, "I write so that you may know how one ought to conduct himself in the household of God, which is the church of the living God, the pillar and support of the truth" (1 Timothy 3:15). Truth is the object of our faith. If we know the truth, it will set us free to grow in love of God and others. The church is gifted to accomplish that objective. Gifts are only a means to an end, and never an end in themselves. We are not instructed to seek the gifts, we are instructed to seek the Giver—and He will gift us in the right way, for the right reason, at the right time. "Seek not and forsake not" is the right balance in my opinion, if "forsake not" is accompanied with discernment (see chapter 11). Our responsibility is to yield to the Holy Spirit. How He chooses to gift us is His responsibility.

In 1 Corinthians 14, Paul specifies the proper use of the gifts of prophecy and tongues in public worship. The gift of prophecy was to be desired over the gift of tongues, because the congregation can only be edified by that which they can comprehend with their minds. The gift of tongues was not to be used in public worship unless there was an interpretation. The Holy Spirit never bypasses our minds when He ministers to us. Paul wrote,

> What is the outcome then? I will pray with the spirit and I will pray
> with the mind also; I will sing with the spirit and I will sing with

the mind also…Brethren, do not be children in your thinking; yet in evil be infants, but in your thinking be mature (1 Corinthians 14:15,20).

## The Misuse of Prophecy

A woman came to me all excited one evening with a "word from the Lord." She told me I was supposed to change the direction of my ministry and do a "new thing." I told her I didn't think this "word" was from the Lord. She was disappointed by my response because the "word" she had heard was so clear. But if I was supposed to do this new thing, why didn't the Lord tell me and my board? If the Lord told her to tell me to do something, what does that make her? Isn't that what a medium is? Remember, "There is one God and one mediator also between God and men, the man Jesus Christ" (1 Timothy 2:5). God has not called any of us to function as mediums. She was actually usurping the role of the Holy Spirit, who was sent to guide us.

When God does send a prophet like Nathan to someone like David, it is for the purpose of bringing conviction in order to get him or her back to a righteous relationship with God. Once they are in a righteous relationship with the Lord, the Holy Spirit will guide them. If that woman had heard from the Lord that I was living an unrighteous life and spoke to that issue for the purpose of helping me get right with God, that would be legitimate. Even that needs to be tested and used properly, as I mentioned in the last chapter.

If we are not a witness of any indiscretion we should never confront another for the purpose of discipline. If we are a witness, then we have the obligation to confront the sin for the purpose of winning over a brother or sister. If that isn't successful we can go no further unless there were two or more witnesses.

We will be out of balance if we seek to be filled and led by the Holy Spirit without having a knowledge of God's Word. The Holy Spirit has promised to lead us into all truth, which will set us free and put us on the right path. The church at Corinth had gifts and manifestations of the Spirit, but they were used improperly and were out of balance. The church was exhorted by Paul to get back to the foundation of truth, which had already been laid by the prophets and apostles, and to focus on developing faith, hope and love. They were also instructed in the proper use of the gifts in public worship, because God does everything properly and in order (1 Corinthians 14:40).

A pastor friend of mine received a letter from a former staff member who was dismissed for moral reasons. He was now the pastor of a church he had planted in the same community. The letter contained a prophecy for my friend's church. I asked, "Why would God give a prophetic message to your church through the pastor of another church?" I suggested that they shouldn't listen to it since it would function like a curse. From the time they read it, everything that happened in the church would be evaluated by the prophecy (either to substantiate or invalidate it). The false prophecy would take precedence over the leading of the Holy Spirit. I recommended that he call Jack Hayford and ask for his advice. Jack gave him the same advice. God will always work through the lines of authority that He has established in His Word.

The apostle Paul wrote, "Do not quench the Spirit; do not despise prophetic utterances. But examine everything carefully; hold fast to that which is good; abstain from every form of evil" (1 Thessalonians 5:19-21).

## Keeping Your Faith in Balance

If you accept prophetic utterances as valid for today, I would encourage you to consider these following tests and guidelines:

1. Is the person giving the prophetic utterance living a balanced and righteous life?

2. Are they committed to building God's kingdom or are they enhancing their own status. This is similar to asking, Is Christ being lifted up or are *they* being lifted up?

3. Does the prophetic utterance establish confidence in the Word of God, and is it consistent with a balanced presentation of the Word? Have prophetic utterances become a substitute for the serious and personal study of God's Word? It's a lot easier and quicker to get a "word from the Lord" than it is to "be diligent to present yourself approved to God as a workman who does not need to be ashamed, accurately handling the word of truth" (2 Timothy 2:15). Christian maturity and proper ministry are not a matter of expediency.

4. Does the use of the spiritual gift bring unity to the church and cause the members to build up one another? Be careful in this test,

because those who hold to a form of godliness but deny its power are not in balance either. They will quench the Spirit through censorship, and very little will be accomplished in the church.

5. Last, do the spiritual manifestations bypass the mind? God operates through our mind; Satan bypasses it. If a person enters a medium-like trance, be assured it is occultic. God renews our minds and brings back to our minds all that He has taught us. He can only do that if we have first put the Word of God into our minds. It is our responsibility to think so as to have sound judgment.

## Healing

Surely our griefs He Himself bore, and our sorrows He carried; yet we ourselves esteemed Him stricken, smitten of God, and afflicted. But He was pierced through for our transgressions, He was crushed for our iniquities; the chastening for our well-being fell upon Him, and by His scourging we are healed (Isaiah 53:4-5).

Isaiah 53:4-5 is a prophecy we can all agree upon, but the last line raises a critical question—*is there healing in the atonement?* Yes, but with qualifications. Recall from an earlier chapter where I explained that salvation is past, present, and future when applied to the believer. The gospel affords us many things in this present life, and chief among them is forgiveness of sins and new life in Christ. Some benefits we have now, but others are promised for the future when we will receive a resurrected body. In this present age we live in a mortal and decaying body: "It is appointed for men to die once and after this comes judgment" (Hebrews 9:27). I do not believe that we can claim by faith perfect healing as a promise in this present age. Nor should we ever say that someone lacks faith if they aren't healed. Perfect faith offers no promise for the eternal preservation of our mortal bodies.

I don't think we should limit the concept of healing to only that of physical abnormalities. It is our souls—the inner person—that God wants to heal. Even if our body is physically healed, it will only decay again and eventually return to dust.

However, Jesus did heal those who were physically suffering, and He did give the 12 disciples power and authority over all the demons and to heal diseases (Luke 9:1). In addition the apostle Paul said there are "gifts of healing by the one Spirit" (1 Corinthians 12:9). I don't think we should conclude that the gifts of healing apply only to the physical body. The soul is most in need of healing. However, I do not hesitate to pray for God's healing hand to be upon those who suffer physically, but I can't claim it as an absolute promise either. Whether someone is healed is not determined by any of us—it is determined by "the one Spirit." I hate to see people suffering needlessly, but we must have a balanced answer. Otherwise we will turn people off to God—who would be seen as failing to live up to His reputation when He chooses not to heal.

A great embarrassment to the church are the so-called miracle workers who fill stadiums with people expecting a miracle, which they are supposed to claim by faith. These "miracle workers" can always cover their tracks by saying unhealed people didn't properly exercise their faith. In other words, "It was their fault, not mine." The message of healing usually includes the promise of material prosperity as well. The target audience is usually the poor and uneducated, which makes it twice as shameful. What happens to those who don't get healed or become wealthy when they go back home? Who cares for their souls? Authenticity and integrity are what seekers are looking for, and this is what the church must offer in these perilous days.

### Taking Responsibility to Steward Our Bodies

Nowhere does the Bible suggest that we can eat like pigs, drink too much, use drugs, or smoke and then expect God to heal us when we get sick. It teaches us to do all things in moderation and to exercise self-control, which is part of the fruit of the Spirit. Most people are sick for psychosomatic reasons, and that is where the church can offer a course on healing and the hope for answered prayer according to James 5:13-16:

> Is anyone among you suffering? Then he must pray. Is anyone cheerful? He is to sing praises. Is anyone among you sick? Then he must call for the elders of the church and they are to pray over him, anointing him with oil in the name of the Lord; and the prayer offered in faith will restore the one who is sick, and the Lord will raise him up, and if he has committed sins, they will be forgiven him. Therefore, confess your sins to one another so that you may be healed. The effective prayer of a righteous man can accomplish much.

If the person who is suffering is willing to pray themselves, assume responsibility for their own health, take the initiative by asking for help, and confess their sins, then the prayer of a righteous person will accomplish much. All of our staff have seen incredible answers to prayer after we have helped people resolve their personal and spiritual conflicts through genuine repentance and faith in God.

Suppose a man calls your church and asks for the elders to pray for him. Let's say the elders are godly men who agree to fast for a day before the time of prayer. They have done their part, but what if the man who is asking for prayer is in the bondage of bitterness, along with a host of other issues keeping him from having an intimate relationship with his heavenly Father? Do you really expect God to answer his plea for healing? I don't. Those who may have the gift of healing will be a lot more effective if they help the person live a righteous life. The same follows for those who have the gift of administration. They will accomplish more if their workers are living righteous lives.

If I loved and cared for a sick man I would help him be reconciled to God and then pray for his physical healing. Didn't Jesus tell us to seek first the kingdom of God and then all the other things would follow? Psychosomatic illnesses are due to a troubled soul, and when that is healed our prayers will be far more effective. The church's primary mission is to heal the soul. "We do not lose heart, but though our outer man is decaying, yet our inner man is being renewed day by day" (2 Corinthians 4:16). I don't lose heart when my physical body continues to decay or God doesn't instantly heal it, because my hope does not lie in the preservation of my physical body, it lies in the hope of a resurrected body when I physically die (see 1 Corinthians 15:35-58).

Paul wrote that it is required of us to be good stewards of all that God has entrusted to us (1 Corinthians 4:1-2). There is a tremendous health benefit for those who live a righteous life and have a proper balance of rest, exercise, and diet. When God calls such saints home, they don't cry and wail, demanding that God heal them. They die with dignity and without fear, which impresses the medical field far more than an occasional healing. Such saints say with Paul, "To me, to live is Christ and to die is gain" (Philippians 1:21).

## Deliverance

I received a letter from the senior pastor of an Assemblies of God Church in Singapore. One of his staff wanted to take a group of people to Ephesus (now in Turkey), where a number of Christians were going to gather and "pray out the queen of heaven." Part of the rationale for such an event was based on a paper by one of the leaders of the new apostolic movement. He had taught that the apostle Paul had gone to Ephesus and defeated the goddess Diana.

I don't want to be critical of anyone so I responded simply by asking the pastor a question: Did Paul defeat the goddess Diana, or did Jesus disarm Satan at the cross and Paul go to Ephesus preaching the full gospel, which the people believed and then repented of their worship of false gods and idols? The pastor thanked me and said he was not going on the trip, which was a wise choice, because the event amounted to nothing.

Deliverance ministries, like inner healing ministries, need to think through who is the responsible party and what are they responsible for. It is not our role to defeat the devil. He is already defeated. It is not our role to assume responsibility for those we are trying to help. Personal repentance and faith in God is and always will be the answer in this present church age. You can't put on the armor of God for another person, but you can teach them how to do it for themselves. You can't submit to God and resist the devil for them (James 4:7), but you can help them do it on their own. Christ is the deliverer, we're not.

If you sense that part of a person's problem is demonic, it might seem easier to cast out that demon for them—but what is to prevent the demon from coming back, and maybe with seven more (see Luke 11:24-26)? You cannot believe, confess, repent, forgive, or stand firm for other believers, but you can help them, which is what Paul teaches in 2 Timothy 2:24-26:

> The Lord's bond-servant must not be quarrelsome, but be kind to all, able to teach, patient when wronged, with gentleness correcting those who are in opposition, if perhaps God may grant them repentance leading to the knowledge of the truth, and they may come to their senses and escape from the snare of the devil, having been held captive by him to do his will.

The following letter from a pastor illustrates the above passage very well, and I hope it brings some encouragement to you as it did to me.

> I thank the Lord and you for the materials you have created. It is wonderful to use something that works for all sorts of people with

all sorts of problems. I stumbled on to your material last year. I was using it for Sunday school, and God was using it to prepare us for working with a severely demonized man. In preparation for taking him through the Steps to Freedom in Christ the elders and I went through the Steps first. I personally had the bondage to sin broken in my own life. My wife found freedom from her family's occultic background.

I'm in a new church now. Not much happened in the first two months, but without advertising or promoting, God has sent 12 people to me to go through the Steps. There has been a great work of God in people's hearts. Two elders resigned to get their lives straightened out. One has been having an affair for the last two years. He told me that his hypocrisy didn't bother him until after I came. It was the Lord! Not me! I'm honored that God has utilized me to touch lives. I'm taking him and his wife through the Steps next week.

I took the other elder and his wife through the Steps last week. He was in bondage to pornography, masturbation, and strip joints when he was on business trips. It was wonderful to see both elders find their freedom, renew, and deepen their relationships. What a joy and privilege to encourage people as they go through the Steps to Freedom.

One of our Sunday-school teachers has been experiencing nighttime terror and demonic dreams. Through God's "chance events," she told my wife about these difficulties. I took her and her husband through the Steps two weeks ago. When we came to forgiveness I had to teach, exhort, and encourage her for over an hour, and I had to physically put the pencil in her hand. It took her another 30 minutes to write the first name. But eventually she made a decision and went for it. God is so good! The next Sunday there was so much joy, peace, and freedom on the face of both herself and her husband.

## Discussion Questions

1. Why do you or don't you believe there are apostles and prophets today?

2. How were false prophets identified in the Old Testament?

3. Have you personally seen the standards given in Jeremiah 23 violated in your church experience?

4. How were false prophets and teachers indentified in the New Testament?

5. How does it make you feel to know that there have been and will be false prophets and teachers even in our churches?

6. In what ways can we improperly overreact to the warnings about false teachers?

7. What is the primary purpose for the gift of prophesy?

8. How can it be misused or counterfeited?

9. Is there healing in the atonement? Why or why not?

10. How should we respond to those who are sick and asking for prayer?

11. Why does the author keep reminding us to be concerned about who is responsible for what?

12. How would you help a person who you suspect is paying attention to a deceiving spirit, or being held captive by Satan to do his will?

Part Two:

# Living in Harmony with God

*Christ did not stand in need of our service when He ordered us to follow Him. Rather, He thereby bestowed salvation upon us. For to follow the Savior is to be a partaker of salvation…Thus, also, service to God profits God nothing; nor has God any need of human obedience. Rather, He grants to those who follow and serve Him life, incorruption, and eternal glory. He bestows benefits upon those who serve Him, because they served Him. He bestows benefits on His followers, because they follow Him. However, He Himself does not receive any benefit from them. For He is rich, perfect, and in need of nothing.*[25]

IRENAEUS (C, 180)

# Chapter Six

# Intimacy with God

*I count all things to be loss in view of the surpassing value of knowing
Christ Jesus my Lord, for whom I have suffered the loss of all things,
and count them but rubbish [refuse] so that I may gain Christ.*

PHILIPPIANS 3:8

*It is not that I flee them [the commands of the law] as base things, but
that I prefer what is superior. Having tasted the grain, I throw away
the refuse. For refuse means the denser and harder part of the chaff. It
carries the grain but is discarded once the grain has been collected.*[26]

THEODORET'S COMMENTARY ON THE EPISTLE TO THE PHILIPPIANS

If anybody could qualify to have a relationship with God on the basis of
the Old Covenant and a natural Jewish heritage, the apostle Paul would
be the leading candidate. He was a "Hebrew of Hebrews" (Philippians 3:5)
and "as for legalistic righteousness, faultless" (verse 6 NIV). He was a zeal-
ous defender of the faith and knew all *about* God, but until the Lord struck
him down on the Damascus road, he didn't *know* God at all. He had an
Old Covenant relationship with God, but not a personal one. His conversion cost him everything he had worked for. He lost his social status, his
friends, his reputation, his position in the synagogue, and his respect in
the Jewish community. But to him that was rubbish compared to knowing
Christ Jesus his Lord.

The most important belief we can have is a true knowledge of God and
who we are in relationship to Him. According to the Westminster Shorter
Catechism, "God is a Spirit, infinite, eternal, and unchangeable in His being,
wisdom, power, holiness, justice, goodness and truth." That's a fairly comprehensive definition that helps us know *about* God, but can we actually

*know* God? Personally? Scripture declares that God is incomprehensible: "How great is God—beyond our understanding! The number of his years is past finding out" (Job 36:26 NIV). We cannot fully comprehend the Infinite One, yet we can truly know Him as our Heavenly Father. Paul prays that "the God of our Lord Jesus Christ, the glorious Father, may give you the spirit of wisdom and revelation, so that you may know Him better" (Ephesians 1:17 NIV).

God has made Himself known to us through His Word, but the written Word by itself can only give us knowledge *about* God. The ultimate revelation of God is Jesus, His Son. Jesus said, "Anyone who has seen me has seen the Father" (John 14:9 NIV). It is through Christ, the Living Word, that we personally know our heavenly Father: "No one knows the Son except the Father, and no one knows the Father except the Son and those to whom the Son chooses to reveal him" Matthew 11:27 NIV). That may sound like only some are chosen to know Him, but Jesus said,

> I say to you, "ask, and it will be given to you; seek, and you will find; knock, and it will be opened to you. For everyone who asks, receives; and he who seeks, finds; and to him who knocks, it will be opened" (Luke 11:9-10).

God has revealed Himself and shared how we can have a personal relationship with Him through Jesus His Son, and how we can live with Him, walk with Him, and have fellowship with Him. That being the case, stop reading for a moment and reflect on your own personal relationship with God. How close are you to your heavenly Father? At this very moment you are as intimate with God as you have chosen to be. I am going to describe four levels of intimacy with God and start with the outer level of intimacy.

## The Outer Level of Intimacy with God

In Exodus 19, "Moses went up to God, and the LORD called to Him from the mountain saying, 'Thus you shall say to the house of Jacob and tell the sons of Israel'" (verse 3). What followed was the Mosaic covenant, which was conditional:

> If you will indeed obey My voice and keep My commandments, then you shall be My own possession among all the peoples, for all the earth is Mine; and you shall be to Me a kingdom of priests

and a holy nation. These are the words that you shall speak to the sons of Israel (verses 5-6).

Moses shared what he heard and the people said, "All that the LORD has spoken we will do!" (verse 8). Give them credit for their willingness to be obedient. Their relationship was not personal, however. It was a law relationship.

Moses gathered all the people, who were to consecrate themselves. On the third day the Lord would come down on Mount Sinai in the sight of all the people. Moses was also instructed to set bounds for them. They were not to go up on the mountain or touch the border of it lest they die. "Moses brought the people out of the camp to meet God, and they stood at the foot of the mountain. Now Mount Sinai was all in smoke because the LORD descended upon it in fire; and its smoke ascended like the smoke of a furnace, and the whole mountain quaked violently. When the sound of the trumpet grew louder and louder, Moses spoke and God answered him with thunder" (verses 17-18).

It is reasonably safe to say there were no atheists in the camp that day— but why the boundary? The answer is in Exodus 20:18-20:

> All the people perceived the thunder and the lightning flashes and the sound of the trumpet and the mountain smoking; and then when the people saw it, they trembled and stood at a distance. Then they said to Moses, "Speak to us yourself and we will listen; but let not God speak to us, or we will die." Moses said to the people, "Do not be afraid; for God has come in order to test you, and in order that the fear of Him may remain with you, so that you may not sin."

It was a test, and it revealed two characteristics of those who occupy the outer level of intimacy. First, their orientation toward God is to avoid punishment. Many people sitting in our churches are satisfied to know that they are saved from the pit of hell. They have their fire insurance, and that is all they want. So they go on living the natural life with very little interest in pursuing their relationship with God. After all, who wants to approach a consuming fire?

Also, they prefer a secondhand relationship or experience with God. The Israelites wanted Moses to speak to God for them and they would hear from God through Moses. That is like saying today, *Pastor, would you pray for me and study for me? Let me know what God says on Sunday morning.* How sad is that? Maybe the real tragedy is the pastors who are willing to settle for that in their own congregations. Assuming the congregation is connected with God, they focus on instructing them how to live, hoping they will obey. Those who want an intimate relationship with God will start looking elsewhere, and those who stay are the ones unsure of their salvation or who fear that leaving will seal their fate (they want to avoid punishment). One such pastor told me that he would not share with his people who they are in Christ, because the knowledge of their freedom would take away their motivation to stop sinning. According to him we should lie about our identity in Christ and motivate people with fear instead of love.

## Sinners in the Hands of an Angry God?

When I was in the eighth grade our school had a program called "religious day instruction." Every Tuesday afternoon they shortened the classes so we could go the last hour to the church of our choice. It wasn't forced religion. Students could go to study hall if they wanted. I chose to go to the church of my mother's choice! But one nice fall afternoon I decided to skip religious day instruction and play in the nearby park instead. I came back to the school in time to catch the school bus and thought I had got away with my deception.

I did not. The principal called me in the next day and chewed me out. He finished his lecture by saying, "I have arranged for you to be off Thursday and Friday from school." Suspended from school for two days for skipping religious day instruction? I was shocked. I wasn't looking forward to going home and sharing that news. I had some alternative thoughts while riding the school bus on the way home. Thoughts like, *Get up tomorrow and pretend you're sick for the next two days.* Or, *Do your chores and pretend that you got on the bus and then go hide in the woods for the rest of the day.* I didn't think I could pull either one off, so I decided to take my medicine. But I was not looking forward to seeing my authority figures.

I chose to confess to my mother because I thought there would be some mercy there. "Mom," I said. "I got suspended from school for two days because I skipped religious day instruction." She responded with a surprised, "What?" Then her expression changed and she said, "Oh Neil, I forgot to tell you. We called the school yesterday to ask if you could be off for two days to help us pick corn." Incredible! I could have gotten away with my indiscretion, but God had arranged it so there would be no secrets between me and my parents.

If I had known that my absence on Thursday and Friday was already excused, would I have dreaded going home? On the contrary, I would probably have run up the lane and gladly sought out my parents. The apostle Paul said, "Having been justified by faith, we have peace with God through our Lord Jesus Christ" (Romans 5:1). If you grasped that, you would go running to your heavenly Father. "There is no fear in love; but perfect love casts out fear, because fear involves punishment, and the one who fears is not perfected in love" (1 John 4:18).

Too many Christians live as though they're walking on glass—and if they make one wrong move the hammer of God will fall on them. Dear Christian, the hammer has fallen. It fell on Christ. We are not sinners in the hands of an angry God, we are saints in the hands of a loving God, who is calling us to come to His presence with confidence and boldness (Ephesians 3:12). Therefore, "Let us draw near with a sincere heart in full assurance of faith, having our hearts sprinkled clean from an evil conscience and our bodies washed with pure water" (Hebrews 10:22).

## The Second Level of Intimacy

> Moses went up with Aaron, Nadab and Abihu, and seventy of the elders of Israel, and they saw the God of Israel; and under His feet there appeared to be a pavement of sapphire, as clear as the sky itself. Yet He did not stretch out His hand against the nobles of the sons of Israel; and they saw God, and they ate and drank (Exodus 24:9-10)

When you climb the mountain of God, notice how quickly the numbers fall off. These 70-plus servants saw only a manifestation of God, because nobody living in a natural body can look fully upon God. We look forward to receiving a resurrected body and seeing God face-to-face, but that will only happen for us when we exchange the natural and perishable body for the spiritual and immortal body (1 Corinthians 15:53). These people had a life-changing encounter with God, but they slid back down the mountain. They were told to wait while Moses and Joshua went farther up. But they got tired of waiting.

They walked back down and built themselves a golden calf (see Exodus 32). Aaron instructed the people to tear off their gold jewelry. He melted it, and with it he made a golden calf and said, "This is your god, O Israel, who brought you up from the land of Egypt" (verse 4). The temptation is to think that we can buy our way out of anything. In truth, money can end physical poverty for a while, but it cannot end the poverty of the soul. Impersonal gods don't have to be served, and backsliders find it tiresome to wait upon the Lord.

"Is there a god?" is not the question for those at this level of intimacy. The question they are asking is more one of relevance. Have you ever wondered why God doesn't settle once and for all the question of His existence? Why doesn't He show Himself for who He is? Suppose He did provide scientific proof to the whole world that He exists. He could communicate to everyone that at a certain date and time He would make himself known to them all in a way that was undisputable. What if He told everyone in advance that He was going to present Himself in a visible way so that the whole world could see Him in the clouds? Photographs could be taken of His appearance, and nobody could ever refute the evidence of His existence.

At first the whole world would be astounded. Every television station would be showing the footage and broadcasting testimonies of those who saw God. Dramatic changes in the way people live would probably be the initial result, but it wouldn't be long before people would settle back to their old routines of work and play. Imagine a father showing his son a picture of God and saying, "Look, son, God exists." To which the son replies, "So?" What difference would it make? What would change in the way we live?

In reality, everything should change the moment we enter into a relationship with God. God has taken up residence in our lives. Christ dwells in our hearts through faith (Ephesians 3:17). We have been given the Holy Spirit, and Jesus said,

> He will glorify Me, for He will take of Mine and will disclose it to you. All things that the Father has are Mine; therefore I said that He takes of Mine and will disclose it to you (John 16:14-15).

The major work of the Holy Spirit is to disclose God's presence to us and to testify with our spirit that we are children of God (Romans 8:16). Assured of salvation, we learn to walk by faith in the power of the Holy Spirit. We learn to accept one another, just as Christ has accepted us (Romans 15:7). We learn to be merciful as God has been merciful to us, and to forgive others as we have been forgiven. We love because He first loved us. We stop going to work just to earn a living. At our places of employment we start doing our work heartily, as for the Lord rather than for men, because it is the Lord Christ whom we serve (Colossians 3:24). We daily practice the presence of God, because He is omnipresent and His presence affects everything we do and say.

To worship God is to ascribe to Him His divine attributes. We don't worship Him for His sake. He doesn't need us to tell Him who He is. We worship Him for *our* sake, and for the sake of our relationship with Him. Worshipping Him in Spirit and in truth stops us from thinking we can hide from Him, because He is omnipresent. It also stops the hypocrisy, because God is omniscient, "able to judge the thoughts and intentions of the heart. And there is no creature hidden from His sight, but all things are open and laid bare to the eyes of Him with whom we have to do" (Hebrews 4:12-13).

That is why we are instructed in 1 John 1:7 to walk in the light and have fellowship with one another. Walking in the light is not moral perfection, because the following verse says, "If we say we have no sin, we are deceiving ourselves and the truth is not in us" (verse 8). Confession of sins and walking in the light are essentially the same practice, which is to be open and honest with God about our moral condition—that is, no hypocrisy. We can do that because we are already forgiven. The presence of God in our lives changes everything!

## The Third Level of Intimacy

> The LORD said to Moses, "Come up to Me on the mountain and remain there, and I will give you the stone tablets with the law and the commandments which I have written for their instruction." So Moses arose with Joshua his servant, and Moses went up to the mountain of God (Exodus 24:12-13).

Why Joshua? What was unique about Joshua that enabled him to take the next step up the mountain of God? After the golden calf debacle Moses pitched the tent outside the camp of the Israelites and called it the tent of meeting (Exodus 33:7). Those who sought the Lord went to the tent.

> When all the people saw the pillar of cloud standing at the entrance of the tent, all the people would arise and worship, each at the

entrance of his tent. Thus the LORD used to speak to Moses face
to face, just as a man speaks to his friend. When Moses returned
to the camp, his servant Joshua, the son of Nun, a young man,
would not depart from the tent (33:10-11).

Level two Christians fulfill their obligations to God and then go on
about their business. Level three Christians don't want to depart from God.
They have tasted the goodness of God, and know there is more of Him to
seek after. Having been a seminary professor I have seen the difference in
my students, some of whom simply came to fulfill the degree requirements
to enable their "professional" journey. They are satisfied with just getting a
diploma. But a small number of my students weren't so easily satisfied. They
would stay after class and ask questions. They wanted more than information. They wanted a relationship.

Another biblical example is the passing of the mantle from Elijah to
Elisha. God had directed Elijah to anoint Elisha as a prophet in his place
(1 Kings 19:16). The two were leaving Gilgal when "Elijah said to Elisha, 'Stay
here please, for the LORD has sent me as far as Bethel.' But Elisha said, 'As
the LORD lives and as you yourself live, I will not leave you.' So they went
down to Bethel" (2 Kings 2:2).

At Bethel there were a few "sons of the prophets" who invited Elisha
to stay with them since his master, Elijah, would be taken away from him
that day. These "sons of the prophets" had made no name for themselves.
They were living off the reputation of their fathers. This colorless conformity
to the status quo might have offered Elisha some job security, but that is
not what he was looking for. He was seeking what Elijah had, which was
God's anointing.

Then Elijah told Elisha to stay in Bethel while he went to Jericho, but
Elisha was not about to do that. So the two went to Jericho and there were
some more "sons of the prophets" who offered Elisha the same "opportunity"
to stay with them, and Elijah encouraged Elisha to do so as he was going to
the Jordan River. By now you should know Elisha's response…and so the
two men went to the Jordan River, but this time the sons of the prophets
followed them.

At the river Elijah took off his mantle and struck the water. The river
parted and "the two of them crossed over on dry ground" (2 Kings 2:8).
Elijah then said to Elisha, "'Ask what I shall do for you before I am taken

away from you.' And Elisha said, 'Please, let a double portion of your spirit be upon me'" (verse 9). He was asking for twice as much. He was asking for the birthright, which was given to a firstborn son. Elijah told him he had asked for a hard thing, but it would be given to him if he saw Elijah taken from him that day. As they were walking and talking together the chariots of God took Elijah to heaven in a whirlwind, and his mantle fell to the ground.

Elijah had just taken Elisha as far as one man can take another, which is to the wrong side of the Jordan River. To further clarify the significance of that, recall that Jacob had labored on that side of the Jordan River after he ran from his father, Isaac. For 14 years he bargained for one wife and got another as he struggled relating to his father-in-law. Fed up with it all, he finally picked up his two wives and livestock and headed for home to face his father and brother. At the Jordan he sent his family and livestock across the river and that night he wrestled with the angel of the Lord (Genesis 32:24, see also Hosea 12:4), agonizing in prayer.

Jacob struggled with this pre-incarnate appearance of Christ until dawn started to break. At first he struggled to get away. But at the crack of dawn he looked into the face of pure love. Now he was holding on to this "man," asking for a blessing. The Lord touched the socket of his thigh so that he would know forever that this was no dream, and asked him his name, and he said Jacob. "Your name shall no longer be Jacob, but Israel; for you have striven with God and with men and have prevailed" (verse 28). Jacob named the place Peniel, which means the face of God. On the east side of the Jordan he was Jacob, but when he limped across to the other side he was Israel. He had discovered God for himself.

Now Elisha finds himself stranded on the wrong side of the Jordan. Elijah could have taken him back to the other side, but it would be the God of Elijah who did it. Elisha would have to discover God for himself, as we all have to. We can go only so far with the God of our parents, pastors, and friends. Elisha picked up the mantle and struck the water saying, "Where is the LORD, the God of Elijah?" (2 Kings 2:14). The water parted and he walked across. The sons of the prophets offered to search for his master, but Elisha refused. Because on the other side of the river Elijah was his master, but on this side of the Jordan God was his master.

God does not favor one of His children over another. All have been invited to His presence. We have our favorites, but God doesn't. It may appear that he favors one over another, but it only seems that way because some have chosen to draw near while others haven't. The blessing comes to those who hold on, who linger at the meetings, who go the extra mile to meet their Creator.

## The Fourth Level of Intimacy

Finally, there was only one person who continued up the mountain of God. What was there about Moses that afforded such intimacy with God that He would speak to him face-to-face? Four issues stand out, and they constitute a challenge to all of us.

### Humility

The first is humility. It is recorded in Numbers 12:3 that "the man Moses was very humble, more than any man who was on the face of the earth." I don't think that was the case from the beginning. Moses was raised in the courts of Pharaoh. This privileged position was orchestrated by God and would likely have prompted more pride than humility.

After Moses had risen to a strong position of political power, God placed a burden on Moses' heart to set His people free. Did God put him in that high political position in order to accomplish that task? That's a natural conclusion, but you don't set God's people free from any human position, political or otherwise. God works through our position in Christ to set captives free. Moses tried to accomplish God's work using his own strength and resources…and he failed. He spent the next 40 years tending his father-in-law's sheep on the back side of the desert.

Then one day this broken man turned aside to see a marvelous sight. A bush was burning, but not being consumed. Moses had once been on fire for God, but he had burned out trying to serve God by his own strength and resources. He realized that the bush continued to burn because God was in it. God, not Moses, would set his people free. God just wanted Moses to be the instrument He worked through, and the same is true for us. Pride is serving God in our own strength and resources. Humility is letting God work through us to accomplish His purposes.

### Freedom from Selfish Ambition

Second, Moses was free from selfish ambition. After the people had built their own god,

> The Lord said to Moses, "I have seen this people, and behold, they are an obstinate people. Now then let me alone, that My anger may burn against them and that I may destroy them; and I will make of you a great nation" (Exodus 32:9-10).

I wonder how many Christian leaders would pass that test today. The people deserved judgment, and God Himself said he was going to carry it out. Many of us would be happy to let God alone in that case and feel blessed by His choice.

It is one thing to come up with that idea ourselves. I'm sure many pastors have thought at some time, *My people are obstinate. I may not ask God to judge them, but I kind of hope He does. Then I could start over again with God's blessing.* It is another thing when God expresses that desire and choice. So how did Moses respond?

> Then Moses entreated the Lord his God, and said, "O Lord, why does Your anger burn against Your people whom You have brought out from the land of Egypt with great power and with a mighty hand? Why should the Egyptians speak, saying, 'With evil intent He brought them out to kill them in the mountains and to destroy them from the face of the earth'? Turn from Your burning anger and change Your mind about doing harm to Your people" (Exodus 32:11-12).

Moses was more concerned about God's reputation than he was his own. He didn't want to build his own kingdom. He wanted to build God's kingdom. He wasn't trying to make a name for himself. Moses was about proclaiming the great I AM, who had sent him back to Egypt to be an instrument in His hand. What name could we make for ourselves that would be more significant than being called children of God? What values rank higher than being eternally related to the One who "upholds all things by the word of his power" (Hebrews 1:3)?

### Having the Right Goal

Third, Moses had the right goal. He had the formidable task of leading five million grumbling Israelites across a barren land for 40 years. There would be no running water, sinks, commodes, showers, bedrooms for privacy or kitchens for cooking. They would have a one-course meal of manna day after day after day. Babies would be conceived and delivered. Disputes would have to be settled and criticism deflected. Then Moses said to the LORD:

> "See, You say to me, 'Bring up this people!' But You Yourself have not let me know whom You will send with me. Moreover, You have said, 'I have known you by name, and you have found favor in My sight.' Now therefore, I pray You, if I have found favor in Your sight, let me know Your ways that I may know You, so that I may find favor in Your sight. Consider too, that this nation is Your people." And He said, "My presence shall go with you, and I will give you rest" (Exodus 33:12-14).

Trekking around the Sinai Peninsula for 40 years is not my idea of rest, but God actually did give Moses rest. The quality of a rest is determined by how you feel after it is over. Forty years later Moses was standing on Mount Nebo looking into the Promised Land, which he never got to enter. "Although Moses was one hundred and twenty years old when he died, his eye was not dim, nor his vigor abated" (Deuteronomy 34:7). Resting in God is not an abdication of responsibility, nor the cessation of labor. Biblical rest is knowing God and His ways and practicing His presence.

Jesus said, "Come to Me, all who are weary and heavy-laden, and I will give you rest. Take my yoke upon you and learn from Me, for I am gentle and humble in heart, and you will find rest for your souls. For My yoke is easy and My burden is light" (Matthew 11:28-29). Weariness comes from carrying our own load. Many stress-related illnesses that plague the world indicate an alienation from God and His ways. Knowing God and His ways actually bring us rest for our souls. The writer of Hebrews says, "There remains a Sabbath rest for the people of God" (4:9).

> Therefore let us be diligent to enter that rest, so that no one will fall, through following the same example of disobedience. For the Word of God is living and active and sharper than any two-edged sword, and piercing as far as the division of soul and spirit, of both joints and marrow, and able to judge the thoughts and intentions of the heart. And there is no creature hidden from His sight, but all things are open and laid bare to the eyes of Him with whom we have to do (Hebrews 4:11-13).

The Word of God mentioned above is not referring to our Bibles. Jesus is the Word the author of Hebrews is referring to. The previous context in Hebrews clearly establishes that Jesus is the subject, the one who is greater than the angels and greater then Moses. Knowing that God has infinite knowledge of us is what prompts the warning not to harden our hearts. There is no condemnation for those who are in Christ Jesus (Romans 8:1). We are forgiven—and knowing the vile nature of our flesh, which is fully known to God—this should spawn gratitude and humility.

There is nothing hidden that won't be revealed. Secret sin on earth is open scandal in heaven. On the other hand, "There will be more joy in heaven over one sinner who repents than over ninety-nine righteous persons who need no repentance" (Luke 15:7). Covering up our sins drives us from God. Repentance draws us closer.

A lady poured her heart out to me after a Sunday morning service. The self-disclosure gnawed at her for the rest of the day. She called me Monday morning as soon as she thought it was appropriate and said, "I can't believe all the things I told you about myself yesterday. What do you think of me?" I said, "Well, I love you for sharing that with me. How else could I help you?" There was a pause, and then she said, "Well, I have a lot more to share with you then." Full disclosure happens naturally when doing so results in acceptance and resolution of past abuses and indiscretions.

### The Desire to See God Glorified

Finally, Moses desired to see God glorified. "Moses said, 'I pray You, show me Your glory!'" (Exodus 33:18), and God did. Moses couldn't see God's face, but His glory passed by and Moses got to see His back. It transformed Moses, and his countenance radiated the glory of God, which slowly faded from his face. Such unusual encounters with God leave lasting impressions on our souls, but not necessarily our physical bodies, which are still destined to decay. Such encounters are not normative, and the lasting physical impression may be blinding, such as happened to Saul, who became Paul, or a limp, as in the case of Jacob, who became Israel.

I was asleep in my hotel room in Israel when I was suddenly awakened by an overwhelming sense of God's presence. I saw and heard nothing, but I felt weightless and oh-so-good. I was speechless, and all I kept saying in my mind was *It's too good. Is this what it will be like in the presence of God? It's too good.* I have never forgotten that experience, and I don't know why God revealed Himself to me that way. No great decision or anointing came from that encounter. It just left me with an impression of God's goodness I have never forgotten.

### New Testament Intimacy with God

The Gospels also tell of the masses who came to see Jesus. Some came out of curiosity to see what all the fuss was about, and others came for healing. Out of compassion Jesus did heal the sick, and then told some of them not to tell anyone. If the Lord's ministry was attested to by signs and wonders, why would he say, "Don't tell anyone?" Because Jesus didn't come to heal the sick, restore sight and hearing to the blind and deaf, or to feed the 5000. He knew the fickle nature of our fallen humanity. If He dealt only with their physical needs, that is all they would come to Him for, as do some people today.

Then why did Jesus heal and help people? He did it because it was His nature to do it. "Seeing the people, He felt compassion for them" (Matthew 9:36). How wonderful it is for us to know that God is moved by compassion...

| | |
|---|---|
| for the crowds and the sick | Matthew 14:14 |
| for the hungry | Matthew 15:32 |
| for the enslaved | Matthew 18:27 |
| for the blind | Matthew 20:34 |
| for the leper | Mark 1:41 |
| for those without a shepherd | Mark 6:34 |
| for those who grieve | Luke 7:13 |
| for the abused | Luke 10:33 |
| for the prodigals of this world | Luke 15:20 |

To those who questioned Him about dining with sinners, Jesus said, "Go and learn what this means: I desire compassion, and not sacrifice" (Matthew 9:13). We have become partakers of His divine nature (2 Peter 1:4), and those who are closest to Him will also be moved by compassion. Jesus cares about all our needs, but He came to walk to the cross and die for our sins, and to be resurrected so we could have new life in Him. He reconciled us to God so that we may know Him and the power of His resurrection.

From the masses He chose to send out only 70 to proclaim the kingdom (Luke 10:1). Then there were the 12 disciples who followed and assisted

Jesus in His public ministry. Of the 12 only Peter, James, and John went with Jesus up the mountain to pray (Luke 9:28) and became witnesses to the transfiguration. Finally, "There was reclining on Jesus' bosom one of His disciples, whom Jesus loved" (John 13:23). John was the only disciple who stayed with Jesus all the way to the cross. "When Jesus then saw His mother, and the disciple whom He loved standing nearby, He said to His mother, 'Woman, behold, your son!' Then He said to the disciple, 'Behold, your mother!' From that hour the disciple took her into his own household" (John 19:26-27).

Jesus entrusted Mary to John, who chose to go the final mile with God. There remains a vacant place upon the bosom of Jesus for all those who consider intimacy with the Father the most precious possession of all. He is the King of kings, the Lord of lords and the great I AM. But to those who know Him personally, He is our Father, our Savior, our Lord, our Wonderful Counselor, our Great Physician, and our Friend.

## Discussion Questions

1. What is the difference between knowing *about* God and *knowing* Him?

2. What has been your understanding of who God is before and after salvation? How has it changed?

3. Does your present orientation toward God draw you closer or keep you away?

4. How relevant is your relationship with God in your daily experience?

5. Why do we worship God?

6. What is the difference between going to church and doing a Bible study out of duty as opposed to seeking God?

7. How do you measure up to Moses in humility?

8. How free are you from selfish ambition?

9. Do you have the right goal in life?

10. Do you desire for God to be glorified?

11. How would you describe the "Sabbath rest" that remains?

12. What do you love most about God?

# Chapter Seven

# The Will of God

*Only if God is reinstated in the heart of the world will He*
*furnish mankind and its leaders with ethical guidance*
*through the dangers and pitfalls of the space age.*[27]

Wernher von Braun

The phone rang shortly before noon. The congregation of the church had extended a call for me to be their senior pastor. I was on staff at an exciting ministry where I had worn several hats. I started out being the college pastor, picked up the youth ministry, and finally became the minister of adult education in a large multi-staffed church. Now I was asked to be the senior pastor in a struggling church plant that met in the rented facilities of a Seventh-Day Adventist Church.

The church was six years old. The founding pastor had left after four years, leaving them without a shepherd for two years. They had pieced together a couple of acres that were irregularly shaped in a residential area. Nobody was too excited about the property, but land was at a premium in this coastal community of Southern California. I had my doubts about the possibility of ever building there.

Six months into the ministry I sensed that God was going to do something in our church that could not be explained by hard work or human ingenuity. I even shared my impressions with the congregation.

While I was studying in my office one day, my secretary told me a realtor wanted to see me. He was representing a construction firm looking for space to build houses. He had tracked us down to see if we would be willing to sell our fragmented property.

Given the difficulty of finding available property, I told him we weren't interested in selling. He asked if we especially wanted that property, or if we would be willing to build somewhere else. I felt a little uncomfortable speaking for the church, but I didn't like the property or its location. We chatted for a while, and he left with the impression that we would be willing to sell the property if he could find something better for us.

A week later he had located a piece of property he thought would be much better for us. To my surprise he showed me five vacant acres situated perfectly in the cross-section of our community. He thought the price would be reasonable since it had been tied up in litigation. A bank had repossessed the property and had been holding it for ten years while paying the taxes. I asked him to give us a bid for our old property.

I informed our board, and they were as pleased and surprised as I was that such property was still available. The church met, and we all agreed to offer a bid for the property, not to exceed $500,000. This was a middle-to upper-middle class coastal community in 1978, so we all had our doubts that we could actually purchase that size property for such a low price. We started negotiations with the bank by making an offer of $400,000. We were all pleasantly surprised to receive an offer of $325,000 for our old property. For $75,000 we could double our acreage and move to a much better location.

Then, on a Friday morning, I heard from the bank that they had turned us down. I drove to the bank to retrieve our bid, and I asked if the person responsible for the property was there. He was and he invited me into his office. I felt led to say, "We are just a nickel-and-dime operation, and I am authorized to counter-offer $425,000. Are we wasting our time?" He said that three vice-presidents, of which he was one, had to agree on such a sale, and one of the other two was present. He excused himself to talk with him. Less than five minutes later he came back with a signed and amended contract for $425,000. I was elated and so was the church. For $100,000 we were getting what was unimaginable weeks earlier.

⌒

While waiting for the contracts to close, we put together a building committee and started making plans for this "gift from God." Days before we were supposed to close on our old property, the realtor paid me another visit with some very bad news. The contractor he represented was backing out of the deal. Could he do that? I asked. The realtor thought he legally could, and shared how sorry he was. "I have represented him for 25 years and he has never done that before," he said. "I think he is having some family problems. His daughter has multiple sclerosis and has been living with them since her husband left her."

I shared the bad news that Sunday morning with the board, and they were quite upset. Several wanted to take legal action against the contractor. I was deeply disappointed in them, and said I would have no part in any such litigation. Our ministry was to help hurting people, not sue them! The next Tuesday I was holding my regular visitation evangelism class, and I sensed the Lord leading me to visit the contractor whom I had never met. To my surprise, his phone number and address were listed in the phone book.

I drove up to the address, doubting I would have any chance to see him in this upscale community, since most of the homes were behind gates. To my surprise, his wasn't! The house was huge; I wasn't sure where the front door was. As I was walking by the kitchen window their maid saw me and asked through the open window what I was doing there. I said I was there to see the contractor. He wasn't home, she said, but his wife and daughter were, and she invited me in. In their large master bedroom, I met the wife and the daughter, whose physical impairment was obvious.

I introduced myself and said, "I have never met your husband, but we had a business deal that fell through. I sensed he was a hurting person, and I wanted to come by to see if I could do anything to help." I found out that the mother and daughter were attending a religious cult, but I noticed they were reading Chuck Colson's book *Born Again*. An hour later I had the privilege to lead both of them to Christ.

I fairly flew off that mountain of affluence in my pastoral limousine, which was a VW Bug. The next day the realtor called and said, "I don't know what you did yesterday, but the deal is back on. However, he has lowered his offer to $300,000." We gladly accepted because it was still a very good deal.

It was a test. God wanted to give us that property, but He wanted to know what we would do with it. There were 8000 people who lived within a four block radius of that location, and He wanted us to be a beacon of light for the lost.

But we weren't finished with roadblocks yet.

Shortly thereafter I had lunch with another realtor, who was also the third-term mayor of the city. I asked him about the possibility of getting a building permit for a church on the new location. He shared that our parcel was one of four such plots that had been in litigation for about ten years. A large contracting firm had wanted to build low-income housing, and the city had quickly rezoned to stop that from happening. So this prime property had sat vacant for ten years, with neither side moving. He advised us to sell, because he had serious doubts about our ever being given permission to build. That could have been a lethal blow to my faith about what I believed to be God's leading, since the mayor knew the real-estate market and the politics of that community far better than I did.

About the same time I received another caller at our church office. This man was a lawyer who represented the large construction firm. They were about to make a deal with the city to stop the litigation if they would let them build condominiums. They owned the other three plots and wanted to buy ours, which I informed them was not for sale. However, they offered us $750,000, and I was beginning to wonder if I was in the wrong business!

The construction company proceeded to make presentations to the planning committee, and we attended with great interest. There were some serious zoning questions that affected how residential housing interfaced with commercial businesses in the area. During one meeting, a council member pointed out that it would be a lot easier if we would exchange our five acres with one of the five-acre plots the construction company owned. The lawyer came to us with an offer. They would exchange their five acres for ours, clear the property of all debris, give us fill dirt for a low spot, and $200,000 cash. We agreed, especially since our architect said the new property was much better located.

Now we were starting our building program with the property debt-free, the ground cleared (which took two dump trucks a week of hauling), and $75,000 cash in our pockets. Halfway through construction, our contractor told us he'd been playing golf the previous weekend and an old friend had asked him about his work. He'd said, "I'm building a church building," and had shared with him the location. His friend said, "You are not going to believe this. Their pastor struck a deal for that property for $425,000 a couple years back, and that very afternoon I submitted a bid of $600,000 for the same property."

God is still building His church and guiding His children. There is nothing I want more than to be in the center of God's will and be guided by Him. Do you know what God's will for your life is? Do you want to know? Those are not simple questions, and not every believer is prepared to answer them.

## Defining God's Will

Bruce Waltke wrote, "The term 'God's will' is tough to define. It is often used in Scripture to refer to God's eternal plan and decree:"[28] In that sense, God sovereignly rules over all His creation, and His eternal plan "hastens toward the goal and it will not fail" (Habakkuk 2:3). He is the King of kings, and He rules over His kingdom. What He has said will come to pass. Jesus instructed His children to pray, "Your kingdom come. Your will be done, on earth as it is in heaven" (Matthew 6:10). What is presently happening in heaven is not what is happening on earth, and Scripture reveals at least one reason why.

In ages past, Lucifer rose up against God and led a rebellion against His sovereign rule. It is believed that a third of the angels (demons) followed his lead and were all thrown out of God's presence. The Lord created Adam and Eve to have dominion over all the earth, but they sinned and lost their relationship with their heavenly Father. Because of the fall, Satan became the rebel holder of authority and the "ruler of this world" (John 16:11), and "the prince of the power of the air" (Ephesians 2:2). God's plan (will) is to defeat Satan and destroy His works (1 John 3:8), bring salvation to the descendants of Adam, and reestablish His kingdom. It *will* be established.

What is God's will for our personal lives? According to Paul, it is our sanctification (1 Thessalonians 4:3)—that is, we are to conform to His image. We are to be holy as He is holy (1 Peter 1:16). His plan is that Christ will "present to Himself the Church in all her glory, having no spot or wrinkle or any such thing; but that she would be holy and blameless" (Ephesians 5:27). To be in God's will, we must believe what He says is true and live by faith according to His Word, and become what He created us to be.

There is a difference between the concepts of knowing God's will and that of divine guidance. There are no instructions in Scripture for making career choices, choosing mates, or selecting places of residence. How then can we know whether we should be carpenters, plumbers, or engineers, live in St. Louis, or marry Susie or Alan? The answer is that God's will is more related to what *kind* of employee, spouse, or citizen we should be. However, He provides divine guidance for His children and equips us with the mind of Christ so we can make decisions that are consistent with His will. His Holy Spirit will guide us in our decision-making process. "All who are being led by the Spirit of God, these are sons of God" (Romans 8:14).

In many cases we get the cart before the horse. We want to know what God wants us to do…before we become who God wants us to *be*. You have to be God's child before you can be led by His Spirit. Godly people who live out their calling have made the choice to put character before career, maturity before ministry, and being before doing. God is far more concerned about who you are than what you do, because what you do is shaped by who you are.

## God Prepares Hearts

God has known us from the foundation of the world and prepares us for His will very early in life. I remember as a young child sitting in church listening to the minister and thinking, *I can do that*. Years later, while attending a military church service, I had the sense that God was calling me into ministry. I even informed my parents in a letter that I was considering becoming a minister.

It's not uncommon to sense a call into the ministry, at an early age. Yet in my case, the unusual part is that I did not become a Christian until two years *after* my military service. God prepares hearts even before we belong to Him. It's consistent with His sovereignty that He actively works in the lives of His people from the beginning to the end of time. Paul wrote that "we are His workmanship, created in Christ Jesus for good works, which God prepared *beforehand* so that we would walk in them" (Ephesians 2:10).

Despite my earlier sensing of being called to ministry I became an aerospace engineer instead. Was I now outside of the will of God, or was God using that experience to prepare me for ministry? After four years in the aerospace industry, I again clearly sensed God's call to full-time ministry. I left a successful career and enrolled at the Talbot School of Theology. From the beginning of our Christian experience, my wife and I have trusted God to lead us concerning where we should serve. Consequently, we have never sought a position in ministry. I was asked to be a club director with Youth for Christ, and was later invited to be a candidate for the position of minister to young adults at a church. Finally I was called to be a senior pastor and then invited by the dean at Talbot School of Theology to be a seminary professor.

I never applied for, sent a resume for, or personally sought any of those positions. In each case, I believe God clearly led me. When I started my walk with God, I had no desire to be a senior pastor and certainly not a seminary professor. My own sense of giftedness and direction became evident as I grew in the Lord. My most difficult decision was to leave Talbot School of Theology and start Freedom in Christ Ministries, which has become a global ministry.

## A Matter of Shaping

When I left engineering school, I had no desire to pursue any more formal education. But as I began to mature in the Lord, my desire to read and learn increased. The Lord was shaping my life in ways I never would have anticipated. Since then I have completed two master's degrees and two doctoral degrees. Anybody who knew me in high school would have to acknowledge that as a miracle. I have come to deeply believe that God sovereignly governs the affairs of His children. He gently guides our steps as we choose to walk with Him.

My purpose for the rest of this book is to help you walk closely with God, and share with you what I have learned about divine guidance. I will do my best to draw a fine line on issues that are clearly taught in Scripture, but I will cover some issues in broad strokes. To our finite minds, there will always be a degree of mystery about the Infinite One. Some questions will remain unanswered and some issues will seem ambiguous until the Lord returns. It is not God's will for us to know everything and lean on our own understanding. It is His intention that we be completely dependent upon Him.

I cannot answer all the questions I have in my own mind, much less yours. I am deeply sensitive to the possibility of leading one of God's lambs down a wrong path. After all, it's a bit presumptuous for any mortal to tell another mortal how God guides. My prayer then is that you will keep an open mind and search the Scriptures with me. The Bible is the only infallible source for faith and practice, not Neil Anderson or any other pastor or seminary professor.

I encourage you to "be diligent to present yourself approved to God as a workman who does not need to be ashamed, accurately handling the word of truth" (2 Timothy 2:15). If I help some of you stay on the narrow path of truth in your walk with God, I will be pleased. If I help others get back on the path, I will be thrilled.

## The Essential Prerequisite

In the first century people were questioning Christ. Some were saying, "He's a good man." Others were saying, "He leads the people astray" (see John 7:12). How could these people know whether Jesus truly was the Messiah and if His teaching was authoritative?

Sensing their need, Jesus set forth seven standards of divine guidance, starting in John 7:17. His first admonition was "My teaching is not mine, but His who sent me. If any man is willing to do His will, he will know of the teaching, whether it is of God or whether I speak from Myself" (John 7:17). The essential prerequisite, then, to know the will of God, according to Jesus, is a willingness to do the will of God even before you know what it is.

Jesus gave us an example to follow in His steps (1 Peter 2:21). He showed us how a person who is spiritually alive could live in this fallen world. It isn't always easy. Jesus agonized in His darkest hour: "Father, if You are willing, remove this cup from Me; yet not My will, but Yours be done" (Luke 22:42). The Lord Jesus Christ modeled a life of total dependence upon God the Father: "My food is to do the will of Him who sent me and to accomplish His work" (John 4:34).

## The Heart of God's Will

Please keep in mind that God's will is that we conform to His image and become the person He created us to be. The only person that can keep that from happening is ourself. Paul wrote, "Those whom He foreknew, He also predestined to become conformed to the image of His son" (Romans 8:29) and in 1 Timothy 1:5, "The goal of our instruction is love from a pure heart and a good conscience and a sincere faith." God's will is that we live in a righteous relationship with Him and in harmony with one another.

Many Christians want to know what God's plan is for their future. Suppose God's plan for your life is on the other side of a closed door. You will be tempted to ask, "What is it?" Why do you want to know what is on the other side? So you can decide whether or not you want to go through it? If you really want to live out your calling in life, then you have to solve something on this side of the door. If God is God, then He has the right to decide what is on the other side of the door. If we don't give Him that right, then we may never know what He had planned for us.

What happens, however, if you walk halfway through but keep your foot in the door just in case you don't like what you see and decide to go back? It's going to be awfully hard to continue walking with God if your foot is stuck in the door. Jesus said, "No one, after putting his hand to the plow and looking back, is fit for the kingdom of God" (Luke 9:62).

When I left engineering to attend seminary, I stayed on part-time as a consultant. I was keeping my foot in the door. After one semester I realized what I was doing and closed the door behind me. That was a critical choice, because I was tempted for the next five years to go back to my secular profession. In my early years of ministry I often thought I had borne more fruit as an engineer than I was in a ministry position—which was actually probably true at that time.

Hope is the present assurance of some future good. Hope gives us the courage to live responsibly, righteously, and confidently today. The critical issue concerning hope of the Lord's second coming has little to do with when He comes, because we have been clearly told we will not know the day or the hour. But it has everything to do with the assurance that He *will* come some day. Our proper response to that certainty is explained by the apostle Peter: "What sort of people ought you to be in holy conduct and godliness" (2 Peter 3:11). Jesus said, "Seek ye first His kingdom and His righteousness, and all these things will be added to you. So do not worry about tomorrow" (Matthew 6:33-34). Biblical prophecy should enhance our hope for the future. What God has decreed in His sovereignty *will* come to pass.

Does that mean we aren't supposed to make any plans for the future or establish any goals for our ministry or work? No, I believe we should prayerfully plan ahead with James 4:15 in mind: "You ought to say, if the Lord wills, we will live and also do this or that." It is appropriate to set goals as long as they aren't gods. A proper goal gives us direction so we know how we should live today. Christians should live one day at a time and trust God for tomorrow.

I have taught church leadership and management classes, and I firmly believe in setting goals and making plans. But a biblical vision for the future and godly goals for ministry or work have no value if they don't provide direction for our lives today. A goal for tomorrow that doesn't prioritize present activities is nothing more than wishful thinking. We make plans for tomorrow in order to establish meaningful activities for today. We need to stay on the course we believe God has called us to, and give Him the right to change our direction and plans any time He chooses.

## Making the Most of Every Opportunity

There are two important concepts about divine guidance that are essential to understand if we are going to be the people God has called us to be. The first is "Bloom where you are planted." Be the best you can be at your present assignment, and stay there until God calls you elsewhere.

I have heard seminary students say, "There are no openings to serve at my church!" My response is, "Oh, yes—there are." Their church is probably begging for someone to teach third-grade boys. "But anyone can teach third-grade boys," they reply. "I had something bigger in mind. Is there an opening in the Trinity?" The following poem speaks to that issue:

> Father, where shall I work today?
>     And my love flowed warm and free.
> Then He pointed out a tiny spot,
>     And said, "Tend that for Me."
> I answered quickly, "Oh no, not that.
>     Why, no one would ever see,
> No matter how well my work was done,
>     Not that little place for me!"
> And the word He spoke, it was not stern,
>     He answered me tenderly,
> "Ah little one, search that heart of thine,
>     Art thou working for them or me?
> Nazareth was a little place,
>     And so was Galilee."[29]

I advise those seminary students to take advantage of the opportunities available. Teach those third-grade boys and decide to be the best teacher you can be. You may start with only three little boys, but at the end of the year you may have twelve boys excited about God. Then one day the chairman of the Christian education committee says, "We need some new life on our committee." Another member on the committee is aware of the fruit you are bearing and says, "There's this guy having a great ministry with our third-grade boys. We should ask him to be on the committee."

Now that you are on the Christian education committee, decide to be the best committee member you can be. It won't be long before they recognize your initiative and further observe your fruit. A vacancy appears on the church board. Someone else has recognized your work and says, "We could use this person on the board." Now you should become the best possible board member you can be. Then the church starts looking for an intern, and guess who people suggest? When you show yourself faithful in little things, they start considering you for a full-time pastoral position. Now you become the best youth pastor, small-group pastor, or college minister you can possibly be. Before long you'll be bearing so much fruit that other churches will start inquiring about your availability. There are *many* open doors for those who will bloom where they are planted.

When D.L. Moody found new life in Christ, he looked for some opportunities to teach at a church, but no one wanted to use the uneducated man. So he started his own Bible study in a shoe store, and it wasn't long before kids were coming out of the woodwork. People couldn't help but notice him because he was bearing fruit, and that was the beginning of an incredible ministry.

Paul said, "I thank Christ Jesus our Lord, who has strengthened me, because he considered me faithful, putting me into service" (1 Timothy 1:12). Show yourself faithful by exploiting the opportunities around you. The needs of people are everywhere, so what are you waiting for? You don't need a church position to serve God.

### Don't Wait Around

That's an elementary concept, but too many Christians bide their time waiting for the "big opportunity" that never comes. Don't be like the pressured volunteer who taught third-grade boys, who at the end of the year had the same three boys he started with—boys looking forward to getting a new teacher who cared about them. Jesus is saying to those who bloom where they were planted, "Well done, good and faithful slave. You were faithful with a few things, I will put you in charge of many things; enter into the joy of your master" (Matthew 25:21). If you aren't responsible in your present assignment and taking advantage of the opportunities that God has already provided, don't expect God to call you elsewhere.

When I was a pastor, a man in our congregation often expressed frustration with his job. For 20 years he had been working as a construction worker, and he hated it! Frustrated with his career, he wondered why God wouldn't call him out of there.

I asked him if he had ever expressed dissatisfaction about his job with his fellow employees who weren't Christians. He said, "Oh, sure. I complain right along with the rest of them." I continued, "What do you suppose that does to your witness?" He was a little startled by my question. I then added, "Do you realize that God has you exactly where He wants you? When you assume your responsibility to be the person God created you to be and bloom where you are planted, He may open a new door for you."

The Holy Spirit must have brought conviction because this man became a missionary at work. He started to be concerned for the needs of his co-workers and their families and began to share his faith. Within six months a new opportunity arose and he left construction work, because he had decided to bloom where he was planted.

## God Guides a Moving Ship

That fact that God can only guide a moving ship is the second major concept that we need to know about God's guidance. He is the rudder, but if the ship isn't under way it can't be directed. Willingness to obey His will gets the ship moving.

When I was in the Navy I was assigned to a destroyer. We had just passed through the Panama Canal on our way to San Diego when we had a flame-out in the middle of the night. The "oil king" (the man responsible for even distribution of the oil on board the ship) had allowed a compartment of oil to be pumped dry. In a short time the boilers went cold for lack of fuel, and we lost all our power. Within minutes our ship was doing 30 and 40-degree rolls. A ship without power is helpless in the sea. The helmsman could do nothing, because the rudder only works if the ship is under way.

In Acts 15:36, Paul decided to revisit the churches he helped establish on his first missionary trip. The churches were being strengthened and increasing in number (Acts 16:5). Luke records,

> They passed through the Phrygian and Galatian region, having been forbidden by the Holy Spirit to speak the word in Asia; and when they had come to Mysia, they were trying to go into Bithynia, and the Spirit of Jesus did not permit them; and passing by Mysia, they came down to Troas. And a vision appeared to Paul in the night: a

certain man of Macedonia was standing and appealing to him, and saying, "Come over to Macedonia and help us" (Acts 16:6-9).

If God wanted Paul to go to Macedonia in the first place, why didn't He make it easier and faster by having Paul travel by land to Caesarea and sail to Macedonia? Apparently the Lord wanted Paul to strengthen the churches he had already established first, then break new ground in what is now known as Greece. Paul didn't know that when he started his second missionary journey. The Lord starts us on a life course and keeps us there until we have fulfilled a certain purpose. When that has been completed and when we have learned what He wants us to know, He changes the course of our lives and we head off on a new direction. Like a good river pilot, He steers us away from troubled waters, and like a good coach, He never puts us in the game until we are ready.

If God wanted me to start Freedom in Christ Ministries, why didn't He do it when He called me out of engineering? He didn't, because I wasn't ready for it. Instead He guided me through a variety of experiences—farm boy, sailor, wrestling coach, aerospace engineer, campus pastor, youth pastor, minister of adult education and senior pastor, and finally seminary professor. All the time I was gaining experience and developing character. Every new assignment was a stretching experience; each one had a greater responsibility.

I strongly believe in divine guidance. Isaiah wrote, "The LORD will continually guide you" (58:11). However, the context reveals prerequisites that have to be satisfied. The Israelites were seeking God's leading through fasting (verse 3), but God revealed that their fasting was a farce that ended in strife (verse 4). The Israelites were like the person who sought to be a sprinter by simply suiting up for the race. Repentance should have been the result of their fasting. The Lord wanted them to set the captives free and meet the needs of the poor around them (verses 6-7). If your striving to do God's will leads to repentance, "Then your light will break out like the dawn" (verse 8).

## Abandonment to God's Will

One man probably spoke for many when he told me, "I'm so used to running my own life, I'm not sure I *want* to trust someone else, or I'm not sure I *can* trust someone else. Besides, God would probably haul me off to some mission field I can't stand." But if we did give our heart to the Lord and God did call us to the mission field, by the time we got there we wouldn't want to be anywhere else.

Do you believe that the will of God is good, acceptable, and perfect for you? Isn't that the heart of the issue? In the Lord's Prayer we are taught to approach God with the request that His will be accomplished on earth. It makes no sense to so petition God if we are not predisposed to do His will.

In the last half of the nineteenth century, George Mueller founded the Bristol Orphan Home. It has become known all over the world as one of the most remarkable monuments of human faith and divine guidance in history. Year after year, without a single advertisement to the public or appeal to Christian friends, hundreds of children were fed, clothed, and educated. The home was maintained simply through prayer and faith. Mueller wrote,

> I seek in the beginning to get my heart in such a state that it has no will of its own in regard to a given matter. Nine-tenths of the trouble with people is just here. Nine-tenths of the difficulties are overcome when our hearts are ready to do the Lord's will. When one is truly in this state, it is usually but a little way to the knowledge of what His will is.[30]

If you desire "what's on the other side of the door" and believe it is something previously planned by your loving, omniscient, omnipotent, and omnipresent heavenly Father, and if you are willing to accept it before you know what it is, then you are well on your way to an adventuresome life.

## Discussion Questions

1. What questions come to your mind after reading the story that began this chapter?

2. What is God's will for your life? Explain your answer.

3. Is God's plan for your life more related to who you are or what you do? Explain your answer.

4. How do you think God has shaped your life in preparation for that plan that He has had for you from the beginning of time?

5. Why do people want to know the future?

6. What is keeping you or has kept you from completely trusting God with your life?

7. Share from your own experience a time when you have bloomed where God has planted you. Has there been a time when you failed to bloom where you were planted because you were looking elsewhere?

8. Why can't God guide us if we are not presently serving Him with what we already know and have?

9. Who or what is keeping you from being the person God called you to be?

# Chapter Eight

# The Glory of God

*Christ could not be described as being man without flesh, nor the Son
of man without any human parent. Just as He is not God without
the Spirit of God, nor the Son of God without having God for His
Father. Thus the origin of the two substances displayed Him as man
and God. In one respect, He was born; in the other respect He was
unborn. In one respect, fleshly; in the other spiritual. In one sense,
weak; in the other sense, exceedingly strong. In one sense, dying; in the
other sense, living. This property of the two states—the divine and the
human—is distinctly asserted with equal truth of both natures alike.*[31]

TERTULLIAN (c. 210)

*The Father Himself placed upon Christ the burden of our iniquities. He
gave His own Son as a ransom for us; the holy one for the transgressors,
the blameless One for the wicked…For what other thing was capable
of covering our sins than His righteousness?…O sweet exchange! O
unsearchable operation! O benefits surpassing all expectation! That
the wickedness of many should be hid in a single righteous One, and
that the righteousness of One should justify many transgressors.*[32]

LETTER TO DIOGNETUS (c. 125–200)

In the vast ocean of eternity there was a tidal wave of time that began with
the incarnation of Christ and ended with His crucifixion. God stepped
out of eternity into time in order that we might step out of time into eternity. His example set the bar so high that it is beyond the grasp of human
achievement. The incarnation was the sternest possible rebuke to our pride.
We cannot fully comprehend the example of Christ who "emptied Himself, taking the form of a bond-servant, and [was] made in the likeness of

men" (Philippians 2:7). He went from the highest state of being to the lowest state of human existence, becoming a helpless infant born in a manger to humble parents with no social status. For you and me to become a slug doesn't come close to approximating the descent. "The Word became flesh, and dwelt among us, and we saw His glory, glory as of the only begotten from the Father, full of grace and truth" (John 1:14).

Our Lord's time came to an abrupt end at the crucifixion, which was the sternest possible rebuke to our selfish nature. "We know love by this, that He laid down His life for us; and we ought to lay down our lives for the brethren" (1 John 3:16). Can you imagine what life on earth would be like if we all believed the words of the apostle Paul and lived according to Philippians 2:3-5?

> Do nothing from selfishness or empty conceit, but with humility of mind regard one another as more important than yourselves; do not merely look out for your own personal interests, but also for the interests of others. Have this attitude in yourselves which was also in Christ Jesus.

## The Question of Motive

We learned from the last chapter that the predisposition of our wills predetermines our knowledge of God's will. Continuing on in the same passage, Jesus raises an additional question of motive: "He who speaks from himself seeks his own glory; but He who is seeking the Glory of the one Who sent Him, He is true, and there is no unrighteousness in Him" (John 7:18). True disciples of Jesus glorify the One who called them. Those who know God's will and are guided by Him do all to the glory of God. Conversely, if we cannot glorify God by what we are thinking, doing, or planning, then it can't be God's will.

This subjugation is perfectly modeled in the Godhead. Notice first the example of Jesus: "I proceeded forth and have come from God, for I have not even come on My own initiative, but He sent Me" (John 8:42). In talking with His Father, Jesus said,

> I glorified You on the earth, having accomplished the work which You have given Me to do...Now they have come to know that everything You have given Me is from You; for the words which You gave Me I have given to them; and they received them, and

truly understood that I came forth from You, and they believed that You sent Me (John 17:4,7-8).

The Holy Spirit functions in the same way according to John 14:16 and 16:13-14:

> I will ask the Father, and He will give you another Helper, that He may be with you forever; that is the Spirit of truth…When He, the Spirit of truth, comes, He will guide you into all the truth; for He will not speak on His own initiative, but whatever He will speak, He will speak; and He will disclose to you what is to come. He will glorify Me, for He will take of Mine and will disclose it to you (John 16:13-14).

According to John 20:21 this directive also applies to us: "As the Father has sent Me, I also send you." Granted, that was said to the apostles, but we have all been commissioned to make disciples. God-sent Christians are called to glorify their heavenly Father by going. Those who go on their own initiative seek their own glory. Do you want to be true? Then glorify the One who sent you! Paul asked,

> Do you not know your body is a temple of the Holy Spirit who is in you, whom you have from God, and that you are not your own? For you have been bought with a price: therefore glorify God in your body (1 Corinthians 6:19-20).

I have counseled a lot of hurting Christians who struggle with the concept of doing all to God's glory. They reason, *God gave me lousy parents. I had no money for a decent education. I've been mistreated by others my whole life. Now God wants me to stroke His ego and build His kingdom! How is this menial existence glorifying to God? When is it my turn?* They may give lip service to God on Sunday morning, but it isn't natural to glorify Him if we believe it was He who dealt us the bad hand.

Defeated Christians struggle giving glory to another when they are desperately in need of affirmation themselves. Some believers have a worm theology, thinking that God is everything and they are nothing. How is He being glorified if His children grovel in a pitiful existence, living defeated lives? New Age teaching can be deceptively attractive to those who have been beaten down all their life. "You are God and all you have to do is realize it. Then you can achieve whatever you perceive." What drivel!

## The Cry of the Hurting

Many Christians think of doing the will of God as a tiresome duty with no immediate personal benefits. Giving glory to God seems like bowing to a king who demands homage from poor peasants who are forced to scramble for the crumbs that fall from His table. Give glory to God? For what? Such is the thinking of defeated and often deceived people.

I recall one of my very best students at seminary. If I had had to pick a rising star in evangelical circles, this man would have been at the top of my list. He was an excellent student, and he was an outstanding communicator with a winsome personality. Upon graduation he accepted the challenge of a small pastorate, but he failed morally. After attending one of my conferences this very gifted, intelligent, and personable man wrote me this following letter:

> I've always figured I was just a no-good, rotten, dirty, stinking sinner, saved by grace yet failing God miserably every day. And all I could look forward to was a lifetime of apologizing every night for not being the man I know He wants me to be. "I'll try harder tomorrow, Lord."
>
> As a firstborn son, I spent my life trying to earn the approval of highly expectant parents. I've related to God the same way. I felt He just couldn't love me as much as other, "better" believers. Oh sure, I'm saved by grace through faith, but I'm just hanging on until He gets tired of putting up with me here and takes me home to finally stop the failure in progress. Whew, what a treadmill!
>
> Neil, when you said that in our new identification in Christ we're not sinners but saints, you totally blew me away. Isn't that strange— that a guy could go through a good seminary and never latch on to the truth that he is a new creation in Christ?
>
> This has been so helpful and liberating to me. I'm beginning to grow out of my old ways of thinking about myself and about God. I don't constantly picture Him as disappointed in me anymore. If He can still love me, be active in me, and find use for even me, after I've failed Him as badly as I have, then surely my worth to Him can't be based on my performance. He just plain loves me. Period!
>
> What a new joyful walk I'm experiencing with Him. Praise God. I have been so deeply touched by the realization of who I am in Christ that I am taking our people through a study in Ephesians

to learn who we are in Christ and what we have as believers in Christ. My preaching is different, and our people are profiting greatly by being built up in strength and confidence. I can't tell you how gracious the Lord has been to me, allowing me to try again. Each day of service is a direct gift from God, and I bank each one carefully in heaven's vault for all eternity to the honor and glory of my Savior.

## Suffering from a Wrong Concept of God

A distorted concept of God and of ourselves is the Christian equivalent of mental illness. It robs us of our victory in Jesus. I counseled a sharp couple who had driven several hundred miles with the hope that I could help them resolve the conflicts going on in their home. He was a successful man—a superintendent of a public school district. He attended church regularly and, by all external evidence, appeared to be a pillar of the community. But he was struggling with compulsive thoughts, explosive anger, and incredible nightmares that left him depleted every morning. Within hours we were able to resolve his personal and spiritual conflicts, and he found his freedom in Christ.

He waited several months before he sent me the following letter. He wanted to be sure that what happened would last:

> I never really understood the relationship God wanted to have with me. I saw God as an omnipotent but distant and stern father. You helped me realize that God is like a real father in how He loves me, meaning that He wants me to enjoy His presence and live a fulfilling life on this earth. I used to see Him as an aloof disciplinarian, a benevolent disciplinarian—but nevertheless a disciplinarian. I knew that I was to have a personal relationship with Him, but I had no way of knowing what that meant.
>
> I equated my own earthly father's attitude toward a father/son relationship to the kind of kinship that would be appropriate between God and myself. I was dead wrong. God not only wants to see me obediently happy, but He also takes joy in my accomplishments. I have struggled with my purpose in life. What did it matter whether I achieved anything? If all my achievements were the result of God's will, and all the credit belonged to Him, it followed in my small mind that I was nothing but a non-efficacious vessel of the Almighty.

Of course I was willing to accept that concept, as I believed it to be biblical. But I was wrong, and I was basing my belief system on a non-scriptural foundation. My downfall was inevitable. There was no way I could experience joy with this belief. Humility was very important to me. But it meant taking no personal satisfaction for a job well done. Without some sort of personal satisfaction for one's endeavors, much of life is missed, and God does not want this. He wants me to do good things and take pleasure in doing them well. Just as an earthly father is pleased when his son does well, so too is God pleased when His children do His will.

This revelation instilled a great deal of meaning in my life. I now have a new concept of God's love and my place in His divine plan. I have meaning, and what I do has meaning. I can take pleasure in doing good things without risking the sin of pride. Now I see the truth—that God is a loving and caring Father. He gave me a will that I am supposed to use to please Him, and that is exactly what I intend to do.

If you perceive God as a distant judge who has little regard for your well-being, you are probably going to stay away from Him. But if you perceive Him as a loving Father, you're going to draw near. Your motive for serving Him is not to gain His approval, because you are already approved in Christ. You don't have to perform for Him in order to be accepted; you are already accepted in the Beloved. That is why you joyfully serve Him. You don't have to labor in the vineyard for the purpose of getting His attention and earning His love. God has known you from the foundation of the world, and He already loves you. Christians will naturally (supernaturally) give glory to God when they know who He really is and what He has freely given them.

### God's Glory Revealed

So what is the glory of God? And how do we glorify God in our bodies? Not by joining a health club with the hope of developing an attractive body. Not by running five miles every day, or eating the perfect foods or dieting to the point where we look like an emaciated model. In such cases, one would have to ask, "For whose glory are you doing these things?"

Don't get me wrong. I believe we should take care of God's temple, but not for the sake of drawing attention to ourselves. According to 1 Corinthians 9:27, we are told to buffet our body and make it our slave so as not to be disqualified from preaching. In other words, don't lose your witness and ability to serve because you don't take care of yourself. Your body is to serve you, not the other way around. Staying healthy and fit is part of being a good steward.

The glory of God is the manifestation of His presence. Recall from the last chapter that Moses said, "I pray You, show me Your glory" (Exodus 33:18). God allowed Moses to witness an unusual manifestation of His presence. The Lord said to Moses,

> You cannot see My face, for no man can see Me and live...Behold there is a place by Me and you shall stand there on the rock. And it will come about that when My glory is passing by, that I will put you in the cleft of the rock and cover you with My hand, until I have passed by. Then I will take My hand away and you shall see My back, but My face will not be seen (Exodus 3:20-23).

God also manifested His presence over the Ark of the Covenant in the Holy of Holies:

> The LORD said to Moses, "Tell your brother Aaron that he shall not enter at any time the holy place inside the veil, before the mercy seat which is on the Ark lest he die, for I will appear in the cloud over the mercy seat" (Leviticus 16:2).

Consider the progressive departure of the glory of God from the temple as revealed in the book of Ezekiel:

1. In Ezekiel 8:4-6, the glory is present in Jerusalem.

2. In Ezekiel 9:3, the glory of God moves to the threshold of the temple, then returns to the sanctuary.

3. In Ezekiel 10:4, the glory moves back to the threshold.

4. In 10:18-19, the glory moves to the east gate.

5. Then in Ezekiel 11:23 the glory of the Lord goes up from the midst of the city and stands over the mountain which is east of the city.

6. Then, "Ichabod"—the glory has departed, ushering in 400 silent years.

Suddenly the glory of God makes an appearance: "The Word became flesh and dwelt among us, and we beheld His glory, glory as of the only begotten from the Father, full of grace and truth" (John 1:14). Jesus was a manifestation of God's presence. Jesus said, "He who has seen Me, has seen the Father" (John 14:9). We glorify God by manifesting His presence, and we do that when we bear fruit. "By this is my Father glorified, that you bear much fruit, and so prove to be my disciples" (John 15:8).

## Right Behavior for the People of God

The natural person is inclined to believe that they are a nobody, therefore they should compete, scheme, achieve, and get ahead—"make something of themselves." If they appear good, accomplish something, or achieve social status, then they are finally somebody. But tragically they climb the ladder of "success" only to discover that it's leaning against the wrong wall. The Bible teaches that we are already somebody important to God and this world. Peter wrote,

> ...Coming to Him as to a living stone, rejected by men but choice and precious in the sight of God...But you are a chosen race, a royal priesthood, a holy nation, a people for God's own possession that you may proclaim the excellencies of Him Who has called you out of darkness into His marvelous light. For you once were not a people, but now you are the people of God. You had not received mercy, but now you have received mercy (1 Peter 2:4,9-10).

After that affirmation Peter wrote, "Submit yourselves, for the Lord's sake, to every human institution" (verse 13), and "Servants, be submissive to your masters" (verse 18). Concerning husband-and-wife relationships, he wrote, "In the same way, you wives be submissive to your own husbands" (1 Peter 3:1). Submitting to God's authority does not diminish who we are. We affirm our identity when we become like Christ and yield to His will.

One of my seminary students wrote me this note:

> What really struck me was the concept that we are saints and not sinners. I remember how surprised I was when I took Greek and saw that a Christian is often called *hagios* ("holy one"). I was so steeped in the idea that I was a totally depraved sinner. The concept of who we are in Christ didn't break through until I read your book *Victory over the Darkness*.

I'm still adjusting to the lofty concept that my real self is holy instead of wretched. I have been saved more than 12 years, and I have never really appreciated what happened to me at my conversion. I always knew that my future destiny was secure, but I didn't understand that I was truly a brand-new creation in Christ Jesus.

## Why Live Below Your Privileged Position?

Suppose you are a prostitute. One day you hear that the king has decreed that all prostitutes are forgiven. That would be great news if you were a prostitute! But would it necessarily change your behavior or your self-perception? Probably not. You might dance in the streets for a while, but chances are you would continue in your same vocation. You would understand yourself to be nothing more than a forgiven prostitute.

How would you respond, however, if the king not only forgave you but made you his bride? You are now a queen. Would that change your perception of yourself? Would it change your behavior if you were the queen and married to the king? Why would you want to live like a prostitute if you were the queen?

I wonder how many Christians fully understand what it means to be the bride of Christ! You are far more likely to promote the kingdom if you are the "queen," as opposed to being a forgiven prostitute. We are not caterpillars destined to crawl for the rest of our lives. We are redeemed butterflies. It makes no sense to crawl around in some false humility when we have been called to mount up with wings as eagles.

The skeptic protests "I would be filled with pride if I believed that." My reply is that you're defeated if you *don't* believe it! Humility is not putting yourself down when God is trying to build you up. Self-abasement has the appearance of wisdom, but it has no value against fleshly indulgence according to Colossians 2:23. Humility is confidence properly placed. We follow Paul's advice and "put no confidence in the flesh" (Philippians 3:3), and put our confidence in God, the one who is "working in you both to will and to work of His good pleasure" (Philippians 2:13).

The Lord knew we would struggle with our understanding of who we are in Christ. So He inspired Paul to write,

> I pray that the eyes of your heart may be enlightened, so that you will know what is the hope of His calling, what are the riches of the glory of His inheritance in the saints (Ephesians 1:18).

I have been burdened by the fact that many Christians don't really know who they are in Christ, nor do they understand what it means to be a child of God. I desire for every believer to know how Christ meets all our needs according to His riches in glory. Our most critical needs and those most wonderfully met in Christ are the "being" needs. Our greatest "being" need was life—and Jesus came to give us eternal life (John 10:10) and a new identity. We are children of God (John 1:12; 1 John 3:1). The needs for acceptance, security, and significance can only be met in Christ, as follows:[33]

### In Christ

*I am accepted:*

| | |
|---|---|
| John 15:15 | I am Christ's friend. |
| Romans 5:1 | I have been justified. |
| 1 Corinthians 6:17 | I am joined to the Lord and I am one spirit with Him. |
| 1 Corinthians 6:20 | I have been bought with a price. I belong to God. |
| 1 Corinthians 12:27 | I am a member of Christ's body. |
| 2 Corinthians 5:21 | I have been made righteous. |
| Ephesians 1:5 | I have been adopted as God's child. |
| Ephesians 2:18 | I have direct access to God through the Holy Spirit. |
| Ephesians 2:19 | I am of God's household. |
| Ephesians 2:19 | I am a fellow citizen with the rest of the saints. |
| Ephesians 3:12 | I may approach God with boldness and confidence. |
| Colossians 1:14 | I have been redeemed and forgiven of all my sins. |
| Colossians 2:10 | I am complete. |

*I am secure:*

| | |
|---|---|
| John 1:12 | I am a child of God (Galatians 3:26-28). |

| | |
|---|---|
| Romans 8:28 | I am assured that all things work together for good. |
| Romans 8:35 | I cannot be separated from the love of God. |
| Romans 8:1 | I am free from condemnation. |
| Romans 8:33 | I am free from any condemning charges against me. |
| 2 Corinthians 1:21 | I have been established, anointed, and sealed by God. |
| Ephesians 1:13-14 | I have been given the Holy Spirit as a pledge, guaranteeing my inheritance to come. |
| Colossians 1:13 | I have been delivered from the domain of darkness and transferred to the kingdom of Christ. |
| Colossians 3:3 | I am hidden with Christ in God. |
| Philippians 1:6 | I am confident that the good work that God has begun in me will be perfected. |
| Philippians 4:13 | I can do all things through Him who strengthens me. |
| 2 Timothy 1:7 | I have not been given a spirit of fear, but of power, love, and a sound mind. |
| Hebrews 4:16 | I can find grace and mercy in time of need. |
| 1 John 5:1 | I am born of God and the evil one cannot touch me. |

*I am significant:*

| | |
|---|---|
| Matthew 5:13 | I am the salt of the earth. |
| Matthew 5:14 | I am the light of the earth. |
| John 1:12 | I am God's child (Romans 8:14-16; 1 John 3:1-3). |
| John 15:1,5 | I am a branch of the true vine, a channel of His life. |

| | |
|---|---|
| John 15:16 | I have been chosen and appointed to bear fruit. |
| Acts 1:8 | I am a personal witness of Christ's. |
| 1 Corinthians 3:16 | I am God's temple. |
| 1 Corinthians 12:27 | I am a member of Christ's body. |
| 2 Corinthians 5:17-18 | I am a minister of reconciliation for God. |
| 2 Corinthians 6:1 | I am God's coworker (1 Corinthians 3:9). |
| Ephesians 1:1 | I am a saint. |
| Ephesians 2:6 | I have been raised up and I am seated with Christ. |
| Ephesians 2:10 | I am God's workmanship. |
| Philippians 3:20 | I am a citizen of heaven (Ephesians 2:6). |

We are not accepted, secure, and significant because of what we have done. Our needs are met because of what Christ has done for us. Therefore we have no right to boast or be prideful. Knowing who he was became a primary motivation for Paul to serve God: "By the grace of God I am what I am, and His grace toward me did not prove vain, but I labored even more than all of them, yet not I but the grace of God in me" (1 Corinthians 15:10).

We will "labor even more" when we understand the tremendous identity and position we have in Christ. A pastor's wife attended my conference and discovered who she was as a child of God. She found her freedom in Christ and wrote, "I crave to share Jesus with people out of my own love for Him, whereas before it was largely an 'I should' activity."

Too many Christians continually struggle to become somebody they already are, which only leads to futility. If we fail to understand or accept who we are in Christ, then no amount of self-effort or works can possibly accomplish what He has already accomplished for us. When we see ourselves from God's perspective, and know who we are in Christ, we are free to serve our loving heavenly Father. We experience His guidance as we glorify Him.

The world is filled with hurting people who suffer injustices, as well as the consequences of their own bad choices. Blaming others will not bring satisfaction or justice. God has offered a far better way. He binds up the brokenhearted and sets the captives free. Those who understand their freedom in Christ supernaturally glorify the Lord, because it is Christ in them the hope of glory (Colossians 1:27). Their liberated life is a manifestation of His presence within them.

## Questions for Discussion

1. Why is the example of Christ such a rebuke to our pride and selfishness?

2. How does the Godhead model subjugation without inferiority?

3. Why isn't it "natural" to give glory to God when we feel defeated, disadvantaged, and disillusioned?

4. In your walk with God, can you personally identify with the testimony of the superintendent of schools? How?

5. What is the glory of God?

6. How can we glorify God in our bodies?

7. Have you been a victim of "worm theology"? Explain.

8. Is God trying to build you up or put you down? Which one has your Christian experience been a model of?

9. How has Christ met all your needs according to His riches in glory?

10. When and how did you discover who you are in Christ?

# Chapter Nine

# The Word of God

*Tradition referred, in the first place, to the so-called* consuetudines ecclesiae *[church customs], things like keeping Sunday holy, turning to the east to pray, the customs of fasting, the various dedications and blessings, and other such things that determined the concrete form of Church piety in the later Middle ages. All those many things, some of them uplifting, some astounding, that had made the Church of the later Middle ages into a rambling, complex house, full of corners and angles, were justified with the term "tradition" and legitimatized as a constituent part of concrete Christian reality. In the light of his experience of a God who judged and forgave people, Luther, who had been seized by the simplicity of the gospel, with its explosive force, could only see petty trifling in all that—things by which people were deceived about the actual abyss of their existence and which pacified them superficially. More than that, he saw in this the return of the law, the setting of human regulations above God's word, against which Paul had relentlessly struggled—and which had now once more become a fact of life in the Church.*[34]

Would it please you, shock you, or disturb you to know that the quote above is from Pope Benedict XVI? Many evangelicals have been led to believe that only Protestants hold to the authority of God's Word. That, of course, is not true. Roman Catholics and Eastern Orthodox both claim the Bible to be the Word of God. The major difference between Protestants and Catholics is the concept of Tradition. In addition to the Bible, Roman Catholics and Eastern Orthodox Christians also hold to the authority of the Church, as expressed in teachings and practices which are not based upon the Bible but upon historical decisions by church councils and/or the Papacy. Martin Luther chose to retain Roman Church Tradition as long as it agreed with Scripture. Other reformers chose to do away with the traditional teachings of the Roman Church unless they were mandated by Scripture, which is the position of most evangelical churches.

## The Distortion of God's Word

In the time of Christ, legalistic traditions had set aside the commandments of God, and the people found themselves in bondage to manmade laws and religious practices. Jesus paid no attention to them, which infuriated the religious establishment. He came to demonstrate and fulfill God's Word as the authoritative standard for faith and practice.

Every generation has distorted God's Word to some extent by adding to it or skewing it. We are fallible people trying our best to teach the infallible Word. That is why conservative Protestant, Catholic, and Orthodox seminaries teach the original languages of Hebrew, Greek, and Aramaic. The intention is to stay as close to the original as possible. Unfortunately, human traditions still creep in, and theological biases influence our understanding. The question we need to ask ourselves is, have we distorted the truth of God's Word or set it aside for the sake of church and family traditions or personal convenience?

In the apostle John's Gospel, Jesus was attacked by the Jews for healing a man on the Sabbath. They even accused Him of having a demon. He confronted the issue of tradition:

> "Did not Moses give you the law, and yet none of you carries out the law? Why do you seek to kill Me?" The multitude answered, "You have a demon. Who seeks to kill You?" Jesus answered and said to them, "I did one deed, and you all marvel. On this account Moses has given you circumcision (not because it is from Moses, but from the fathers), and on the Sabbath you circumcise a man. If a man receives circumcision on the Sabbath that the Law of Moses may not be broken, are you angry with Me because I made an entire man well on the Sabbath?" (John 7:19-23).

Jesus argued that the Mosaic Law required circumcision on the eighth day. If a child was born eight days before the Sabbath, then the law required that he be circumcised on the Sabbath. If it is lawful to circumcise a child on the Sabbath, why not bring healing to the whole person on that day?

Jesus was never one to beat around the bush. In essence He was saying, "Moses gave you the rule book, and none of you are following it! Not only that, but some of you are seeking to kill Me." The last charge was a fact, recorded earlier in John 5:18: "The Jews were seeking all the more to kill Him, because He not only was breaking the Sabbath, but also was calling God His own Father, making Himself equal with God."

The accusation that Jesus had a demon resulted from the Israelites' bewilderment that He could discern the nature of their hearts. Blinded to the truth, they concluded that Jesus received His information by occult practice. They believed that demons were capable of communicating secret knowledge to people. This is the means by which all spiritual mediums function. That is why we cannot ignore the warning by Paul in 1 Timothy 4:1: "The Spirit explicitly says that in the latter times some will fall away from the faith, paying attention to deceitful spirits and doctrines [teachings] of demons."

## False Guidance: Wrongly Using the Word

God did not take false guidance lightly. Mediums and spiritists were to be stoned to death (Leviticus 20:27). Those who received their counsel were to be cut off from the rest of the people (Leviticus 20:6). When King Ahaziah of Israel fell through the lattice in his upper chamber, he sent messengers to inquire of Baalzebub, the god of Ekron, whether he was going to recover from his sickness. But the angel of the Lord said to Elijah, "Arise, go up to meet the messengers of the king of Samaria and say to them, 'Is it because there is no God in Israel that you are going to inquire of Baalzebub the god of Ekron?'" (2 Kings 1:3) The message he did receive from God was that he would surely die, and he did.

Isaiah warned God's people about the occult and told them to return to God's Word (8:19-20):

> When they say to you, "Consult the mediums and the spiritists who whisper and mutter," should not a people consult their God? Should they consult the dead on behalf of the living? To the law and to the testimony! If they do not speak according to this word, it is because they have no dawn.

Even though the Hebrew nation was given the law and the prophets, they still sought after false gods, turned away from the commandments of Moses, failed to heed the warnings of the prophets, and severely distorted God's Word.

In the New Testament, Jesus affirmed the validity of the law and the prophets and warned against distorting that truth. He said in Matthew 5:17-19,

> Do not think that I came to abolish the law or the prophets; I did not come to abolish, but to fulfill. For truly I say to you, until heaven and earth pass away, not the smallest letter or stroke shall pass away from the law, until all is accomplished. Whoever then annuls one of the least of these commandments, and so teaches others, shall be called least in the kingdom of heaven; but whoever keeps and teaches them, he shall be called great in the kingdom of heaven.

The church is warned in James 3:1, "Let not many of you become teachers, my brethren, knowing that as such we shall incur a stricter judgment." There are severe penalties for those who distort God's Word. It must be kept in the highest regard since it is the only infallible source for understanding the will of God.

Matthew 23 reveals that Jesus considered the religious establishment of His day as the least in the kingdom of God, calling its leaders (among many other things) "blind guides" (verse 24). The Pharisees seated themselves in the seat of Moses (verse 2) and thus shut people off from the kingdom of heaven (verse 13).

## Rightly Using God's Word

It goes beyond the scope of this book to tackle the problem of hermeneutics (principles of biblical interpretation). I do want to identify several issues, however, that affect the way we understand and apply the Bible to life. Hopefully then we will be able to see how we stray from the truth—and fall prey to Satan's half-truths and lies.

### Systematic Interpretation

First, if our interpretation of Scripture is right, it must be *systematic*. Individual parts need to be seen in the context of the whole. There are two potential hindrances that keep the average person's theology from being systematic.

- *Many Christians don't have the opportunity to see the whole picture.*

They come to church weekly and receive one piece in a very large puzzle. Occasionally they miss a week, so they have a few pieces missing. Then they try to put the puzzle together without the benefit of looking at the box top. Many individual pieces remain separate from the whole.

- *We interpret the pieces through the grid of our own limited perspective.* To illustrate this point, hold up your hand in front of you with your palm facing you. Now have someone who sees only the back of your hand describe what they see. Eventually, they will mention fingernails. But from your perspective you don't see any fingernails, so you say, "Wait a minute—there are no fingernails on my hand. How can there be any fingernails when I don't see them? Are we looking at the same hand?" You are looking at the same hand, but from different perspectives.

There are many truths that we may have never personally encountered. We will have a better understanding of the truth if we add another person's perspective. That's why God inspired four Gospels. All four wrote about the life, death, burial, and resurrection of Christ. But all four are different. One author saw Jesus as the fulfillment of messianic prophecies and presented Him as King. Two saw Him as the suffering servant and the Good Shepherd. Another saw Jesus as the Son of God, the great I AM. Which one is correct? All four! If you want a complete picture, you have to read all four.

### Grammatical/Historical Interpretation

Second, a conservative hermeneutic takes into account the *grammatical, historical method of* biblical interpretation, which include the four following principles.

- First principle: *God has revealed Himself in time and place.* It has been my privilege to study in Israel. I have seen Jerusalem, the remains of the temple, the Jordan River, and the Sea of Galilee. The basis of the Christian faith is rooted in geography and history. History is "His story" fleshed out in our three-dimensional world. That is not the case with many cults, which base their faith in unknown times, places, and events.

- Second principle: *The self-disclosure of God was an unfolding process.* It occurred over a time span of 1400 years. It wasn't complete until John received his vision on the island of Patmos and wrote the book of Revelation. God is still guiding His people, but it will never be in opposition to what He has already revealed. The Holy Spirit is first and foremost the Spirit of truth (John 14:17). Jesus said, "When He, the Spirit of Truth, comes, He will guide you into all truth" (John 16:13). When Jesus prayed, He said, "I do not ask You to take them out of the world, but to keep them from the evil one" (John 17:15). Then He said, "Sanctify them in the truth; Your Word is truth" (verse 17). The primary work of the Holy Spirit is to establish God's presence within us and lead us into all truth. He opens the spiritual eyes of our hearts so we can understand His Word.

  Most conservative biblical scholars do not believe God dictated the Bible, in the sense that He told human beings what to write by some audible means. That would be like the occultic practice of automatic writing, which requires the writer to function as a medium. An occultic medium or a New Age channeler seeks a passive state of the mind. Instead, God worked through the minds of the prophets and apostles and superintended their choice of words. We have a reliable text inspired by God that comes through the personalities of the writers.

  The guidance of God does not bypass our responsibility to think or to search the Scriptures. God's guidance works through the discipline of our study and applies it to our daily walk. We need to be like the Bereans, who were considered "noble-minded" because they examined the Scriptures daily to "see whether these things were so" (Acts 17:11).

- Third principle: *The grammatical, historical method of interpretation means that we seek to understand what God's message meant to the hearers at that time.* This requires some understanding of the culture and language of the people who lived at the time of Christ and when the prophets spoke. For instance, a slave in Palestine at the time of Christ did not suffer the same indignities that American slaves did. Many slaves at the time of Christ were better off than people who didn't have a master.

- Fourth principle: *A historical, grammatical method of interpretation takes the literary context into account.* Nothing has meaning without context. Who wrote the book, and why was it written? What is the major point of the passage under consideration? We should never isolate a passage, text, sentence, or word from its literary context. If you are puzzled by a verse then go back to the nearest antecedent (that is, what is the context right before the verse?). There is only one true interpretation, but there may be many applications.

Some applications in the contemporary church border on the bizarre. A "prophetess" had a "vision" after reading Isaiah 35:8, which reads, "A highway will be there, a roadway, and it will be called the Highway of Holiness." She concluded that the passage was referring to Interstate Highway 35, which divides the eastern United States from the western part. I saw an early morning news program that showed a bunch of Christians praying with great fervor along I-35. The wry smile on the face of the reporter said it all. The rest of the verse reads, "The unclean will not travel on it, but it will be for him who walks that way, and fools will not wander on it." The redeemed will travel safely on the *highway of holiness* to worship in Jerusalem. I hope you are not tempted to look at Isaiah 40 to see if there is a reference to Interstate 40, which divides our country the other way!

## Why the Message of the Bible Gets Distorted

God has given us His Word as an infallible guide to life. The following five hindrances can affect our understanding and application of it.

**1. We can make doctrine an end in itself.** If we do this, we will distort the very purpose for which it was intended. According to 1 Timothy 1:5, "The goal of our instruction is love from a pure heart, a good conscience, and a sincere faith." If our doctrine is correct, it will enable us to have a loving relationship with God and others. If the truth has touched our hearts, it should set us free and transform our lives. We can intellectually acknowledge the truth, and yet be the same old person we always have been. Intellectual knowledge by itself "makes arrogant, but love edifies" (1 Corinthians 8:1).

**2. We can let the intellect guide our faith instead of letting faith renew our intellect.** After affirming to his readers that we have become partakers of God's divine nature, the apostle Peter wrote, "For this very reason also, applying all diligence, in your faith supply moral excellence, and your moral excellence, knowledge" (2 Peter 1:5). We have turned this order around. Christopher Hall explains:

> A primary dictum of the Western theological tradition, channeled through the conduit of Augustine and Anselm, had been that faith led to understanding. This was a faith in Christ grounded in personal self-awareness of sin and cognizant of the continual lure of self-deception, rooted in the intrinsic authority of Scripture and the divinely inspired revelation it communicated, and nurtured by the church's history of reflection on the meaning of God's word to humanity.

> The Enlightenment perspective stood this approach on its head. Understanding would lead to a mature faith, rather than the reverse. Hence, those aspects of the Christian tradition that failed to meet the standards of human reason—liberated, autonomous reason—were regarded with suspicion and for many ultimately discarded. Is it surprising that the resurrection, incarnation, Trinity, miracles and other revelatory gifts soon became negotiables?[35]

Human reason can supplant faith. Wisdom says, "Trust in the LORD with all your heart and do not lean on your own understanding. In all your ways acknowledge Him, and He will make your paths straight" (Proverbs 3:5-6). The alternative is to be like little children who say to their father, "I don't know why I have to do that." The wise Father says, "Trust me and do as I say, and someday you will know why."

**3. We can memorize Scripture and still not think scripturally.** Rote memory without understanding or appropriation has no impact on our lives. We have to incarnate the Word of God. We have to *own* it. Thinking about Scripture is not the same thing as thinking scripturally.

**4. We can hear the Word and not do what it says.** The Great Commission instructs us to go into the world, make disciples, and teach them to observe all that Christ commanded. It's in the observation (obedience) that we really learn. Average people retain about 10 percent of what they hear. They retain about 20 percent of what they see, but more than 80 percent of what they hear, see, and *do*. Not much is accomplished when we educate people beyond their obedience. Jesus said, "If you know these things, blessed are you if you do them" (John 13:17). The apostle James wrote,

> The one who looks intently at the perfect law, the law of liberty, and abides by it, not having become a forgetful hearer, but an effectual doer, this man shall be blessed in what he does (James 1:25).

**5. We can "neglect the commandment of God, and hold to the tradition of man" (Mark 7:8)—and think we are doing God's will.** The problem is that long-established practices and time-honored faith get blended together in people's minds. If the young pastor advocates a different religious practice than what the old guard is used to, they will think he is fooling with their faith and will fiercely resist any change. You can add your own horror stories of church splits and terminated pastors because somebody's traditions were being violated even though the Word of God wasn't.

## A Timeless Message for a Changing Culture

The world at the beginning of the twenty-first century is changing at an alarming rate. People are under tremendous stress to keep up with the rapid rate of change. The ecclesiastical challenge is to give anxious people the timeless message of Christ and present it in a contemporary way that relates to a changing culture.

Some of the older and "mature" saints who sit on the boards and committees in our evangelical churches resist change. They are comfortable with the form of worship, style of music, and methods of teaching that brought them to Christ and helped them mature. It almost becomes their God-appointed purpose in life to maintain the status quo. New ideas and changing practices make them feel uncomfortable. We need God's guidance if we are going to preserve both the old and the new wine as we navigate the twenty-first century.

Jesus came to fulfill the law and establish a New Covenant. The Jewish community was bound by legalism and enslaved to their traditions, and they vigorously opposed Jesus when He confronted their time-honored traditions. His mission was to move His chosen people from law to grace and reconcile them with the Gentiles within a three-year public ministry, though He had no official status in the political or religious communities. Machiavelli wrote in *The Prince*, "There is nothing more difficult to take in hand, more perilous to conduct, or more uncertain in its success, than to take the lead in the introduction of a new order of things."

In my first pastorate, I had the privilege of leading our church from rented facilities to the acquisition of new property and buildings. (I told some of the story in chapter 7.) That was just one of many changes I attempted to bring about. We revised the church's constitution to change our form of church government. The previous pastor had been more formal and conservative in style, while I was more of a simple-faith country boy.

All the board members were at least 20 years my senior, and most were charter members. Many of them would agree that the new property and government were better than what they had before, but when I left the church I had "bullet holes" all over my body! In all of this I learned something about the process of change while studying for my first doctorate.

After responding to a call to teach at Talbot School of Theology, I had the privilege of helping an established church work through an organizational change. The founding pastor had been there for 30 years, and he had led the church from a small Bible study to more than a thousand attendees. The organizational structure of the church had evolved with little planning or purpose. In the reorganization we went from 24 committees to 7 without any dissension. So it can be done! The major key in this case was the cooperation and credibility of the pastor.

Since God is leading us in the twenty-first century, we must learn how to adapt our ministry to a changing culture. Jesus taught and modeled some timeless principles that we must understand before we consider revising established practices. Therefore, let's examine how Christ responded to pharisaic traditions that conflicted with Scripture.

## When Religious Traditions Become Pharisaic Practices

One of the many beautiful things about Jesus is His universal appeal. If you are an ultraconservative, you will love the fact that He changes not: "Jesus Christ is the same yesterday and today, yes and forever" (Hebrews 13:8). If you are a flaming liberal, you will love the way He refused to participate in pharisaic practices, particularly the customary traditions of fasting, ritual washings, and observations of the Sabbath. The fact that Jesus was willing to suffer the rejection of the establishment clearly shows that there is something greater at stake than simply getting one's own way. There are three criteria that determine whether a stand for truth should be made against religious traditions:

**1. Don't conform to religious traditions if they place people under an unnecessary burden (Luke 11:37-41).** The Law of Moses called for cleansing after touching an unclean animal or a corpse and for ceremonial cleansings for religious practices. To those laws the rabbis added many petty rules to guard against any possible defilement. God probably had hygiene in mind, but the Pharisees elevated the laws for cleansing to a higher religious significance. They reasoned, "If we have contact with anything impure, we are impure, and therefore we must be cleansed by washing. The water must also be pure, and if the water must be pure, then the vessel carrying the water must be pure," and so forth.

The Talmud, a collection of ancient rabbinical writings, relates the story of Rabbi Akiba, who was imprisoned. Rabbi Joshua brought him some water, but the guard spilled half of the container. There was too little water to both wash and drink, and Rabbi Akiba faced the possibility of death for lack of water if he chose to wash. He reasoned, "He who eats with unwashed hands perpetuates a crime that ought to be punished by death. Better for me to die of thirst than to transgress the traditions of my ancestors!"

Any preoccupation with trifles as matters of conscience will make one either a moral imbecile or an intolerable hypocrite. Jesus responded harshly to such reasoning: "You blind guides who strain out a gnat and swallow a camel!" (Matthew 23:24). The Lord cautions that the weightier matters of the law (such as justice and mercy) are overlooked when attention is focused on strict observance of religious practices. This leads to a corresponding negligence of the eternal laws of God. Jesus told the people to pay more attention to cleansing their hearts and not be like their leaders, who cleansed only their hands.

The laws of God are not restrictive, they are protective. The rules of any institution should ensure the freedom of each individual to reach their God-given potential. They should serve as a guide so we don't stray from our purpose, and they should protect us from those who abuse the system.

The principle that Jesus modeled could be stated as follows: If people are commanded to follow a traditional practice that makes life more difficult and no longer contributes to the purpose of the organization, then we must not participate as a matter of religious conscience. Jesus simply didn't observe such traditions, and He defended His disciples for not observing them as well.

**2. Don't conform to religious practices if the traditions distort the law they are intended to serve (Luke 6:1-11).** In His ministry, Jesus often violated the traditional instructions surrounding the observance of the Sabbath, because they were a clear distortion of God's law. A common practice—born out of a desire to protect a known law or principle—is to establish additional rules to keep us from breaking the law or violating the principle. The problem is, it doesn't take long for the fences around the laws to become laws themselves.

For instance, we are not to be unequally yoked in marriage (2 Corinthians

6:14-15). To ensure that this doesn't happen, we build a fence that says, "You can't associate with or date non-Christians." That may be advisable in some cases, but don't make it a law. It won't be long before we can't associate with non-Christians. That would make fulfilling the Great Commission an even more formidable task!

A common practice in many churches, left over from the Prohibition era, is to require total abstinence from alcohol. Again, that may be wise in many cases, but the Bible doesn't teach that. It prohibits strong drink and drunkenness and teaches that all things should be done in moderation. You can argue for abstinence in some cases if having a drink causes a weaker brother to stumble. If you believe you should never drink alcohol, you would eliminate some important medications. In some cultures refusing a glass of wine may even be a stumbling block.

Years ago, a neighbor I had led to Christ found out I was home with a terrible cold. This Italian Catholic came by that evening with a "hot toddy" to cure me. Being a Baptist pastor, should I have accepted this act of love? I'll leave you with the tension of not knowing whether I did drink it or not, but I will admit to this: I slept like a baby that night!

The point is, we can easily distort the true Word of God by adding our own traditional practices and making them equal with His Word. We may need to stand against such pharisaic practices as the Lord did, or we will find ourselves in bondage to man-made traditions.

**3. Don't conform to religious traditions that are contrary to the will of God (Mark 7:6-9).** Time devoted solely to the traditions of man is often morally corrupt time. For every commitment to the traditions of man there is a corresponding decrease in the commitment to the commandments of God. Remember the Lord's words: "You nicely set aside the commandment of God in order to keep your tradition" (Mark 7:9). It is often easy to see this in others, yet difficult to see it in ourselves. Santa Claus at Christmas and the Easter Bunny at Easter are obvious, but what isn't obvious are the little traditions that churches and Christians keep observing year after year, although their purpose is no longer evident. Such practices take time away from what we should be doing.

We cannot ignore the clear example of Jesus. If the Word of God is being abused or distorted in any way, if traditional practices no longer serve their purpose or add to people's burdens, we should take an active stand against them.

## Changing Christian Practices for Effective Ministry

It must grieve God when ministries are impeded because well-intentioned people resist the inevitable and needlessly fight change.

I used to tell my students that the greatest assets they would have in ministry are mature saints. But the greatest liability they would have is saints who got old but didn't mature. All they want to do is censor. They are no more loving or kind than they were 20 years ago. They don't bear fruit—they often prevent it. They should have learned to restrict their freedom for the weaker brother, but instead they are the weaker brothers.

Another major problem is when Christian leaders act impulsively as change agents without giving thought to what the consequences will be to the fellowship. If loss of unity is the price of change then the price is probably too high. We must be diligent to preserve the unity of the Spirit (Ephesians 4:3). Such agents of change need to keep in mind that patience is a fruit of the Spirit. Change for the sake of change profits nothing. To those who needlessly resist change and to those who want to be effective change agents, I offer four suggestions.

The Mosaic law required an annual fast on the Day of Atonement. By the time of Zechariah, there were four days of fasting per year. In Jesus' time, strict Jews were fasting twice a week (Luke 18:12). John's disciples were fasting, but the Lord's disciples weren't. The Pharisees wanted to know why. Jesus used this occasion to share four principles that are timeless and critical:

> They said to Him, "The disciples of John often fast and offer prayers; the disciples of the Pharisees also do the same; but Yours eat and drink." And Jesus said to them, "You cannot make the attendants of the bridegroom fast while the bridegroom is with them, can you? But the days will come; and when the bridegroom is taken away from them, then they will fast in those days." And He was also telling them a parable. "No one tears a piece from a new garment and puts it on an old garment; otherwise he will both tear the new, and the piece from the new will not match the old. And no one puts new wine into old wineskins; otherwise the new wine will burst the skins, and it will be spilled out, and the skins will be ruined. But new wine must be put into fresh wineskins. And no one, after drinking old wine, wishes for new; for he says, 'The old is good enough'" (Luke 5:33-39).

**1. Jesus taught that Christian practices should be appropriate for the**

**situation.** Jesus didn't condemn or condone the fasting of John's disciples but by the same token it was all right for His disciples if they didn't fast. It wasn't necessary while He was with them. The day would come when He wouldn't be with them, and then it would be appropriate to fast. It's not a question of ritual, but of purpose.

It's always appropriate to ask *why* we're doing what we are doing. "Because we've always done it that way before" is unacceptable. Christian practices continue for years after outliving their purpose until someone with enough courage asks, "Why are we doing that?"

The greatest avenue for productive change comes when we clarify the purpose of any existing ministry or group. I worked with the leaders of an adult group and helped them create a purpose statement. Redefining their purpose lead to some major changes in their fellowship. Within two years they had doubled in attendance. Asking "Why?" forced them to evaluate their purpose and ministry, and precipitated necessary changes.

**2. Jesus taught that Christian practices should be consistent with the inward condition of the heart.** Holding to external practices that no longer correlate with the heart is repugnant to God. Jesus clearly spoke against praying in vain repetitions and putting on a gloomy face while fasting.

Consistency cries for an affirmative answer to the question, "Is it real?" The Christian community searches for truth while the world searches for reality. These are large overlapping circles, but I'm convinced that we must be real in order to be right. The need for change is most evident when Christians sit week after week carrying on their worn-out traditions in utter hypocrisy.

Form always follows function, but people have a tendency to fixate on the form. Those who have a real Christian experience are the ones who are free to change their Christian practices that are not specifically given in Scripture. They are committed to the substance of their faith, not the form. True believers find their security in the changeless Christ, not in changeless traditions.

It's also important to understand that organizational renewal will not bring spiritual renewal. When the spiritual tide is out, every little tadpole wants his own little tide pool to swim in. When the spiritual tide is in, the fish swim in one big ocean where every move is synchronized. If the spiritual tide is in, almost any program will work. If the spiritual tide is out, then no program will work.

**3. Jesus taught that the forms of our Christian practice need to change.**
To make this point, the Lord carefully chose His metaphors. The garment
and the wineskin are the external dress and the container. They do not
represent the substance of our faith. They represent the religious customs,
practices, and traditions in which the substance of our faith is packaged.
Jesus said the garment needs mending and the old wineskin is old! What
worked before isn't working anymore. Times change, cultures change—and
what was effective 20 years ago may not be today. What doesn't change is
truth, the object of our faith.

We need to keep asking tough questions: "Is it relevant?" "Do our
Christian practices relate to our culture?" The older generation is the
stable force in our churches. They are faithful and many are mature.
They often represent the financial stability every church needs. They also
make up the boards and committees that determine the style of ministry, and they have a natural tendency to perpetuate long-established
practices because they are still meaningful to them…but maybe not to
the younger generation.

The struggle to change is more sociological than spiritual. Why is it
that a good Bible-believing church that faithfully carries out its ministry
struggles to hold onto its young people, when down the street a contemporary ministry rents a store building and has four times more young people
in a matter of months? Because the contemporary ministry down the street
relates to the culture of the youth. We don't have to compromise our faith
in order to change the style of worship, since no form is given in the New
Testament. We just need to worship in Spirit and in truth.

**4. Jesus taught that Christian practices should preserve the old and
the new wine.** The old wine is superior to the new wine. It has matured
through the aging process. Mature saints are wise, gentle, reverent, and
good. Because of the quality of their vintage, they make a strong argument
for resisting change. Even Jesus conceded to loving the old wine of Jewish
piety: "And no one, after drinking the old wine wishes for the new; for he
says, 'The old wine is good enough.'" But its supply will run out!

New wine can be bitter and harsh. But can we object to its existence?
Can we deny the need for new forms of worship, new styles of music and
art, and even new methods of instruction? We may not desire it because it
is strange and novel, but wisdom says not to spurn, spill, or spoil it or we
will not have any successors to our ministry.

## The Unity of the Spirit

A final principle asks the question, "Does it unify?" The unity of the Spirit is already present since He resides in every one of His children. It is everyone's responsibility to practice unity by tolerating the preferences of others and accepting the diversity of the body as a good thing. The task is difficult, but not impossible.

If we are to accomplish our purpose, we must ask ourselves four questions:

- Why are we doing what we are doing?

- Is it real?

- Does it relate?

- Does it unify?

God is leading us in the twenty-first century. Some changes are necessary. Others should wait. We need to pray that God will give us the wisdom and power to change ourselves first and then our ministries so that we can be fruitful instruments in His hand.

## Questions for Discussion

1. In your church experience, what traditions have you practiced or seen practiced that have no basis in God's Word?

2. How does God's concern about false guidance differ from the modern world's concern?

3. What hinders the average Christian from having a good systematic understanding of Scripture?

4. How would you summarize the grammatical, historical method of biblical interpretation?

5. How can we distort the Word of God? Which way are you most likely to struggle with? Why?

6. What may need to change in our church practices, and what should never change?

7. Following the example of Jesus, when *shouldn't* we conform to religious practices?

8. Christian practices should adhere to the following four principles. Can you illustrate present practices that either coincide or conflict with them?

   • appropriate for the situation (Why?)

   • consistent with the inward condition of the heart (Is it real?)

   • changeable when necessary (Does it relate?)

   • able to preserve the unity (Does it unify?)

# Chapter Ten

# The Providence of God

*Not a single thing that has been made, or that will be made, escapes
the knowledge of God. Rather, through His providence, every
single thing has obtained its nature, rank, number, and special
quality. Nothing whatever has been produced (or is produced) in
vain or by accident. Instead, everything has been made with precise
suitability and through the exercise of transcendent knowledge.*[33]

IRENAEUS (C. 180)

A devout Christian heard an urgent news report on his radio that a flash
flood was within minutes of entering the peaceful valley where he lived.
Immediately he went to his knees, recommitted his life to the Lord, and
prayed for safety. The words were still on his lips when he became aware
that water was seeping under his door. He retreated to the second floor, and
finally onto the roof of his house.

While he sat on the roof, a helicopter flew by, and the pilot asked over
the loudspeaker if they could lift him off. "It's not necessary since I have
the Lord's protection," he replied.

Moments later the house began to break up, and he found himself cling-
ing to a tree. A police boat, braving the waters, approached him for rescue,
but he assured them the Lord would save him. Finally, the tree gave way
and the man went to his death.

Standing before the Lord, he said, "Lord, I'm glad to be here, but why didn't
you answer my prayer for safety?" The Lord responded, "Son, I told you over
the radio to get out of there. Then I sent you a helicopter and a motorboat!"

God created the universe, and He accomplishes His purposes by working through that which He created. The *providence of God* refers to His

direction and care over all creation. Keep in mind that God "upholds all things by the word of His power" (Hebrews 1:3). He is the ultimate reality, and if He somehow disappeared so would all creation. It is inconsistent with Scripture to believe that God works only through "miraculous" interventions that lie outside the realm of His created order. How God accomplishes His purposes while keeping His covenant to work through obstinate people like us is the real miracle.

We fulfill our purpose when we live in harmony with Him. We do that by knowing Him and His ways and living accordingly by faith. Patrick Reardon comments on His providence:

> The doctrine of providence is asserted in the biblical thesis that "all things work together for good to those who love God" (Romans 8:28). This "working together" of historical events under divine governance for particular and interrelated purposes is a mystery, of course, but a mystery in two senses.

> First, divine providence is a mystery in the sense that it is humanly inscrutable, exceeding even the furthest reaches of our thought, and is known only by faith. That is to say, it pertains to divine revelation. It is not the general, natural [revelation]…but a special providence revealed by God's particular interventions in the structure of history. For this reason Holy Scripture never attempts to explain it. Although the Bible affirms divine providence, it teaches no theory of the matter.

> Second, divine providence is also a mystery in the sense that we are initiated into it. It is rendered accessible, that is, to our revelatory experience of it, the discernment of which is a gift of the Holy Spirit. It is particular and personal, sensed through the coherent structure of events. For this reason Holy Scripture not only confirms divine providence, but also portrays the mystery of it through narratives about events.[37]

One such narrative is the remarkable story of Joseph in the book of Genesis. As you read his story you intuitively know that all things are working together for good, but don't know how. Every time Joseph tells the truth, he seems to suffer setbacks. His brothers throw him in a well to die, but he is brought back out and put on a caravan to Egypt. He is promoted from slavery to a favored position in the house of an official. Then he is thrown in prison, only to be brought out to interpret the dreams of the king, which leads the way for his family to be reunited in Egypt. Of all this Joseph concludes, speaking to his ill-intentioned brothers, "It was not you who sent me here, but God" (Genesis 45:8).

Sometimes the Bible uses a narrator to reveal the providential nature of a story. For instance, divine providence is illustrated in the story of David's escape from Saul at the hill of Hachilah (1 Samuel 26): "They were all asleep, because a sound sleep from the LORD had fallen on them" (verse 12). In the context of Absalom's revolt, the narrator says, "The LORD had purposed to defeat the good advice of Ahithophel, to the intent that the LORD might bring disaster on Absalom" (2 Samuel 17:14).

In the New Testament we are directed to focus on God's providential care when we are anxious. In the Sermon on the Mount, Jesus said we are not to worry about tomorrow, since our heavenly Father cares more about us than He does about the lilies of the fields and birds of the air, which we know by observation He is also taking care of. His providential care does not mean we won't face trials and tribulations. It means we have the assurance that He is present with us, and that nothing can happen to us apart from His knowledge, presence, and love.

God never sees our problems as permanent. They will seem so from the perspective of time, but not so from an eternal perspective. Paul wrote, "I consider that the sufferings of this present time are not worthy to be compared with the glory that is to be revealed to us" (Romans 8:18). "For our light and momentary troubles are achieving for us an eternal glory that far outweighs them all" (2 Corinthians 4:17).

The opening question of the Heidelberg Catechism (1563) goes to the heart of divine providence. It begins by asking,

> "What is your only comfort in life and death?" Answer: "That I, with body and soul, both in life and death, am not my own, but belong to my faithful Savior Jesus Christ who…so preserves me that without the will of my Father in heaven not a hair can fall from my head; yea, that all things work together for my salvation."

## Providence and Personal Responsibility

How God works all things together for our good will remain a mystery for us, but it does not preclude the need for us to assume responsibility for our own attitudes and actions. Reliance on providence is not fatalism.

Foreknowledge does not mean that all events are pre*determined,* they are just pre-*known.* Given God's sovereignty and mankind's responsibility, there will always be some tension between "letting it happen" and "making it happen." Calvinists lean to the former, and Arminians to the latter. Your decision as to whether it all depends upon God or whether it all depends on you will have a major impact on how you live.

Keep in mind that the sovereignty of God works in conjunction with our wills, and we will be held accountable for the choices we make. Consequently there will always be some anxiety concerning the decisions we have made or are about to make. This is why it is likely that some of us will be tempted to seek signs of confirmation from God. There is also the temptation to think that God is present only when something phenomenal happens. "God was 'really' at the church service last night." "The Lord must have been with him!" But the truth is, the Lord is omnipresent. He is in every church service and in the life of every believer—always. We live with the promise that He will never leave nor forsake us.

From the wisdom literature we read that "the mind of man plans his way, but the Lord directs his steps" (Proverbs 16:9). Therefore, it behooves us to be transformed by the renewing of our minds and thus prove that the will of God is good, acceptable, and perfect (Romans 12:2). God is the manufacturer, and He has given us the Manufacturer's instruction book in the form of the Bible. If we want to know how we are supposed to function in this world, shouldn't we consult the Manufacturer's Handbook? If God gave us a watch, would we be honoring Him more by asking what time it is or by simply looking at the watch?

## The Way God Works

I believe in miracles, and I believe every one recorded in the Bible. I believe our entire Christian experience is a miracle. It simply cannot be explained by natural means. If God didn't primarily guide us through His Word (which never changes) and if He didn't take into account the fixed order of the universe, then how could we ever have any stability or security? How could we make any concrete plans if God didn't stay consistent (immutable)?

I challenge you to take an exhaustive concordance and look up references for the words *way* and *ways* in connection with God. You will discover that He is not capricious—that is, impulsive or without plans. He has clearly established His ways, and He is faithful to them. Let me illustrate with just a few references:

- Moses said, "If I have found favor in Your sight, let me know Your ways, that I may know You" (Exodus 33:13).

- "You shall keep the commandments of the LORD your God, to walk in His ways and to fear Him" (Deuteronomy 8:6).

- John the Baptist said, "Make ready the way of the Lord" (Mark 1:3).

- Jesus said, "I am the way" (John 14:6).

God has revealed His ways, and we are to walk in them. The mystery is, how does He work through human responsibility and the natural order of the universe to bring about His will? Somehow He orchestrates human affairs in such a way as to guarantee the outcome of the ages. What impresses me more than His miraculous interventions is His timing.

Notice how Jesus responded to those who insisted on a sign:

> Some of the scribes and Pharisees answered Him saying, "Teacher, we want a sign from You." But He answered and said to them, "An evil and adulterous generation craves for a sign; and yet no sign shall be given to it but the sign of Jonah the prophet" (Matthew 12:38-39).

Satan tempted Jesus to produce a sign. He said, "If You are the Son of God, throw Yourself down" (Matthew 4:6). Jesus responded, "You shall not put the Lord your God to the test" (Matthew 4:7). Jesus was saying that the sign we need is the Word of God. We are to use the Word to guard against Satan's temptations to force the Lord to prove Himself. God tests us in order to strengthen our faith, but the devil tempts us in order to destroy our faith.

## Providence Antagonists

The sovereignty of God is being contested by all those who rebel against Him. The prime instigator of that rebellion is Satan, who persuaded a third of the angels to follow him. Those fallen angels now make up a hierarchy of demons by which Satan attempts to rule this world. According to Paul, we were all under his dominion at one time:

> You were dead in your trespasses and sins, in which you formerly walked according to the course of this world, according to the prince of the power of the air, of the spirit that is now working in the sons of disobedience. Among them we too all formerly lived in the lusts of the flesh, indulging desires of the flesh and mind, and were by nature children of wrath, even as the rest (Ephesians 2:1-3).

The natural person believes they are their own god, but Scripture reveals that they are actually living according to the god of this world. Remember that Jesus came to undo the works of Satan (1 John 3:8), which he primarily accomplished at the cross. God is now accomplishing His purpose through the church, as Paul testifies:

> To me, the very least of all saints, this grace was given, to preach to the gentiles the unfathomable riches of Christ, and to bring to light what is the administration of the mystery which for ages has been hidden in God who created all things; so that the manifold wisdom of God might now be made known through the church to the rulers and the authorities in the heavenly places. This was in accordance with the eternal purpose which He carried out in Christ Jesus our Lord, in whom we have boldness and confident access through faith in Him (Ephesians 3:8-12).

Stop for a moment and consider the implications of the above passage. The eternal purpose of God is to make His wisdom known through the church to the rulers and authorities in the heavenly places (the spiritual realm). How well are we doing? Most Westerners don't even believe in a personal devil, and many Christians are scarcely aware that "our struggle is not against flesh and blood but against the rulers, against the powers, against the world forces of this darkness, against the spiritual forces of wickedness in the heavenly places" (Ephesians 6:12).

### Assuming Our Responsibility

I am amazed that God has chosen to work through us. Knowing my own fallibility, I would have bypassed Neil Anderson. There is obviously a purpose for God choosing to use us, which will be fully revealed some time in the future—and I am sure it is to our benefit.

In this present age we can't grow without Christ, but we won't grow if we don't assume our responsibility either. God has instructed us to "think so as to have sound judgment," and make wise decisions consistent with His Word. This cooperative process based on our union with God was explained by one Church Father, Clement of Alexandria, as follows:

> Many things in life take their rise in some exercise of human reason, having received the kindling spark from God. Some examples are health by medicine, soundness of body through gymnastics, and wealth through trade. Now, all these things truly have their origin and existence through divine providence—yet, not without human cooperation as well.[38]

For the rest of this chapter, I will analyze seven ways in which Christians typically seek God's guidance, and then I will conclude with ten keys to making wise decisions. Keep in mind that the guidance of God brings with it peace of mind, not anxious states of mind. In other words, there is peace in the center of God's will, and anxiety (which literally means "double-mindedness") outside His will.

## Seven Commonly Employed Means of Seeking God's Guidance

### 1. Conscience

There is an old axiom that says, "Let your conscience be your guide." The conscience is a function of our minds and is not always reliable. Our minds were originally conformed to this world, so our consciences can be poorly formed. A conscience will always be true to its own standard, but that standard isn't necessarily consistent with God's Word. Until we come to Christ, our standard is the moral values we assimilated from our environment. Many people are thus falsely guided by a guilty conscience—which may not be indicative of true guilt.

Those who develop an oversensitive psychological guilt often become perfectionists who labor under repeated condemnation. The Bible says, "There is no condemnation for those who are in Christ Jesus" (Romans 8:1). These people aren't led; they are driven and constantly seek affirmation. They have a tendency to be man-pleasers and lean toward legalism. On the other hand, those who have been raised with no moral boundaries seem to have no conscience at all. They slide toward license. Since our minds were conformed to this world we need to renew them in such a way that what we believe is in accordance with truth.

Concerning nonmoral issues, Paul wrote,

> The faith which you have, have as your own conviction before God.
> Happy is he who does not condemn himself in what he approves.
> But he who doubts is condemned (Romans 14:22-23).

We should be very cautious about going against our own conscience, and we shouldn't be a stumbling block for those who hold different standards on nonmoral issues. Neither should we allow a faulty conscience to convict us in matters we approve for others. We are to restrict our freedom if it causes a weaker brother to stumble, and we never have the right to violate another person's conscience. Paul declared, "I also do my best to maintain always a blameless conscience both before God and before men" (Acts 24:16).

## 2. Fleeces

"If the sun is shining in the morning, I'll know it's God's will."

"If he's there when I open the door, I'll know he's the one."

"If I pass the class on world missions, I'll be a missionary."

This kind of thinking is all too common in Christian circles. Such propositions are commonly referred to as "fleeces." The term *fleece* comes from the Old Testament story of Gideon.

In Judges 6, Gideon is called by God to deliver Israel from the Midianites. Gideon questions whether God is even for Israel (verse 13), and he doubts his own ability (verse 15). So he asks God for a sign (verse 17). God gives him one, then tells him to take the family ox and tear down the altar of Baal. Gideon is afraid to go during the day, so he goes at night. Then he questions again whether God will deliver Israel. This time he puts a lamb's fleece on the ground. If God will deliver the nation, then the lamb's fleece will be wet in the morning and the ground around it will be dry.

The next morning it was as he requested. That ought to have satisfied him, right? Wrong! Wanting to be doubly sure, and hoping God wouldn't get too angry, Gideon asks Him to do it again, but this time with the opposite results (the fleece dry, and the ground wet). Not exactly the stuff heroes are made of—but God still answers Gideon's request. Then He reduces Gideon's army to 300 men! Humanly speaking, that was not enough men to win the upcoming battle with the Midianites.

God wanted to show that He, not man, is the deliverer. He chose an insecure man and reduced his army to nothing so the victory would clearly be His. The fleece wasn't a means of demonstrating faith—it was just the opposite. And it certainly wasn't used to determine God's will. He had already told Gideon what to do. Gideon was questioning His will, just as we do when we ask for a fleece when He has already shown us His will.

### 3. Circumstances

One temptation is to assume that something is God's will if the circumstances are favorable and it isn't God's will if the circumstances are unfavorable. I would estimate that more Christians are "guided" by the circumstances of life than by any other means, next to the Bible. And yet, of all the possible means of guidance, this is the least authoritative and trustworthy.

I shared earlier my experience of pastoring a church that purchased new property and went through a building program. Through most of the process the circumstances didn't seem favorable. Twice I sat with the mayor, who was also a local realtor, and asked him if he thought our plans were feasible. He advised us not to purchase the land, and he didn't think the city would allow us to build if we did. He knew real estate and the political climate better than anyone in the city.

In the providence of God, purchasing the land increased our assets by literally millions, and the city planning commission voted 7 to 0 in favor of our building plans. Circumstances influence our planning, but God directs our paths. Make sure you follow Him, not the tide of circumstances.

I once heard a motivational speaker say, "I don't like to recruit Christians because when the going gets tough they quit, concluding that it must not be God's will." Generally speaking, I believe that Christians should live *above* life's circumstances and not be guided by them. Establishing God's kingdom on earth is an uphill climb with a lot of obstacles. Also, be careful about applying too much significance to unusual circumstances or coincidences, such as, "It must be God's will. Why else would that book be lying there!" It *could* be God guiding you, but it could also be just a book lying there. I have counseled many people in spiritual bondage who make bizarre associations or attach far too much significance to irrelevant events.

### 4. Godly Counsel

Proverbs 11:14 says, "Where there is no guidance, the people fall, but in abundance of counselors there is victory." No one person has a complete perspective on all issues, and no one person perfectly knows the truth. God has structured the church in such a way that we need each other. I have made some dumb decisions that would never have been made if I had consulted someone else. Be careful, however, not to consult with only those who are predisposed to agree with you. We all need meaningful friends who care enough about us to speak the truth in love.

The counsel of others does have to be weighed, however. In Acts 21 the apostle Paul was warned by others not to go to Jerusalem. Disciples in Tyre "kept telling Paul through the Spirit not to set foot in Jerusalem" (verse 4). Then a prophet named Agabus gave a visual demonstration by binding himself and saying, "This is what the Holy Spirit says: 'In this way the Jews at Jerusalem will bind the man [Paul] who owns this belt and deliver him into the hands of the Gentiles'" (verse 11). Everyone began begging him not to go. Paul responded,

> "What are you doing, weeping and breaking my heart? For I am
> ready not only to be bound, but even die at Jerusalem for the name
> of the Lord Jesus." And since he would not be persuaded, we fell
> silent, remarking, "The will of the Lord be done!" (Acts 21:13-14).

The disciples and Agabus were probably hearing from the Lord, but their conclusion wasn't right. The Holy Spirit wasn't trying to prevent Paul from going; He was preparing Paul for coming persecution. Paul correctly chose not to take the easy way out.

The famous missionary Hudson Taylor often went against advice of others, and the resulting circumstances nearly destroyed him. But he, more than anyone else, opened China to the gospel. People can tell you the truth, but draw the wrong conclusions. We need to discern our own motives as well as those of the people we seek counsel from. Unbiased opinions from spiritually sensitive people will lead to better decisions.

## 5. Gifts and Abilities

After I taught a class on spiritual gifts, a young man asked me, "Is my gift prophecy or exhortation?" Knowing him very well, I was careful in my response. "I don't think either one is your gift. If anyone ever had the gift of helps, you have it. I have seen you respond to the needs of others, and you always seem ready to help."

A look of disappointment came over his face. "I knew it!" he responded. He was struggling with a poor sense of worth, and probably thought if he had some other gift he would be more worthy. I told him, "You will never be fulfilled trying to become somebody you aren't."

No one person has all the gifts and talents. For that reason alone we can be assured that God didn't intend our identity and sense of worth to be based on gifts and talents. Our identity and sense of worth comes from knowing who we are in Christ and our growth in character.

Every child of God has the same identity and the same opportunity to grow. When our identity is firmly established in Christ and we are growing in grace, then we use our gifts and talents to edify others with proper motives.

God has known us from the foundation of the world. He has entrusted us with certain life endowments. He will certainly lead us in a way that makes best use of our gifts and talents. It is our responsibility to take advantage of opportunities as they become available. Tragically, many people go to the grave with their music still in them, never contributing to the symphony of God's work. They don't reach their potential or take the risks that faith requires. You can hang on to the security of the tree trunk, but the fruit is always on the end of the limb.

## 6. Duty

Much of our Christian calling is simply a matter of duty. You don't need some special leading to live a responsible life. You don't need a subjective confirmation for every decision. There will be a lot of times when we don't "feel led" to do things we know we should do. You may not feel like getting out of bed some mornings, but life goes on, and the wise ones are those who simply do their duty. You don't need any special leading to love your spouse or discipline your children. Scripture tells us to do it, so we do it. Hopefully we do so in the power of the Holy Spirit, rather than according to the flesh. "If you know these things, you are blessed if you do them" (John 13:17).

## 7. Desires

Some people are led by their natural desires, which can be nothing more than carnal living. I believe God wants to give us the desires of the heart...if our hearts are right. I have seen my desires change as I have matured in the Lord. After engineering school I had very little desire to read until I came to Christ. Now I read volumes.

After I received Christ, I wanted to serve Him full-time. I had completed engineering school and was prepared to do anything God wanted—except to go back to school. Within a year I could hardly wait to get to seminary. It was the best educational experience of my life, and the first one I ever enjoyed. Since then, as I said earlier, I have finished four more degrees. Also, I never had a desire to write a book until my wife and I went through an experience of great brokenness described in chapter 12. I have nearly lost count of the number of books I have written since then.

Saying you have no desire to do what you have been called to do is no excuse for not doing it. Those who are truly seeking God will desire to be in His will regardless of what it is. "Blessed are those who hunger and thirst for righteousness, for they shall be satisfied" (Matthew 5:6). Do you believe that? I do, because I don't believe anything else satisfies. You can never satisfy the desires of the flesh. The more you feed the flesh, the bigger it grows.

## Ten Keys to Wise Decision-Making

At the end of the chapter there is a checklist entitled "Ten Keys to Wise Decision-Making." It represents the grid I use when I make decisions. The first five keys are generic, and they apply to all decisions concerning God's will. The final five relate more to divine guidance.

**1. Have I prayed about it?** The Lord's Prayer begins with a petition for His will. Prayer was never intended to be a fourth-down punting situation in which we ask God to bail us out of our hasty decisions. It was intended to be a first-down huddle. We aren't supposed to ask God to bless our plans; we're supposed to ask God for His plans. God could just give us what we need, but He taught us to pray, "Give us this day our daily bread." Prayer demonstrates our dependency upon God.

**2. Is it consistent with the Word of God?** In our culture, ignorance is no excuse, since resources abound. Every Christian home should have a concordance, a Bible dictionary, a good commentary, and a study Bible with notes. Most communities in America have a pastor within driving distance or one who is reachable by phone. Godly pastors love to share what God has to say about a given matter.

We also have many Christian radio programs with great Bible teachers. Some programs invite people to call in with questions. Christian bookstores sell books on every conceivable subject. You will make wise decisions if you consult the Bible and these godly resources.

**3. Can I do it and be a positive Christian witness?** Asking that question years ago prompted me to give up bridge and golf when I was a young Christian. There is nothing morally wrong with either, but they were ruling my life. I was too competitive to be a good witness. Now that I have matured a little, I can play golf again!

A seminary student once asked me about a job he had been offered. It would take care of some financial needs, but he had some reservations concerning the sales pitch he was required to use. I asked him if he could use the sales technique and be a positive witness for Christ. He didn't take the job.

That simple question will govern a lot of behavior. Several spin-off questions can be helpful: *Would I do that if Jesus were physically present and watching? Would I go to that movie if Jesus were my escort? Can I tell that joke from the pulpit?* And of course, *What would Jesus do?*

**4. Will the Lord be glorified?** Can I do this and give glory to God? In doing it, would I be glorifying Him in my body? Am I seeking the glory of man or the glory of God? Am I doing this to be noticed by others, or am I seeking to please the Lord? Those who are truly sent by God seek to glorify Him in all they do.

**5. Am I acting responsibly?** God doesn't bail us out of our irresponsibility. He will allow us to experience the consequences of irresponsible choices. But when we are faithful in little things, He will put us in charge of greater things. Don't get ahead of God's timing or you will be over your head in responsibilities. Seek to develop your life and message, and God will expand your ministry.

**6. Is it reasonable?** God expects us to think. His guidance may transcend human reasoning, but it never excludes it. God doesn't bypass our mind; He operates through it: "Do not be children in your thinking; yet in evil be babes, but in your thinking be mature" (1 Corinthians 14:20). We are warned in Scripture not to put our mind in neutral. We are to think and practice what we know to be true (Philippians 4:8-9).

**7. Does a realistic opportunity exist?** Closed doors are not meant to be knocked down. If you have a hopeless scheme, let it go. If it isn't God's timing, wait. If a realistic opportunity exists, and all the other factors are in agreement, then step out in faith. God may open a window of opportunity, but it will close if not taken advantage of. The faithless man asks, "What do I stand to lose if I do?" The faithful man asks, "What do I risk losing if I don't?"

**8. Are unbiased, spiritually sensitive associates in agreement?** Be careful not to consult only those who will agree with you. Give your advisors permission to ask hard questions. Don't be afraid of "no" answers. If something isn't God's will, don't you want to know that before you make the mistake of acting impulsively?

**9. Do I have a sanctified desire?** Don't think that being in the will of God must always be an unpleasant task. The joy of the Lord should be our strength. I find my greatest joy in serving God and being in His will. But don't get the idea that if everything is wonderful you must be in the will of God. Is this a desire to satisfy a lust of the flesh, or a Spirit-filled desire to see God's kingdom established and people helped?

**10. Do I have a peace about it?** This is an inner peace. In the world you will have tribulation, but in Christ we have the assurance of overcoming the world. Is the peace of God guarding your heart and your mind?

If you have been able to answer yes to all ten of these key questions, then what are you waiting for? Step out in faith as the following person does:

> I am part of the "Fellowship of the Unashamed." I have Holy Spirit power. The die has been cast. I've stepped over the line. The decision has been made. I am a disciple of His. I won't look back, let up, slow down, back away or be still. My past is redeemed, my present makes sense and my future is secure. I am finished and done with low living, sight walking, small planning, smooth knees, colorless dreams, tame visions, mundane talking, chintzy giving and dwarfed goals!

> I no longer need pre-eminence, prosperity, position, promotions, plaudits or popularity. I don't have to be right, first, topped, recognized, praised, regarded, or rewarded. I now live by presence, lean by faith, love by patience, lift by prayer and labor by power.

> My face is set, my gait is fast, my goal is heaven, my road is narrow, my way is rough, my companions few, my guide reliable, my mission clear. I cannot be bought, compromised, detoured, lured away, turned back, diluted or delayed. I will not flinch in the face of sacrifice, hesitate in the presence of adversity, negotiate at the table of the enemy, ponder at the pool of popularity or meander in the maze of mediocrity.

> I won't give up, shut up, let up or burn up till I've preached up, prayed up, paid up, stored up and stayed up for the cause of Christ.

I am a disciple of Jesus. I must go till He comes, give till I drop, preach till all know and work till He stops.

And when He comes to get His own, He'll have no problems recognizing me. My colors will be clear.[39]

## Questions for discussion

1. How would you describe the providence of God?

2. Why are we often anxious about making decisions?

3. How does God's providence work together with our delegated responsibility?

4. What are the consequences of relying too much on God's sovereignty and failing to assume our responsibility?

5. What are the consequences of thinking we have to make everything happen on our own?

6. Concerning God's kingdom, should we *let* it happen or *make* it happen?

7. For determining God's guidance, how reliable or unreliable are the following (that is, what are their strengths and weaknesses)?

   • conscience

   • fleeces

   • circumstances

   • godly counsel

   • gifts and abilities

   • duty

   • desires

8. Which of the "ten keys to wise decision-making" are you most likely to overlook? Why?

## Ten Keys to Wise Decision-Making

**Discerning God's will:**                                        Yes    No

1. Have I prayed about it?                                    ___    ___

2. Is it consistent with the Word of God?                    ___    ___

3. Can I do it and be a positive Christian witness?          ___    ___

4. Will the Lord be glorified?                               ___    ___

5. Am I acting responsibly?                                  ___    ___

**Discerning divine guidance:**                               Yes    No

1. Is it reasonable?                                          ___    ___

   What makes sense?

   What doesn't make sense?

2. Does a realistic opportunity exist?                       ___    ___

   Factors for:

   Factors against:

3. Are unbiased, spiritually sensitive people                ___    ___
   in agreement?

   Those for:

   Those against:

4. Do I have a sanctified desire?                            ___    ___

   Why?

   Why not?

5. Do I have a peace about it?                               ___    ___

   Why?

   Why not?

# Chapter Eleven

# Spiritual Discernment

*We must carefully discern the thoughts that come on us and set them against the testimonies from the divinely inspired Scriptures and from the teaching of the spiritual teachers, the holy Fathers, so that, if we find them to agree with these witnesses and correspond to them, we may with all our might hold these thoughts fast and boldly act on them. But if they are not in harmony with "the word of truth" we must expel them from us with much anger, as it is written, "Be angry, but sin not." As from something defiling and from the sting of death, so must we flee from the interior assault of passionate thoughts. Accordingly, we need great soberness, great zeal and much searching of the divine Scriptures. The Savior has shown us their usefulness by saying, "search the Scriptures." Search them and hold fast to what they say with great exactitude and faith, in order that you may know God's will clearly from the divine Scriptures and be able infallibly to distinguish good from evil and not believe every spirit.*[40]

SYMEON THE NEW THEOLOGIAN

A wonderful Christian couple, good friends of ours, was being used by the Lord in full-time ministry. Some difficulty developed in their marriage, so they consulted a pastor/counselor. The wife's response after their initial meeting was negative, but they continued with this "counselor" based on his endorsement by some colleagues.

Over the next year their ministry deteriorated. So did our friendship. A short time later their pastor/counselor was exposed for having sex with a number of counselees. The damage he did to several women was incredible. He justified his behavior by explaining, "What we do in the flesh doesn't matter. Only what we do in the Spirit counts!" That is Gnosticism.

My friends were then confronted by the leadership in their ministry with an ultimatum: "Choose your ministry with us or choose him." They chose to stay with the apostate pastor!

They didn't exercise discernment, nor did they judge righteously. "Little children, let no one deceive you; the one who practices righteousness is righteous, just as He is righteous; the one who practices sin is of the devil" (1 John 3:7-8). The authoritarian, arrogant spirit of this "pastor" had some kind of spiritual hold on many, since half his church stayed with him. The wife's initial discernment was correct, but the husband ignored the warning of the Holy Spirit.

Spiritual discernment is our first line of defense, especially when our ability to reason is limited by incomplete knowledge. We will never have the perfect discernment of Jesus, but we can learn from His example and develop our ability to discern good from evil.

## The Discernment of Jesus

While many Jews were questioning whether Jesus was a good man, they couldn't help but marvel at His teaching: "How has this man become learned, having never been educated?" (John 7:15). Jesus responded, "My teaching is not Mine, but His who sent me" (verse 16). After the Sermon on the Mount, the crowds were amazed at His teaching, "for He was teaching them as one having authority, and not as their scribes" (Matthew 7:29). Yet Jesus never held any earthly position of authority.

"But Jesus, on His part, was not entrusting Himself to them, for He knew all men, and because He did not need anyone to testify concerning man for He Himself knew what was in man" (John 2:24-25). It's not hard to know the truth if you are the Truth—and speaking with authority is an unalterable norm for God! Though we don't possess these attributes, we do have the Holy Spirit dwelling within us. If we *are* going to continue the work of Jesus, we must yield to the Holy Spirit and allow Him to lead us into all truth. Then we can know the truth, speak God's word with a greater degree of authority, and discern good and evil. Let's briefly analyze these three functions.

## Guidance from God

> When He, the Spirit of truth, comes, He will guide you into all truth; for He will not speak on His own initiative, but whatever he hears, He will speak; and He will disclose to you what is to come.

He shall glorify Me; for He shall take of Mine, and shall disclose it to you. All things that the Father has are Mine; therefore I said, that He takes of Mine, and will disclose it to you (John 16:13-15).

**1. The Holy Spirit is first and foremost the Spirit of truth, and He will lead us into all truth.** The promise in the passage above has primary reference to the apostles, but its application extends to all Spirit-filled believers (1 John 2:20-27). In His High-Priestly Prayer, Jesus prayed on our behalf, "I do not ask You to take them out of the world, but to keep them from the evil one...Sanctify them in the truth; Your word is truth" (John 17:15,17). Divine revelation is what keeps us from the evil one, not human reasoning or empirical research. The Holy Spirit enables us to understand the Word of God from His perspective.

**2. As we conform to God's image we can speak His Word with greater authority.** Although Jesus had no earthly position of authority, He had a heavenly one. His hearers recognized His authority because of the quality, conduct, and character of His life.

The true shepherd exercises spiritual leadership with the heart of a servant (see Matthew 20:24-28). Spiritual leadership is not based on any earthly position of authority since there is no position lower than a servant. It is based on our position in Christ. We are joint heirs with Christ, seated with Him in the heavenlies.

Our ministry and message will take on a greater degree of authority when our character is Christlike and our message is balanced and true. Servant leaders are subject to the needs of those they are called to lead. The qualifications for spiritual leadership in 1 Timothy 3 and Titus 1 are all character requirements. The indwelling presence of the Holy Spirit is what enables us to grow in grace and speak the truth in love. The apostle Peter wrote,

> Shepherd the flock of God among you, not under compulsion, but voluntarily, according to the will of God; and not for sordid gain, but with eagerness; nor yet as lording it over those allotted to your charge, but proving to be examples to the flock (1 Peter 5:2-3).

The Gospels never record Jesus pulling spiritual rank or saying something like, "Listen, you obstinate people, get your act together and do what I say, because I am God!" Christian leaders who base their authority on their position in Christ and godly character don't lord it over others. They lead by example, and people respect them and their teaching.

The same applies for marriages and parenting. What kind of marriage does a couple have if the husband demands that he be respected because he is the head of the home? Being the head of the home is an awesome responsibility, not a right to be demanded. The spiritual head of a home assumes his responsibility by seeing to the needs of his family. He cannot meet most of their needs, but God can—so his first priority is to lead his family to Christ. A wise husband depends upon God and seeks the perspective of his wife. Enabled by the power and wisdom of the Holy Spirit, he can live a righteous life and lead with loving authority.

**3. The Holy Spirit enables us to discern.** According to John 16:8, He "will convict the world concerning sin, and righteousness, and judgment." The Holy Spirit doesn't take up residence in our lives and then sit passively by while we participate in sin. Since we are alive in Christ, we have become partakers of the divine nature (2 Peter 1:4). We will be convicted internally when we choose to behave in a way that isn't consistent with the Spirit's presence in our lives. The Holy Spirit is not compatible with the world, the flesh, and the devil, and He enables us to discern good from evil.

## How Discernment Works

I don't know of any legitimate Christian who questions the role of the Holy Spirit in leading us to truth, or living a righteous life, or helping us discern good from evil. The questions usually center on how He does it. A passage central to this discussion is 1 Corinthians 2:9-16:

> Just as it is written, "Things which eye has not seen and ear has not heard, and which have not entered the heart of man, all that God has prepared for those who love Him." For to us God revealed them through the Spirit; for the Spirit searches all things, even the depths of God. For who among men knows the thoughts of a man except the spirit of the man, which is in him? Even so the thoughts of God no one knows except the Spirit of God. Now we have received, not the spirit of the world, but the Spirit who is from God, that we might know the things freely given to us by God, which things we also speak, not in words taught by human wisdom, but in those taught by the Spirit, combining spiritual thoughts with spiritual words. But a natural man does not accept the things of

the Spirit of God; for they are foolishness to him, and he can not understand them, because they are spiritually appraised. But he who is spiritual appraises all things, yet he himself is appraised by no man. For who has known the mind of the Lord, that he should instruct Him: But we have the mind of Christ.

I believe we can and should draw the following conclusions from the above passage:

1. A natural man cannot discern what is spiritually true; he can only know his own thoughts and that which he can perceive through his natural senses.

2. The Holy Spirit knows all things and is capable of revealing the nature of God and His will. The Spirit of God knows the thoughts of God, because they are one and the same.

3. We have not received the spirit of the world but the Spirit who is from God. The Holy Spirit makes known to us the things freely given by God.

4. We have the mind of Christ because He indwells us.

5. The Holy Spirit takes words (*logos*), which are not taught by human wisdom but by the Spirit, and combines (brings together, compares, or explains) them. What is actually being combined or compared isn't clear. The original language literally says, "spirituals with spirituals." The NASB translates the phrase, "combining spiritual thoughts with spiritual words." The NIV translates the phrase, "words taught by the Spirit, expressing the spiritual truths in spiritual words."

The apostle Paul wrote: "The flesh sets its desire against the Spirit, and the Spirit against the flesh; for they are in opposition to one another" (Galatians 5:17). They are in opposition because the flesh is a learned independence, while the Spirit is totally dependent upon God the Father. God has given us the responsibility to choose between living according to the flesh, or living according to the Spirit. Carnal Christians choose to live according to the habit patterns and thoughts that were programmed in them over time from the environment in which they were raised, which is their flesh.

Additionally, if they fail to put on the armor of God they may find themselves paying attention to deceiving spirits. The spiritual man has crucified the flesh—and puts on the armor of God and chooses to think upon that which is true. It is our choice as to whether we are going to remain conformed to this world or to be conformed to the image of God.

We are renewed in the spirit of our minds (Ephesians 4:23). The Holy Spirit discloses the mind of Christ in our hearts. In order to be conformed to the image of Christ, we have to be diligent to present ourselves approved to God as a workman who does not need to be ashamed, handling accurately the word of truth (2 Timothy 2:15). When we do, we are transformed by the renewing of our minds. We choose to think the truth, and the Holy Spirit enables our thoughts and renews our minds with the *logos*. Then the peace of God guards our hearts and minds. We let the peace of Christ rule in our hearts by letting the word of Christ richly dwell in us (Colossians 3:15-16). Those who have done so are in a position to discern good and evil.

## Distinguishing Right and Wrong

In a world saturated with deceiving spirits, false prophets, and false teachers, the importance of exercising discernment cannot be overemphasized. In the Old Testament, the Hebrew word *bin* is used 247 times and is translated as "discern," "distinguish," and occasionally "understand." It means "to make a distinction, or separate from." The New Testament counterpart, *diakrino*, also means "to separate or divide." It is used primarily in reference to making righteous decisions. The Holy Spirit enables us to distinguish right from wrong, truth from lies, God's thoughts from man's thoughts.

An incident in King Solomon's life reveals God's thoughts on discernment. David had died, and Solomon had taken his place as king of Israel. Solomon believed he was too young and inexperienced to be the king. "O LORD my God, You have made Your servant king in place of my father David, yet I am but a little child; I do not know how to go out or come in" (1 Kings 3:7). The Lord appeared to Solomon in a dream at night and said, "Ask what you wish Me to give you." Here is Solomon's request and the Lord's response:

> "Your servant is in the midst of Your people which You have chosen, a great people who cannot be numbered or counted for multitude. So give Your servant an understanding heart to judge Your

people to discern between good and evil. For who is able to judge this great people of Yours?" And it was pleasing in the sight of the LORD that Solomon had asked this thing. And God said to him, "Because you have asked this thing and have not asked for yourself long life, nor have asked riches for yourself, nor have you asked for the life of your enemies, but have asked for yourself discernment to understand justice, behold, I have done according to your words. Behold, I have given you a wise and discerning heart, so that there has been no one like you before you, nor shall one like you arise after you" (1 Kings 3:8-12).

This passage reveals several key concepts about discernment.

**1. God gave Solomon the ability to discern because of the purity of his motives.** Solomon wasn't asking for personal gain or an advantage over his enemies. He was asking for the ability to discern good and evil, and God gave it to him. The ability to discern comes from God, and He knows the thoughts and intentions of our hearts. The Lord does not enable us to use His power with wrong motives coming from an impure heart. This is true for the proper use of any spiritual gift. Wrong motives open the door for Satan's counterfeits.

A few years ago, an undergraduate girl was following me around to various speaking engagements. After an evening service at a local church, she was shaking visibly. I saw her plight and asked if I could help. Learning she was a student at our school, I asked her to stop by my office the next day. When we got together, she told me she was seeing one of our Christian counselors. I asked her how that was going, and she replied it was like a game. She could tell everything the counselor was going to do next. When I realized she enjoyed playing mind games with her counselor, I challenged her, "You like doing that, don't you? You like the advantage it gives you over other people." As soon as I exposed the deception, an evil spirit began to speak through her.

She believed God had given her a spiritual gift that enabled her to expose people's sins. She could point to students and say, "That person is struggling with sex, that person with alcohol," and so on. As near as I could tell, she was right. Yet when she found her freedom in Christ, that ability disappeared. It wasn't the Holy Spirit that had been enabling her to discern. It was an evil spirit compatible with the evil spirits that were related to the moral problems in other people. Her goal was to be a Christian counselor and use this "gift" to "help" people. Instead, once she was set free, she went to the mission field. She is helping people, but now by the Spirit of God.

**2. True biblical discernment is on the plane of good and evil.** The "distinguishing of spirits" mentioned in 1 Corinthians 12:10 is the ability to distinguish between a good spirit and an evil spirit. I was working with a young lady who was plagued with compulsive thoughts that contributed to an eating disorder. As she was going through the process of forgiving others, I discerned that it wasn't the girl speaking anymore. "That's not her," I said. There were two other people in the room observing the counseling process, but they didn't sense the change. After the session, they asked how I knew it was the wrong spirit. I really can't explain how I knew, but my discernment was right. The expression on her face changed, and a different voice said, "She will never forgive that person." After finding her freedom in Christ, she too is now working as a missionary.

Spiritual discernment is primarily a function of the Spirit, but it doesn't bypass the mind. Nor does it replace the need to know the truth from the Word of God. Rather, it builds upon the truth already understood in our hearts. The mind wants to know what is wrong, but we may not always know that. In spiritual discernment, the Holy Spirit is simply alerting us that *something* is wrong—like a built-in spiritual alarm.

Let me illustrate. Suppose, when he was young, my son came home and I sensed something was wrong. So I asked him, "What's wrong, Karl?" He said, "Nothing!" Again I asked him what's wrong, and again he claimed nothing was wrong. But my "buzzer" was going off because I was discerning that something *was* wrong. At this point it is very easy to blow the discernment. If we try to be objective, we are likely to guess what we think is wrong (is that being objective?). "Karl, have you been doing such and such again?" If the guess is wrong (and it probably will be), we blow the discernment. The other person will stalk away, mad at us for falsely accusing them.

So what should we do when we don't know what is wrong? We should just share the discernment. "Karl, something is wrong." "No, Dad, nothing's wrong!" "Karl, I know something *is* wrong." He shrugs his shoulders and goes to his room. Is that the end of it? Only if there is no God! The Holy Spirit will convict him of his sins. The Holy Spirit made me aware that something was wrong when I shared my discernment. God now has a direct shot at my son—actually, His son—in his bedroom. Guess what happens in the bedroom? He is being convicted and is probably thinking,

*Dad knows!* I really don't know what's wrong, but my discernment alerted me to the truth that *something* was wrong. I reported only that which I knew. I couldn't discipline him, because discipline has to be based on factual observance—which is why God can discipline him. He disciplines all His children, because He loves them.

When I was pastoring, I would sometimes enter a family's home and sense something was wrong. There was no visible evidence. The people were smiling and friendly. They had a pot of coffee on the stove and had dusted off the Bible. But I could cut the air with a knife. I would know something wasn't right, but early on in my ministry I didn't know what to do about it. In such cases, the temptation is to ignore our discernment and conduct business as usual. But if we discern something is wrong, we should stop and pray for guidance.

## Discernment: An Early Warning System

Discernment is like an early warning system—the first line of defense in the spiritual world. It is not the same as woman's intuition, which is a natural gift many mothers and wives have. All God's children can learn to be discerning. The Holy Spirit will not remain passive in the face of adversity. He is testifying with our spirit and counteracting the influence of the world, the flesh, and the devil. When these influences are incompatible, your "buzzer" goes off. The corollary is also true. We can sense a compatible spirit with others whom we "know" are true believers without a word being spoken.

The ability to discern increases with our maturity according to Hebrews 5:12–6:2:

> Though by this time you ought to be teachers, you have need again for someone to teach you the elementary principles of the oracles of God, and you have come to need milk and not solid food. For every one who partakes only of milk is not accustomed to the word of righteousness, for he is a babe. But solid food is for the mature, who because of practice have their senses trained to discern good and evil. Therefore leaving the elementary teaching about Christ, let us press on to maturity, not laying again a foundation of repentance from dead works and of faith toward God, of instruction about washings, and laying on of hands, and the resurrection of the dead, and eternal judgment.

What the writer of Hebrews identifies as elementary teaching is advanced theology for some people. A good systematic theology is the foundation upon which we build our lives. It is to our walk with God what our skeleton is to our body. It holds us together and keeps us in the right form. But doctrine is never an end in itself. True doctrine governs our relationship with God and our neighbors. You can have a theological relationship with God, and not have a personal relationship with Him. The Spirit gives life to the body (Romans 8:11). Those accustomed to the word of righteousness are sensitive to the personal leading of the Holy Spirit.

Solomon started with a love for God. He "became greater than all the kings of the earth in riches and in wisdom. And all the earth was seeking the presence of Solomon, to hear his wisdom which God had put in his heart" (1 Kings 10:23-24). He had the ability to discern, but moral failure led to his downfall. His wives turned his heart away from God, and he was no longer accustomed to the words of righteousness. His heart was not wholly devoted to the Lord.

Christians can faithfully attend church on Sunday, and the sermon may reach their ears, but not their hearts so as to transform their lives. Their senses will not be trained to discern good and evil. I'm not sure my senses would have been trained if God hadn't called me into the ministry of setting captives free. If we are going to minister in a world of deception, we had better learn to rely upon God and not lean on our own understanding.

## Discernment Is Not a Shortcut to Maturity

The Holy Spirit does more than warn us. He enables us to understand Scripture, and He enhances our spiritual understanding so we can effectively minister to others. As I've matured in the Lord, I find that these kinds of impressions get to the heart of the issue when ministering to others. Such impressions are not a substitute for knowing the Bible, however, and they need to be tested, as I mentioned in an earlier chapter. Our ability to discern grows in proportion to our spiritual maturity and knowledge of God and His ways. God brings to our minds the Scripture we have already put into our hearts through studying His Word. There are no shortcuts to maturity. The Holy Spirit doesn't bypass those portions of Scripture that require us to show compassion, develop trusting relationships, and exercise patience. The spiritual leading of the Holy Spirit works through the whole counsel of God.

Deceiving spirits encourage shortcuts, try to bypass the mind, and seek to create a dependency upon esoteric knowledge (knowledge that does not come through our normal channels of perception or disciplined study). *You won't even have to think. Just go by what you hear in your head.* That's how mediums work. New Age channelers and spiritists are making big money with their esoteric knowledge. Some will even profess to be Christians. Satan gives them enough truth to hook a gullible public.

The apostle John writes, "Beloved, do not believe every spirit, but test the spirits to see whether they are from God; because many false prophets have gone out into the world" (1 John 4:1). This is not an optional exercise for Christians. We are instructed by God to test the spirits. There is only one infallible source of faith and practice, and that's the Word of God. It's the *logos* hidden in our hearts that the Holy Spirit uses to enable us to minister to others.

> Our power to perceive the light of God is, of all our powers, the one which we need most to cultivate and develop. As exercise strengthens the body and education enlarges the mind, so the spiritual faculty within us grows as we use it in doing God's will (*Friends Book of Discipline*).

Let's not waste such a precious resource that God has made available to us—our spirits quickened by the Holy Spirit to be able to discern good and evil, and right from wrong.

## Discussion Questions

1. Why is it so important to determine how righteous a person is before receiving counsel from them?

2. Jesus was able to discern what was in the hearts of men and women. Since the Holy Spirit lives in us, shouldn't all Christians be able to discern good from evil? Why or why not?

3. How does a true shepherd lead?

4. What five conclusions can be drawn from 1 Corinthians 2:9-16?

5. What does spiritual discernment reveal?

6. What are the conditions for a Christian to have spiritual discernment?

7. What are the characteristics of deceiving spirits?

8. How can we improve our ability to discern?

9. Share some times when you sensed a compatible spirit in another person and an incompatible spirit in another person.

Chapter Twelve

# Walking in Darkness

*God, who has made us, knows what we are and that our happiness*
*lies in Him. Yet we will not seek it in Him as long as he leaves us any*
*other resort where it can even plausibly be looked for. While what we*
*call "our own life" remains agreeable, you will not surrender it to Him.*
*What then can God do in our interest but make "our own life" less*
*agreeable to us, and take away the plausible sources of false happiness.*[41]

—C.S. Lewis

Being led by the Holy Spirit and living in His power is a liberating experience for every child of God. Sensing His presence, living victoriously, and knowing the truth are characteristics of a free person. But what if you couldn't sense His presence? What if God, for some reason, suspended His conscious blessings? What would you do if you were faithfully walking in the light and suddenly you found yourself engulfed in darkness?

Job was enjoying the benefits of living righteously when, unexpectedly, it was all taken away. Health, wealth, and family were all gone! If we found ourselves in Job's shoes, our minds would likely spin with many questions:

"What did I do to deserve this?"

"Did I miss a turn in the road?"

"Is this what I get for living a righteous life?"

"Where is God?"

"God, why are You doing this to me?"

Like Job, we may even feel like cursing the day we were born.

My family and I have been through two dark periods in our lives. There were days I wasn't sure if we were going to make it. Both times of testing preceded significant changes in my ministry. If it weren't for the message given in Isaiah 50:10-11, I'm not sure we would have survived those trials:

Who is among you that fears the LORD, that obeys the voice of His servant, that walks in darkness and has no light. Let him trust in the name of the LORD, and rely on his God. Behold all you who kindle a fire, who encircle yourselves with firebrands, walk in the light of your fire, and among the brands you have set ablaze, this you will have from My hand, and you will lie down in torment.

Isaiah is talking about a believer, somebody who obeys God, and yet walks in darkness. Isaiah is not talking about the darkness of sin, nor even the darkness of this world (that is, the kingdom of darkness). He's talking about the darkness of uncertainty, a blanket of heaviness that hovers like a dark cloud over our very being. The assurances of yesterday have been replaced by the uncertainties of tomorrow. God has suspended His conscious blessings. Could this happen to a true believer? What is the purpose for such a dark time? What are followers of Christ to do when the path before them isn't certain?

## Keep on Walking in the Light of Previous Revelation

In the light we can see the next step—the path ahead is clear. We know a friend from an enemy, and we can see where the obstacles are. The Word has been a lamp to our feet. It has directed our steps, but now we begin to wonder if it's true. Darkness has overcome us. We are embarrassed by how feelings-oriented we are. Every natural instinct says, Drop out, Sit down, Stop! But the text encourages us to keep on living by faith according to what we know to be true.

Our first encounter with such a period of darkness came after my wife, Joanne, discovered that she was developing cataracts in both eyes. In the late 1970s they would not do lens implants for anybody under the age of 60. We had no alternative but to watch each of her eyes cloud over until she could barely see. Then they surgically removed the lenses. Thick cataract glasses were prescribed until she could be fitted with contact lenses. This traumatic experience for Joanne lasted for two years.

Living the role of a pastor's wife is pressure enough, but this additional trauma was more then she could bear. So for Joanne's sake, I started to consider another way to serve the Lord other than being a senior pastor. At the time I felt led to pursue my first doctoral degree, even though I had no idea what God had in store for me. Just the assurance that I was putting Joanne ahead of my desire to be a pastor gave her a sense of hope. Since our church was in the middle of a building program, I needed to stay until the project was complete. Within months after we dedicated our new buildings, God released me from that pastorate. I was nearing the completion of my doctoral studies and facing the major task of doing research and writing my dissertation. I also wanted to finish a second seminary degree.

Sensing God's release, I began one of the most difficult educational years of my life. In one year I completed 43 semester units. Seventeen of them were language studies in Greek and Hebrew. In the middle of that year I took my comprehensive exams, and by the end of the year finished my research and doctoral dissertation. I also taught part-time at Talbot School of Theology. It was a difficult year to say the least. But when you take a year off for education, you try to accomplish as much as you possibly can.

We started that year with the assurance that $20,000 would be made available to us interest-free. The plan was to pay off the loan when we sold our home. Not having to sell our house allowed us to keep our children in the same school for that year. After I completed my education, I was confident that God would have a place for us. So I proceeded with a great deal of anticipation of finishing my doctorate and a second master's degree. For the next six months our life unfolded as planned. Then God turned out the lights.

Apparently the second half of the promised $20,000 wasn't going to come in. Having no other source of income, we saw our cupboards become bare. I had no job, and my educational goals were only half completed. I always considered myself a faithful person, but now I was on the brink of not being able to provide for the basic needs of my family. I had been so certain of God's calling six months earlier, but the darkness of doubt and uncertainty had settled in.

It all culminated two weeks before my comprehensive exams. Only 10 percent of the doctoral candidates had passed the previous testing, which had taken place on two consecutive Saturdays. So I was sensing a lot of pressure. If I didn't pass the exams, I couldn't start my research and dissertation. I had already invested three years of my life and $15,000 in the program. Now I didn't even know where my next meal was coming from. I had equity in my home, but interest rates at the time were so high that houses weren't selling.

The tension to create my own light was overwhelming. I looked into a couple of ministry opportunities, but I knew they weren't for me, and I couldn't accept them. The problem wasn't an unwillingness to work. I would have sold hot dogs to provide for my family. I wasn't struggling with pride. I just wanted to know God's will!

I began to wonder if I had made the wrong decision. His leading had been so clear the previous summer. Why was I now walking in darkness? It was as though God had dropped me into a funnel that was getting darker and darker. When I thought it couldn't get much darker, I hit the narrow part! Then, at the darkest hour, God dropped us out of the bottom of that funnel, and everything became clear again.

It was in the middle of my sleep on a Thursday night when the dawn broke. Nothing changed circumstantially, but everything changed internally. I remember waking up with a sense of excitement and joy. My startled wife awoke and wondered what was going on, but she too could sense something had taken place. There was a conscious awareness of God in a remarkable way. No audible voices or visions. God in His quiet and gentle way was renewing my mind. My thought process went something like this, *Neil, do you walk by faith or do you walk by sight? Are you walking by faith now? You believed Me last summer—do you believe Me now? Neil, do you love Me, or do you love My blessings? Do you worship Me for who I am, or do you worship Me for the blessings I bring? What if I suspended My conscious blessings in your life—would you still believe in Me?*

I learned something that evening in a way I had never experienced before. In my spirit I responded, *Lord, You know I love You, and of course I walk by faith, not by sight. Lord, I worship You because of who You are, and I know You will never leave me nor forsake me. Lord, I confess that I doubted Your place in my life and questioned Your ability to provide for all our needs.*

Such precious moments can't be planned or predicted. They're never repeatable. What we have previously learned from the Bible either becomes incarnate—or discarded—during such times. Our worship is purified, and our love clarified. Faith moves from a textbook definition to a living reality. Trust is deepened when God puts us in a position where we have no other choice but to trust Him. We either learn to trust Him during these times, or we end up compromising our faith. The Bible teaches us the rules of faith and knowledge of the object of our faith, but we learn to live by faith in the course of living. This is especially true when circumstances are not working favorably for us. The Lord has a way of stretching us through a knothole, and just before we are about to break in half, suddenly we slip through to the other side. But we will never go back to the same shape we were before.

⟋

The next day everything changed. The Dean at Talbot School of Theology called to ask if I had taken another position. He asked me not to accept anything until we had the opportunity to talk. That Friday afternoon he offered me the position I was to hold for the next ten years. Friday evening, a man from my previous ministry stopped by at 10 p.m. When I asked him what he was doing at our home at that hour of the night, he said he wasn't sure. I invited him in and assured him we would figure out something. I half jokingly asked him if he'd like to buy my house and he responded, "Maybe I would." The next Tuesday he came to our home with his parents and made an offer on our house that we accepted. Now we could sell our house because we knew the destination of our next move.

Nothing had changed externally before that morning, but everything changed internally. God can change in a moment what circumstances can never change. My wife and I had previously made the commitment not to make a major decision when we are down. That alone has kept me from resigning after difficult board meetings or messages that bombed. The point is, never doubt in darkness what God has clearly shown you in the light. We are to keep on walking in the light of previous revelation. If it was true six months ago, it's still true. If we're serious about our walk with God, He will test us to determine if we love Him or His blessings. He may cloud the future so we learn to walk by faith and not by sight or feelings.

Understand that God has not left us, He has only suspended His "conscious" presence so that our faith will never rest on our feelings, be established by unique experiences, or fostered by temporal blessings. If our physical parents found themselves in difficult circumstances and couldn't afford any Christmas presents when we were young, would we stop loving them? Would we stop looking to them for direction and support? If God's ministry of darkness should envelop you, keep on walking in the light of previous revelation.

## Don't Create Your Own Light

*Don't light your own fire* is another lesson we should learn from Isaiah. In other words, *Don't create your own light.* When we don't see it God's way, the natural tendency is to do it our way. Notice the text again, "All you who kindle a fire, who encircle yourselves with firebrands, walk in the light of your fire." God is not talking about the fire of judgment, He's talking about fire that creates light. Notice what happens when people create their own light. "Among the brands you have set ablaze, this you will have from my hand, you will lie down in torment." Essentially God is saying, *Go ahead, do it your way. I will allow it, but misery will follow.*

Let me illustrate this principle from the Bible. God called Abraham out of Ur into the Promised Land. In Genesis 12, a covenant was made in which God promised Abraham that his descendants would be more numerous than the sands of the sea or the stars in the sky. Abraham lived his life in the light of that promise, and then God turned out the light. So many months and years passed that his wife Sarah could no longer bear a child by natural means. God's guidance had been so clear before, but now it looked like Abraham would have to assist God in its fulfillment. Who could blame Abraham for creating his own light? Sarah supplied the match by offering her handmaiden to Abraham. Out of that union came another nation, which has created so much conflict that the whole world lies down in torment. Jews and Arabs have not been able to dwell together peacefully to this day.

God superintended the birth of Moses and provided for his preservation. Raised in the home of Pharaoh, he was given the second-most prominent position in Egypt. God had put into his heart a burden to set his people free. Impulsively Moses pulled out his sword, attempting to help God, and God turned out the lights. Abandoned to the back side of the desert, Moses spent 40 years tending his father-in-law's sheep. Then one day, he turned aside to see a burning bush that wasn't consumed. God turned the light back on.

I'm not suggesting that we may have to wait 40 years for the cloud to lift. In our life span that would be more time than an average person's faith could endure. But the darkness may last for weeks, months, and, for some exceptional people, possibly even years. God is in charge, and He knows exactly how small a knothole He can pull us through. Isaiah wrote, "The One forming light and creating darkness, causing well-being and creating calamity; I am the Lord who does all these" (Isaiah 45:7). Why does God cause calamity?

~

Let me share about our second period of darkness. Five years after Joanne's surgery to remove her lenses from both eyes, her doctor suggested she have a lens implant. So much scientific progress had been made that implanting a lens had become a simple outpatient surgery. At first Joanne was reluctant, and our insurance provider wouldn't pay. They called the surgery cosmetic, but they finally came around. Joanne's doctor and I convinced her it was the best thing to do.

The surgery was successful, but Joanne emerged from the anesthesia in a phobic state. She had been anesthetized in surgery before, so I couldn't understand why she was so fearful now. I certainly could understand her apprehension before surgery, because having your eyeball cut into is not something you look forward to. Just the thought of it can send shivers down your spine. So her emotional state before surgery was somewhat troubled. Could the anesthetic itself have caused her emotional state? Or could the nature of her postoperative care been a factor? The cost for medical care has pushed many hospitals into day surgeries that leave no time for rest or recovery after such a traumatic experience.

The nurses had to ask for my assistance in helping Joanne come out of the anesthetic. I think part of their motivation was to clear the bed for other patients. Joanne was just one of several patients that day. Some people need more emotional care than that. If she had been permitted to gradually recover from her experience and spend at least one night in the hospital, she might have recovered a lot better. Bringing Joanne home that afternoon was an ordeal for both of us. She just couldn't stabilize emotionally.

The possibility of this also being a spiritual battle became evident the next day. Joanne thought she had a foreign object in her that had to come out. This made no rational sense at all, since the surgery had been success-ful. She could see with 20/30 vision. I didn't understand the battle for our minds then as I do today. For instance, I have seen such thoughts with young women struggling with eating disorders. Paul said, "I find then the principle that evil is present in me, the one who wants to do good" (Romans 7:21). They believe they have evil present in them and they have to get it out. That is the lie behind their purging, defecating, and cutting themselves. But the evil is not their blood, feces, or food. The evil that Joanne was fighting was not the physical kind—it was the lie of Satan that came at a very vulnerable moment.

It is painful to recall this, because much of what followed could have been avoided. Joanne's struggle with anxiety led to sleeplessness and finally depression. She went from her eye doctor, to her primary care doctor, to her gynecologist, and finally to a psychiatrist. Since they could not find anything physically wrong with her they assumed she was a head case or a hormone case. They tried hormones, antidepressants, and sleeping pills, but nothing seemed to work. She lost her appetite, and her weight dropped significantly. She was hospitalized five times.

Getting proper medical help was exceedingly expensive. Our insurance ran out, and we had to sell our house to pay the medical bills. For months Joanne couldn't function as a mother or wife. My daughter wasn't sure if she could handle it if her mother were to die. My son withdrew into himself. I got caught in a role conflict like never before. Was I her pastor, counselor, or discipler—or was I supposed to be just her husband? I decided there was only one role I could fulfill in her life, and that was to be her husband. If someone was going to help my wife, it would have to be someone other than myself. My role was to hold her every day and say, "Joanne, this too will pass." I was thinking it would be a matter of weeks, but it turned into a 15-month ordeal. The funnel got narrower and narrower. The words in Isaiah 21:11-12 had great meaning to me:

> One keeps calling to me from Seir, "Watchman, how far gone is the night? Watchman, how far gone is the night?" The watchman says, "Morning comes but also night."

A ministry of hope must be based on the truth that "morning comes." No matter how dark the night; morning comes. It usually is the darkest before the dawn. In our darkest hour, when I wasn't even sure if Joanne was going to live or die, morning came. She had all but given up on any medical hope, but a doctor in private practice was recommended to her. He immediately took her off the medication she was on, and prescribed a much more balanced approach that dealt with depression but also her general health, including nutrition.

At the same time we had a day of prayer at Biola University where I was teaching. I had nothing to do with the program other than to set aside special time for prayer in my own classes. The undergraduate students had a communion service that evening. Since I taught at the graduate level, I normally wouldn't have gone, but work had detained me on campus so I decided to participate. I sat on the gym floor with the undergraduate students and took communion. I'm sure nobody in the student body was aware that it was one of the loneliest and darkest times of my life. I was deeply committed to doing God's will, and I was walking as best I could in the light of previous revelation, but I felt incredibly lonely and frustrated. There was nothing I could do to change Joanne or the circumstances.

## Morning Comes

I can honestly say I never once questioned God nor felt bitter about my circumstances. I have Him to thank for sustaining me. For some time, the Lord had been preparing my heart and leading me into a ministry that binds up the brokenhearted and sets captives free. Somehow I knew that the nature of my ministry was related to what my family was going through, but I didn't know what to do about it. Should I abandon what I was doing to help others, in order to spare my family? God was blessing my ministry in unprecedented ways, but my family wasn't being blessed. He had stripped us of every thing we owned. All we had left was each other and our relationship with God. When He is all you have, you begin to discover that He is all you need. When we had exhausted all our resources, morning came!

If God has ever spoken to my heart, He did in that communion service. There were no voices or visions. It was just His quiet and gentle way of renewing our minds. It didn't come by way of the worship leader's message, or the testimonies of the students; but it did come in the context of taking communion. The essence of my thought process went like this, *Neil, there's a price to pay for freedom. It cost My Son His life. Are you willing to pay the price?* I remember thinking, *Dear God, if that's the reason, I'm willing...but if it's some stupid thing I'm doing, then I pray that You would tell me.* I left that evening with the inward assurance that it was over. The circumstances hadn't changed, but in my heart I knew that morning had come.

Within a week Joanne woke up one morning and said, "Neil, I slept last night." From that point on she knew it was over. She never looked back, and she continued on to full and complete recovery. At the same time our ministry took a quantum leap. What was the point of all this? Why did we have to go through such a trial?

## Brokenness: The Key to Ministry

There are several reasons why God takes some of His children through His ministry of darkness. First, *you learn a lot about yourself during those times.* Whatever was left of my flesh that gave simplistic "advice" such as "Why don't you read your Bible?" or "Just work harder" or "Pray more" was mercifully stripped away. Most people going through dark times want to do the right thing, but many can't—or at least don't believe they can—and they don't know why. We also realize our limitations and deepen our roots in the eternal streams of life while severing ties with temporal answers and props that don't last.

Second, *we learn compassion during God's ministry of darkness.* We learn to wait patiently with people, weep with those who weep, and restrain from instructing those who weep. We learn to respond to the emotional needs of people who have lost hope. Instruction may come later when it is appropriate. I believe I was a caring person before, but nothing like I am now because of God's gracious way of ministering to me.

We had some "friends" like those who tried to help Job advise us in our time of darkness, and I can tell you that it hurts. What Job needed in his hour of darkness was a few good friends who would just sit with him. They actually did for one week, but then their patience ran out. The meaningful help we received was from the church, people who just stood by us and prayed. If God took away every material blessing and reduced our assets to nothing more than meaningful relationships, would that be enough for us?

Some citizens of this world have learned to be content with food and clothing because they have no other choice. Many Americans have too much, and some want more. Paul said, "I know how to get along with humble means, and I also know how to live in prosperity; in any and every circumstance I have learned the secret of being filled and going hungry, both of having abundance and suffering need" (Philippians. 4:12). That is an important lesson to learn.

The final lot of Job was far better than it was at the beginning. The same happened for us. Within two years God replaced everything we lost, and this time it was far better in terms of home, family, and ministry. Be confident that God will make everything right in the end.

Third, *I believe God brings us to the end of our resources in order that we may discover His.* We don't hear enough sermons on brokenness these days. It's the great omission, and that's why we can't fulfill the great commission. In all four Gospels, Jesus taught us to deny ourselves, pick up our cross daily, and follow Him. When it was time for the Son of Man to be glorified He said, "Truly, truly, I say to you, unless a grain of wheat falls into the ground and dies, it remains by itself alone; but if it dies it bears much fruit" (John 12:24). I don't know of any painless way to die to self-rule. Self-sufficiency is the biggest obstacle to overcome if we are going to find our sufficiency in Christ. I do know that denying self is necessary, and that it's the best possible thing that could ever happen to us. "We who live are constantly being delivered over to death for Jesus' sake, that the life of Jesus also may be manifested in our mortal flesh" (2 Corinthians 4:11).

Moses was no good for God in Pharaoh's court. God had to strip him of his earthly possessions and positions before he could be an instrument in His hand. Chuck Colson was no good for God in the White House, but he became a powerful force in prison. I had a lot of hard-earned attributes, including five earned degrees, but I wasn't much good for God until I suffered the loss of all things. I can't set a captive free or bind up the brokenhearted—but God can. Every book I have written and every audio or video I have recorded all came after this experience. That period of brokenness was the beginning of Freedom in Christ Ministries, which has spread all over the world. "No pain, no gain," says the bodybuilder. That's also true in the spiritual realm. Isaiah's second point is simply this, *don't create your own light.* Man-made light is very deceptive.

### A Lesson in Trust

The final point Isaiah makes is, "Let him trust in the name of the Lord and rely upon His name" (50:10). *Walking in darkness is a lesson in trust.* Every great period of personal growth in my own life and ministry has been preceded by a major time of testing. The first led to my appointment to teach at Talbot School of Theology, and the second led to the birth of Freedom in Christ Ministries.

Possibly the greatest sign of spiritual maturity is the ability to postpone rewards. The ultimate test would be to receive nothing in this lifetime, but look forward to receiving our reward in the life to come. This is how the writer of Hebrews expressed it:

> All these died in faith without receiving the promises, but having seen them and having welcomed them from a distance and having confessed that they were strangers and exiles on this earth, for those who say such things, make it clear that they are seeking a country of their own (11:13).

Verse 39 reads,

> All these having gained approval through their faith did not receive what was promised because God had provided something better for us, so that apart from us they should not be made perfect.

If I had known beforehand what my family would have to go through to get where we are today, I probably wouldn't have come this way. But looking back, we can all say, "We're glad we came." God makes everything right in the end. It may not even be in this lifetime, as happened with the heroes of our faith mentioned in Hebrews 11. I believe with all my heart that when this physical life has come to an end, for all those who embraced their heavenly Father as Lord and Savior, they will look back and say that the will of God is good, acceptable, and perfect.

> *It is not the critic who counts, nor the man who points how the strong man stumbled, or where the doer of deeds could have done better. The credit belongs to the man who is actually in the arena, whose face is marred by the dust and sweat and blood; who strives valiantly; who errs and comes short again and again; who knows the great enthusiasms, the great devotions, and spends himself in a worthy cause; who, at best, knows in the end the triumph of high achievement; and who, at the worst, if he fails, at least fails while daring greatly, so that his place shall never be with those cold and timid souls who know neither victory or defeat.*
>
> THEODORE ROOSEVELT

## Discussion Questions

1. What are three characteristics of a free person?

2. Have you ever felt as though God has abandoned you? What did you do?

3. If the assurances of yesterday have been replaced by the uncertainties of tomorrow, how can you get back to the assurances of God?

4. Have you ever doubted in darkness what God has clearly shown you in the light? What would enable you to keep on walking in the light of previous revelation?

5. What may be some of the consequences of creating our own light, judging from the experiences of Abraham and Moses?

6. How difficult is it for you to wait upon the Lord?

7. What is the most important lesson to be learned in God's ministry of darkness?

8. If all you had was God, a few friends, and a close family, would that be enough?

9. How has the ability to postpone rewards helped you do well in school? Work? Church?

# Epilogue

*I desire the bread of God, the heavenly bread, the bread of life—which
is the flesh of Jesus Christ, the Son of God...And I desire the drink of
God, namely His blood, which is incorruptible love and eternal life.*[42]

IGNATIUS (C. 105)

After I had spoken at a conference, a man approached me and said, "I can't
peg you!" To which I responded, "Try Christian." What is there about
us that wants to pigeonhole one another? Labels may help us understand
each other, but too often they provide grounds for acceptance or rejection.

I have never felt comfortable being labeled a Protestant. It sounds like
someone who protests, which is partially true; because a Protestant is a
believer in Christ who isn't Catholic or Orthodox. Protestants have a lot of
options to choose who they feel comfortable associating with (or not), since
there are 20,000-plus denominations, associations, or movements that can
be called Protestant. Sounds vaguely familiar to "In those days there was no
king in Israel; everyone did what was right in his own eyes" (Judges 21:25).
That is not something to boast about. Many Evangelicals, including me, are
tired of the next new fad or popular trend.

Some major movements such as the Reformation, have brought needed
corrections to the body of Christ. The Evangelical movement reaffirmed
the authority of God's Word and ignited the fire of missions and evangelism. The Charismatic movement challenged us to reconsider the role of
the Holy Spirit.

Other movements are short-lived, such as the "seeker-sensitive" movement, which has come and gone. I often wondered, *If you take down all
the crosses and images of Christianity so as to not offend anyone, then what
are they seeking?* The proper response is to be more sensitive to seekers, but

not to be seeker-driven. Another movement has appeared, the "emergent" church, that may awaken the social conscience in some, but where is their journey leading them? The book *Why We Are Not Emergent* is a good read for those who don't want to get bogged down in relativism.[43] Many serious Christians are deeply concerned for the Church and long to be firmly rooted in Christ.

## Examining the Roots

Archbishop Wayne Boosahda is a neighbor and friend of mine who is a key player in the convergence movement (not to be confused with the emergent movement). Arising out of a common desire and hunger to experience the fullness of Christian worship and spirituality, the convergence movement seeks to blend or merge the essential elements in the Christian faith represented historically in three major streams of thought and practice: the Charismatic, Evangelical/Reformed and liturgical/sacramental.[44] Wayne sees Christianity as a river that has many tributaries that branch off in different directions. Some become little streams that end in stagnant ponds and eventually die, while others just disappear into the landscape. Those tributaries that have survived have stayed connected to mainstream Christianity. In other words, they have abided in Christ to one degree or another.[45]

Many evangelicals are not going to embrace the convergence movement because of the strong emphasis on the Charismatic/Pentecostal movement, which has no historical roots before the twentieth century. Pentecostals only recently celebrated the hundredth anniversary of the Azusa Street revival, which is considered by many to be the beginning of Pentecostalism, while the more recent Charismatic movement began in the early 1960s. However, Evangelicals and Pentecostals alike may be interested in what David Neff, the Editor-in-Chief of *Christianity Today,* is doing at Northern Seminary. He and his associates are establishing the Robert E. Webber Center for Ancient Evangelical Future, which is a serious look at the Evangelical connection with the historical Church.[46]

The leaders of the convergence movement do have an ongoing dialogue with the Catholic Church, which cautiously accepts the contribution of the Charismatic movement, as do the Anglicans. Many in England prefer to call it the Renewal Movement. It has touched many Anglican priests, many of whom now refer to themselves as born-again. Charismatic Catholics have also brought renewal to some of their dioceses. I also have had the privilege to share resources with some in the Catholic Church, as illustrated in the following letter:

> Just a quick note to let you know that things are still humming along here in San Antonio [Texas]. We have a Freedom Ministry established at my parish, St. Mark the Evangelist, and at the Catholic Center for Charismatic Renewal, Archdiocese of San Antonio.
>
> Since I last saw you at the "Living Free in Christ" conference in Edmond, Oklahoma (hosted by a Southern Baptist church), we have developed a team of nine people. Two are encouragers, five are prayer partners; three also teach spiritual growth classes and another four facilitate your video series starting this fall at St. Mark's.
>
> All have completed the Steps to Freedom personally and have completed your "Breaking Through to Spiritual Maturity" course. I am as excited now as I was a year ago about what Freedom in Christ Ministry has to offer not only hurting Christians, but those with real problems. We have taken about 150 people through the Steps, and most are doing well.

## Movement Toward the Orthodox and Catholic Churches

In recent decades, many Evangelicals have grown to have a deeper appreciation and openness to some aspects of Roman Catholic and Orthodox tradition. A few have even gone so far as to whole-heartedly embrace these traditions, leaving their evangelical roots behind. During the turbulent 1960s several Campus Crusade for Christ staff started asking the question, "What is the church?" Their search led them to the Orthodox Church. Peter Gillquist shares their journey in his book *Becoming Orthodox*.[47] Gillquist now plays a significant role in the Antiochian Orthodox church in the United States.

The Orthodox Church claims to teach what the apostles have always taught, and I believe that is basically true. They are sacramental, and they would argue that the church has been such from the beginning. While the various segments of the Orthodox Church profess to be in communion with one another, they are governed separately under several different Patriarchs.

Having, for a time, attended an Antiochian Orthodox Church, I can tell you that they are not seeker-sensitive. They have no desire to make you feel comfortable. The service begins with the Bible being elevated, and congregants reverently bow as it passes by from the rear of the church to the front. I cannot help but be impressed with their reverence for God. While I have a lot of respect for the Orthodox Church, I struggle with their traditions and their isolation from the rest of the Christian community. Although there is missionary work and community service going on in it, it appears to be significantly less than what I see in Evangelicalism or the Catholic Church.

Another example is Scott and Kimberly Hahn who were rising stars in the Reformed tradition. Scott was a brilliant student at Gordon–Conwell Theological Seminary, destined to be a major player in conservative Presbyterian circles. He was staunchly anti-Catholic. He is now a Catholic theologian at the Franciscan University of Steubenville, a conservative Catholic school. Scott and Kimberly share their journey in *Rome Sweet Home*, subtitled "Our Journey to Catholicism."[48]

Scott did his doctoral work at Duquesne University. In *Rome Sweet Home*, Kimberly wrote, "Though it was a Catholic institution, he usually found himself being the lone defender of the Catholic Faith in class." Later in the book Scott wrote, "I quickly learned that very few, if any, of my Catholic students really understood their Faith, even the basics."[49] He also related a conversation he had with a man in his parish. He was sharing how he had just attended a conference for Catholic theologians at Steubenville and had experienced the enthusiastic singing, the dynamic biblical preaching, and the warm fellowship. His friend responded, "Scott, personally I think Protestants have all those things because they don't have the Blessed Sacrament. Once you have the Real Presence of Christ in the Holy Eucharist, you don't need all the rest. Don't you agree?"[50]

Scott didn't agree with him and professes a commitment to biblical preaching and teaching, but the response by his friend illustrates one of the problems evangelicals have with the Catholic Church and somewhat with the Orthodox Church as well. But throughout this book I have quoted several of the Church Fathers to illustrate their profound belief that the Word and the sacraments were both necessary for Christians to grow and connect with God.

## The Role of the Word and the Sacraments

Two sacraments, baptism and the Eucharist (the Lord's Supper), are universally recognized in Christendom and are clearly taught in the Bible. The Catholic and Orthodox Churches have added other sacraments, which have not been accepted by Protestants because they lack the biblical precedents of baptism and communion. Historically, in the Catholic and Orthodox Churches, sacraments have been understood to be an outward and visible sign of an inward and spiritual grace. Evangelicals shy away from the word *sacrament* in favor of "ordinances," and are quite divided as to their significance.

The early church believed that baptism was a means to publicly identify with Christ and initiate a convert into the church. That union with God was sustained through the preaching and teaching of God's Word and the celebration of the Eucharist. Eventually, weekly confession was prescribed or encouraged in order that no one participate in the Eucharist in an unworthy manner. Most Lutherans and Anglicans maintained the weekly Eucharist. For many Protestants it is a purely symbolic act, unfortunately, and even meaningless in some cases.

The primary focus of Evangelicals has been the teaching and preaching of God's Word, and they bemoan the lack of biblical instruction in Catholic and Orthodox Churches around the world.

Having traveled around the world, I too can attest that the Catholic and Orthodox Churches have done a poor job of educating their people. The fact that their ecclesiology was developed when most of their congregants couldn't read and before the printing press was invented may have contributed to their long-standing practices. Just visit Russia or Greece and ask the average Orthodox Christian what they believe. Or go to Latin America and ask average Catholics what they believe. Most have been allowed to believe that simply taking the elements of the Eucharist fulfills their obligation.

Such ignorance is less true of the Catholic Churches in the United States, and it would be wrong to conclude that their priests are not educated. In most cases they have more education than an average Protestant pastor. If you were to read the Catechism of the Catholic Church, you'd likely be surprised by how much agreement there is between Evangelicals and Catholics on some of the most essential issues. I painfully confess that I have disagreed (privately) for years with the Catholic Church based primarily from what I have heard from other Protestants. Of course there are some fundamental disagreements, but what we have in common is far greater than what separates us.

Although I would disagree with them on several issues, I have shared the journeys of Wayne Boosahda, Peter Gillquist, and Scott Hahn because they are intelligent and serious Christians who have come to value the historical roots of the church. The Church Fathers have provided a rich heritage, and we owe them a lot for clarifying the Trinitarian nature of God and formulating the canon of Scripture.

I'd encourage you to keep an open mind and be informed by the right sources before you pass judgment. I am an Evangelical because I believe that God's Word should be taught and believed, but as an Evangelical I believe we have not fared well in fostering our union with God after salvation. We seem more inclined to connect ourselves to information revealed in the Bible. How many Protestants have an intimate relationship with God and how many have unresolved conflicts due to a lack of repentance? I believe in the preaching and teaching of God's Word, but just doing that Sunday morning will not be enough to help God's children be fully reconciled to their heavenly Father.

Luke wrote of the early church that "they were continually devoting themselves to the apostles' teaching and to fellowship, to the breaking of bread and to prayer" (Acts 2:42). Teaching is not enough by itself. Breaking of bread in Holy Communion is not enough by itself. Having a nice time of fellowship is not enough by itself. Even prayer is not enough by itself. When Jesus said, "Do this in remembrance of Me," He was not saying we should try to remember Him during our worship services.

The English word *amnesia* comes from the Greek word translated as "remembrance." Putting an "a" (alpha) in front of the word reverses its meaning. When God says, "I will remember your sins no more," He is not saying He will forget them. He couldn't forget them even if He wanted to, because He is omniscient. Those words mean He will not use the past against us. He will remove it as far from Himself as the east is from the west.

Rather, "Do this in remembrance of me" has the opposite meaning. It means that we should take what was accomplished in the life, death, and resurrection of Christ 2000 years ago and apply it to ourselves today and every day, because we are alive in Christ. I hope that all Protestants will help their people prepare better for communion and better celebrate the presence of the living Christ that is within them. A minute of silent prayer will not accomplish that in most cases. I also hope that Catholic and Orthodox Churches will make the commitment to educate their people so they can live by faith and in fellowship with all believers.

# Resources for Growth

If you or your church would like to connect people to God in a living and liberating way through genuine repentance and faith in Him, then I offer you the following plan. Freedom in Christ Ministries began with my books and expanded into a conference ministry with the "Living Free in Christ" conference, which I have shared around the world. That conference is now available as a curriculum for Sunday schools, small groups, home Bible studies, and so on. The course is entitled *Freedom in Christ*. In the United Kingdom it is entitled *The Freedom in Christ Discipleship Course.* Both courses come with a DVD that includes a 30-minute message for each lesson and a teacher's guide that has all the messages written out so leaders can give the message themselves or play the DVD. Finally, there is a Learner's Guide, which includes the Steps to Freedom in Christ. (Each participant should have a copy of the Learner's Guide.)

This curriculum can be the entry point for churches, but it is not an end. For some believers it will be a new beginning on their journey to freedom and wholeness. If they have no additional issues to be resolved, the *Daily Discipler* is written to give them a practical theology that can be digested five days a week for a year. There will be some who need additional help for sexual addiction, chemical addiction, anger, fear, anxiety, depression, and reconciliation with others. Freedom in Christ Ministries has resources for all those, which will be explained later.

The next step is to help marriage partners become one in Christ. The book I offer for that is *Experiencing Christ Together,* which has "Steps for Beginning Your Marriage Free" and "Steps for Setting Your Marriage Free." The book and the "Steps for Beginning Your Marriage Free" are intended for premarital counseling. *Experiencing Christ Together* and the "Steps for

Setting Your Marriage Free" are for Sunday school classes and small-group or home-group studies. There are modified Steps available when only one partner will try.

These marriage steps follow the same reasoning as the individual Steps to Freedom—that is, Christ must be included in the process. We recommend that the book be read or taught first and then a retreat scheduled in the church or elsewhere to process the marriage Steps to Freedom. It takes a full day to work through the marriage steps. It is a powerful process that helps couples resolve their conflicts by the grace of God.

The final step is for the official board of the church and the ministerial staff to resolve the church's conflicts and set the church or ministry free. The book I have written for that is *Extreme Church Makeover,* which explains servant leadership and lays the foundation for corporate conflict resolution. The "Steps to Setting Your Church Free" is a process that the board and staff work through, and that usually requires a day and an evening to process.

Both the marriage and church steps cannot be processed without individual freedom being established first. That is why I recommend that churches start with the *Freedom in Christ* discipleship course. If you have a church full of people in bondage to sex, alcohol, drugs, bitterness, gambling, legalism, and so on, you have a church in bondage. If you have a church full of bad marriages, you have a bad church. The whole cannot be greater than the sum of its parts.

### Discipleship Counseling Training

I have written a book entitled *Restored,* which is an expansion upon the "Steps to Freedom in Christ." This is a book Christians can work through on their own and thus facilitate their own repentance. That is possible because God is the one who grants repentance and is the only one who can bind up the brokenhearted and set the captives free.

We estimate that 85 percent of the participants in a "Living Free in Christ" conference or the *Freedom in Christ* course can work through the Steps on their own. The book *Restored* may facilitate that process to a higher percentage. For those who can't work through the process on their own we offer comprehensive training through books, audio resources, and study guides. It is our prayer that churches that use our material would offer this training on a continuous basis.

The material for training encouragers includes books, study guides (which greatly increase the learning process by helping people personalize and internalize the message), and several series of video and audio resources (each series comes with a corresponding syllabus). Trainees receive the most thorough training when they watch the videos, read the books, and complete the study guides. We recommend two hours per week for 16 weeks. The material should be presented in the order listed:

### Basic Training

**Sessions 1-4**

| | |
|---|---|
| Video/audio: | *Victory over the Darkness* |
| Reading: | *Victory over the Darkness* and Study Guide |

**Sessions 5-8**

| | |
|---|---|
| Video/audio: | *The Bondage Breaker* |
| Reading: | *The Bondage Breaker* and study guide |

**Sessions 9-16**

| | |
|---|---|
| Video/audio: | *Discipleship Counseling* and *Helping Others Find Freedom in Christ Video Training Program* |
| Reading: | *Discipleship Counseling* |

The book *Discipleship Counseling* has further instructions on how to set up a discipleship-counseling ministry in your church. We don't want to add to the workload of any pastoral staff. We firmly believe that discipleship counseling has the potential to greatly reduce their load and equip the layperson to do the work of ministry.

I close with the following encouragement that our U.S. office received by e-mail:

> Dear Sir,
>
> We are full-time missionaries in Tanzania, East Africa, writing you today just because Freedom in Christ Ministries changed our lives some 22 years ago and has continued to be a big part of what we do in Tanzania.
>
> Last week we held a youth camp (18-27 year olds) and we took the entire camp through the Steps to Freedom! It was amazing. Curses were broken, bitterness and hatred toward other tribes were

forgiven, and blinders were taken off so the students could realize who they really are in Christ! Afterward I kept thinking, *I would love to share this with Neil, as he is the one that took me through the Steps to Freedom back in 1986, and I have been FREE ever since.* My story is in one of Neil's books, which was also a part of my healing process.

Setting the captives free is the main reason why God sent me out to Africa five years ago. We appreciate your prayers, as you know Africa is a very spiritual place. We are surrounded with wizards, witch doctors, and demons daily, yet we have peace knowing that we are children of the Most High God. Not to say that life is easy out here, but when you know who you are and have been set free from the enemy, then you can say, "Greater is He who is in me than he who is in the world!"

# Notes

1. *A Dictionary of Early Christian Beliefs* (Peabody, MA: Hendrickson Publishers, 1998), p. 116.

2. *Ancient Christian Commentary on Scripture,* New Testament VIII (Downers Grove, IL: IVP, 1999), pp. 150,151.

3. Quoted by Timothy George in *First Things,* "Religion and Public Life," August/September 2007, p. 21.

4. I have witnessed many attempts to reconcile ethnic groups and other groups that had little lasting effect. I believe that is the case because the individuals had not been first reconciled to God. Any attempt to unite fallen humanity on any other basis than Christ has always failed. Reconciliation requires repentance and forgiveness. Anything less is at best conciliation, which I explain in *The Path to Reconciliation* (Regal Books, 2008).

5. *Ancient Christian Commentary,* New Testament VIII, p. 44.

6. *Ancient Christian Commentary,* New Testament VIII, p. 40,41.

7. Neil T. Anderson, Rich Miller, and Paul Travis, *Breaking the Bondage of Legalism* (Eugene, OR: Harvest House, 2003).

8. These three levels of growth (being firmly rooted, growing in Christ, and living in Christ) are the primary basis for *The Daily Discipler* (Regal Books, 2005), which is a practical systematic theology book. The final section is on overcoming "in Christ" and explains the enemies of our sanctification—namely, the world, the flesh, and the devil.

9. In his book *Revolution* (Tyndale, 2005), Barna claims that 20 million believers are worn out on church and are supposedly finding a vibrant faith beyond the walls of the sanctuary.

10. The information on sexual problems is taken from my book *Winning the Battle Within* (Harvest House, 2008).

11. *Ancient Christian Commentary,* New Testament VIII, p. 29.

12. *Ancient Christian Commentary,* New Testament VIII, p. 29.

13. Having the inquirer pray rather than the counselor is the basis for the Steps to Freedom in Christ, which are now being used all over the world.

14. In my book *Discipleship Counseling* (Regal Books, 2003), I explain who is responsible for what. As a minister of the gospel I can't assume someone else's responsibility, nor can I play God in their lives.

15. *Ancient Christian Commentary,* pp. 181,182. Justin Martyr is comparing the various Hellenistic philosophers with the Old Testament prophets and is claiming that the wisdom of the latter predates that of the former. This argument that biblical truth is older, and thus more venerable, than that of philosophy was commonplace in early Christian apologetics and rested on the assumption generally shared in the ancient world that what was more ancient was more true. The high point of such thinking is the work *Against Celsus* by Origen.

16. Martin Wells Knapp, *Impressions* (Wheaton, IL: Tyndale House Publishers, 1984), p. 32.

17. Knapp, p. 43.

18. Knapp, p. 14.

19. *Ancient Christian Commentary,* p. 290.

20. *Ancient Christian Commentary,* vol. p. 290.

21. *A Dictionary of Early Christian Beliefs,* p. 540.

22. *Catechism of the Catholic Church* (New York: Doubleday, 1995), p. 247.

23. *A Dictionary of Early Christian Beliefs,* p. 540

24. *A Dictionary of Early Christian Beliefs,* p. 540

25. *A Dictionary of Early Christian Beliefs,* p. 309.

26. *Ancient Christian Commentary on Scripture,* New Testament VIII, p. 257.

27. Sherwood E. Wirt and Kersten Beckstrom, *Living Quotations For Christians,* (New York: Harper and Row, 1974), p. 100

28. Bruce K. Waltke, *Finding God's Will,* (Grand Rapids, MI: William B. Eerdmans Publishing Company, 1995), p. 8.

29. Meade McGuire, date and source unknown.

30. George Mueller, *Narratives.*

31. *A Dictionary of Early Christian Beliefs,* p. 356.

32. *A Dictionary of Early Christian Beliefs,* p. 42.

33. Adapted from, Neil T. Anderson, *Who I Am in Christ* (Ventura, CA: Regal Books, 2001), p. 278.

34. Joseph Ratzinger (Pope Benedict XVI), *God's Word,* (San Francisco: Ignatius Press, 2005), p. 42.

35. Christopher Hall, *Reading Scripture with the Church Fathers,* (Downers Grove, IL: InterVarsity, 1998), pp 24-25.

36. *A Dictionary of Early Christian Beliefs,* p. 629.

37. Patrick Reardon, *Christ In His Saints* (Ben Lomond, CA: Conciliar Press, 2004), p. 228.

38. As quoted in Reardon.

39. Authored by an unnamed African pastor who was martyred for his faith. (See http://home.snu.edu/~houlbert/commit.htm.)

40. *Ancient Christian Commentary,* New Testament X, p. 79.

41. C.S. Lewis, *The Joyful Christian: 127 Readings from C.S. Lewis* (New York: Macmillan, 1979), p. 139.

42. *A Dictionary of Early Christian Beliefs,* p. 251

43. Kevin DeYoung and Ted Kluck, *Why We Are Not Emergent* (Chicago: Moody Press, 2008).

44. As an example, the Communion of Evangelical Episcopal Churches (CEEC), Wayne

Boosahda's denomination claims to have an association of 3000 churches worldwide and 1000 churches in the United States (see www.theceec.org).

45. The convergence movement has been influenced by Dr. Robert Webber, who once taught at Wheaton College and in his latter years at Northern Seminary. His original article on the convergence movement is included in his eight-volume set entitled The Complete Library of Christian Worship. It is included on the CEEC website, as well as an article on the history of the Convergence Movement entitled, "The Threefold Cord."

46. See www.ancientevangelicalfuture.blogspot.com.

47. Peter Gillquist, *Becoming Orthodox*, (Ben Lomond, CA, Conciliar Press, 1992).

48. Scott and Kimberly Hahn, *Rome Sweet Home*, (San Francisco: Ignatius Press), 1993.

49. Hahn, pp. 83,119.

50. Hahn, pp. 124,125.

51. The editor is Joseph Cardinal Ratzinger (Pope Benedict XVI) an articulate theologian and scholar.

*Victory over the Darkness* with study guide, audiobook, and DVD (Regal Books, 2000). With over 1,000,000 copies in print, this core book explains who you are in Christ, how to walk by faith in the power of the Holy Spirit, how to be transformed by the renewing of your mind, how to experience emotional freedom, and how to relate to one another in Christ.

*The Bondage Breaker®* with study guide, and audiobook (Harvest House Publishers, 2006) and DVD (Regal Books, 2006). With over 1,000,000 copies in print, this book explains spiritual warfare, what our protection is, ways that we are vulnerable, and how we can live a liberated life in Christ.

*Breaking Through to Spiritual Maturity* (Regal Books, 2000). This curriculum teaches the basic message of Freedom in Christ Ministries.

*Discipleship Counseling* with DVD (Regal Books, 2003). This book combines the concepts of discipleship and counseling and teaches the practical integration of theology and psychology for helping Christians resolve their personal and spiritual conflicts through repentance and faith in God.

*Steps to Freedom in Christ* and interactive video (Regal Books, 2004). This discipleship counseling tool helps Christians resolve their personal and spiritual conflicts through genuine repentance and faith in God.

*Freedom in Christ* (Regal Books, 2008) is a discipleship course for Sunday school classes and small groups. The course comes with a teacher's guide, a student guide, and a DVD covering 12 lessons and the Steps to Freedom in Christ. This course is designed to enable new and stagnant believers to resolve personal and spiritual conflicts and be established alive and free in Christ.

*The Daily Discipler* (Regal Books, 2005). This practical systematic theology is a culmination of all of Dr. Anderson's books covering the major doctrines of the Christian faith and the problems Christians face. It is a five-day-per-week, one-year study that will thoroughly ground believers in their faith.

*Overcoming Addictive Behavior* with Mike Quarles (Regal Books, 2003). This book explores the path to addiction and how a Christian can overcome addictive behaviors.

*Overcoming Depression* with Joanne Anderson (Regal Books, 2004). This book explores the nature of depression, which is a body, soul, and spirit problem, and presents a wholistic answer for overcoming this "common cold" of mental illness.

*Praying by the Power of the Spirit* (Harvest House Publishers, 2003).

*Unleashing God's Power in You* with Robert Saucy (Harvest House Publishers, 2004). A thorough analysis of sanctification, along with practical instruction on how you can grow in Christ.

*Finding God's Will in Spiritually Deceptive Times* (Harvest House Publishers, 2003).

*Daily in Christ* with Joanne Anderson (Harvest House Publishers, 2000). This popular daily devotional is also being used by thousands of Internet subscribers every day.

*Who I Am in Christ* (Regal Books, 2001). In 36 short chapters, this book describes who you are in Christ and how He meets your deepest needs.

*Freedom from Addiction* with Mike and Julia Quarles (Regal Books, 1997). Using Mike's testimony, this book explains the nature of chemical addictions and how to overcome them in Christ.

*One Day at a Time* with Mike and Julia Quarles (Regal Books, 2000). This devotional helps those who struggle with addictive behaviors and explains how to discover the grace of God on a daily basis.

*Freedom from Fear* with Rich Miller (Harvest House Publishers, 1999). This book explains anxiety disorders and how to overcome them.

*Extreme Church Makeover* with Charles Mylander (Regal Books, 2006). This book offers guidelines and encouragement for resolving seemingly impossible corporate conflicts in the church and also provides leaders with a primary means for church growth—releasing the power of God in the church.

*Experiencing Christ Together* with Dr. Charles Mylander (Regal Books, 2006.) This book explains God's divine plan for marriage and the steps that couples can take to resolve their difficulties.

*Christ-Centered Therapy* with Dr. Terry and Julie Zuehlke (Zondervan Publishing House, 2000). A textbook explaining the practical integration of theology and psychology for professional counselors.

*Getting Anger Under Control* with Rich Miller (Harvest House Publishers, 2002). This book explains the basis for anger and how to control it.

*Breaking the Bondage of Legalism* with Rich Miller and Paul Travis (Harvest House Publishers, 2003). An explanation of legalism and how to overcome it.

*Winning the Battle Within* (Harvest House, 2008). This book shares God's standards for sexual conduct, the path to sexual addiction, and how to overcome sexual strongholds.

*The Path to Reconciliation* (Regal Books, 2008). God has given the church the ministry of reconciliation. This book explains what that is and how it can be accomplished.

For more information, or to purchase the above materials contact:

**Freedom in Christ Ministries**
9051 Executive Park Drive
Suite 503
Knoxville, Tennessee 37923
(865) 342-4000

info@ficm.org
www.ficm.org
www.ficminternational.org

## About Dr. Neil T. Anderson

Dr. Neil T. Anderson was formerly the chairman of the Practical Theology Department at Talbot School of Theology. In 1988, he founded Freedom in Christ Ministries, which now has staff and offices in various countries around the world. In 2001, Dr. Anderson stepped down as president of Freedom in Christ Ministries in the United States and now serves on the board of Freedom in Christ Ministries International.

To learn more about books by Neil T. Anderson
or to read sample chapters, log on to our website:

**www.harvesthousepublishers.com**

HARVEST HOUSE PUBLISHERS
EUGENE, OREGON